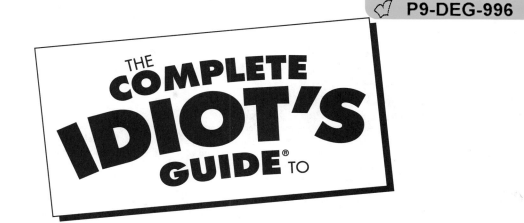

THE COMPLETE IDIOT'S GUIDE® TO

The U.S. Special Ops Forces

by Marc Cerasini

ALPHA

A Pearson Education Company

To my father, John F. Cerasini, who taught me the importance of the printed word.

Copyright © 2002 by Marc Cerasini

THE COMPLETE IDIOT'S GUIDE TO and Design are registered trademarks of Pearson Education, Inc.

International Standard Book Number: 0-02-864373-9
Library of Congress Catalog Card Number: 2002102225

04   03   02   8   7   6   5   4   3   2   1

Interpretation of the printing code: The rightmost number of the first series of numbers is the year of the book's printing; the rightmost number of the second series of numbers is the number of the book's printing. For example, a printing code of 02-1 shows that the first printing occurred in 2002.

Printed in the United States of America

Note: This publication contains the opinions and ideas of its author. It is intended to provide helpful and informative material on the subject matter covered. It is sold with the understanding that the author and publisher are not engaged in rendering professional services in the book. If the reader requires personal assistance or advice, a competent professional should be consulted.

The author and publisher specifically disclaim any responsibility for any liability, loss, or risk, personal or otherwise, which is incurred as a consequence, directly or indirectly, of the use and application of any of the contents of this book.

Publisher: *Marie Butler-Knight*
Product Manager: *Phil Kitchel*
Managing Editor: *Jennifer Chisholm*
Acquisitions Editor: *Gary Goldstein*
Development Editor: *Michael Koch*
Production Editor: *Billy Fields*
Copy Editor: *Krista Hansing*
Illustrator: *Jody Schaeffer*
Cover/Book Designer: *Trina Wurst*
Indexer: *Julie Bess*
Layout/Proofreading: *Svetlana Dominguez, Rebecca Harmon*

For marketing and publicity, please call: 317-581-3722

The publisher offers discounts on this book when ordered in quantity for bulk purchases and special sales.

For sales within the United States, please contact: Corporate and Government Sales, 1-800-382-3419 or corpsales@pearsontechgroup.com

Outside the United States, please contact: International Sales, 317-581-3793 or international@pearsontechgroup.com

Contents at a Glance

Contents

Appendixes

Foreword

If I had to list the three qualities most important to becoming a successful SpecWarrior based solely on the thousands of e-mails I get from the readers of my *Rogue* novels, they would be, first, a facility for using the F-word; second, the belief that it's okay to disregard orders; and third, Special Operations is just another way of saying "Let's shoot huge quantities of hollowpoint ammunition." This book will go a long way to dispel those cartoonish notions.

Roguish readers, take careful note. The *Rogue* novels are *fiction*. This guide to the world of Special Operations tells it like it really is.

Special Warfare, or as I write it, SpecWar, is warfare conducted "outside the box" by small groups of highly motivated and trained Warriors who overcome larger conventional forces. SpecWarriors prevail through audacity, skill, surprise, and grit. SpecWar is as old as history itself. Joshua sent two of his Hebrew "special forces" to sneak and peek inside the city of Jericho before those walls came tumblin' down. Homer wrote about SpecWar in *The Iliad*. Remember Odysseus's Trojan Horse gambit? It was nothing more than the tactical embodiment of Sun Tzu's dictum, "All war is deception."

This book explodes many of the popular fictions about those who succeed in the world of Special Operations. For example, today's SpecWarriors go through rigorous psychological training, because rogues may be terrific characters in novels, but they do not function well on a team. Creative use of the F-word may be fun in a book. In the real world, SpecWarriors must be articulate. What good is a "poop and snoop" mission if you can't describe what you've seen accurately and succinctly. And yes, shooting is important. But so, equally, are academic talents such as math and languages. SpecWarriors have to be able to calculate the formula to plot their free-fall drift when they HALO out of a plane at 35,000 feet, or compute their HARP—High Altitude Release Point—for a HAHO infiltration that can mean a mission's success or failure. The ability of U.S. Special Forces operators to speak Uzbek, Pashto, and Dari made a huge positive difference during the initial days of the Afghanistan campaign, when the indigenous resistance fighters were suspicious of our motives.

Finally, today's American SpecWarrior community—the Army's Special Forces, Rangers, and its SOAR (Special Operations Air Regiment), the Navy's SEALs, and the Air Force's Special Warfare Command—are all the godchildren of an eighteenth-century American Warrior named Robert Rogers. He created a small, mobile, audacious, unconventional force ultimately known as Rogers's Rangers. Indeed, Major Rogers's "Standing Orders," written in 1756 and included in this book, provide the philosophical and operational foundation on which all of America's SpecWar doctrine has been built.

Read them and absorb, Grasshopper. Because the core values of character, integrity, patriotism, and the "Keep it simple, stupid" approach to warfare that Roger preached almost 250 years ago are precisely the same ideals of Duty, Honor, and Country, and the sorts of resourceful, aggressive, uncompromising tactics that both characterize and motivate our twenty-first–century SpecWarriors.

John Weisman
Co-author of the popular *New York Times* best-selling *Rogue Warrior* series; regular contributor to *Soldier of Fortune* magazine

Introduction

According to Gen. Carl Stiner (Ret.)—ex–Green Beret, Vietnam War veteran, and former commander-in-chief of the United States Special Operations Command from 1990 to 1993—even in times of relative peace, there are more than 3,500 active-duty soldiers of the Army's Special Forces operating in over 70 countries around the world. These soldiers are there to protect American lives, property, and interests. Many operate in secret, risking their lives to gather intelligence on hostile nations, train insurgents to overthrow unfriendly governments, prevent the proliferation of weapons of mass destruction, and provide humanitarian relief to struggling countries.

Despite their long tradition of service, the notion of "special operations forces"—elite military units with advanced training, enhanced skills, and special equipment—flies in the face of America's cherished ideal of the "citizen soldier." Many members of the conventional military also regard the "special forces" with suspicion—believing that they rob the so-called "real" military of funding and resources. Yet the stalwart "GI Joe" who willingly takes up arms in a time of national crisis, only to return home to work and family after the conflict ends, is no longer the best candidate for the rigorous requirements of modern warfare—conventional or unconventional.

We live in an era of specialization. Most professionals, including scientists, physicians, and lawyers, have become more specialized as their vocations have become more and more complex. No doctor practicing today can possibly master the comprehensive knowledge, skills, or techniques required to treat *every* disease or injury—medical knowledge and practices have become too numerous and far too complex for one individual to master it all. This is also true of modern warfare. The military arts have evolved so much and so quickly over the past few decades that professional warriors are needed now, more than ever. And though there will always be a place for the citizen soldier in America's military, today's Army, Navy, and Air Force require highly skilled and rigorously trained personnel to perform the difficult and challenging tasks required of them, as the technology and tactics of modern warfare become more and more complicated and specialized.

Sadly, Americans know very little about special warfare operations or the men who carry them out. This guide is meant to be a first step in remedying that situation.

Whom This Book Is For

Written for a layman, this guide will provide an overview of America's Special Operations Forces, an examination of their glorious—and not so glorious—history, a look at their training, and a glimpse at the top secret missions they have carried out in the past, as well as the missions they will be tasked with in the future. Because of the wall of secrecy surrounding *all* special warfare units, and the evolution in training and tactics that goes on constantly, no work on this subject can be considered final or all-inclusive. This volume is no exception, though the author and editors have done their very best to give an accurate and up-to-date account of special warfare units and their activities today.

Those who desire a general study of America's Special Operations Forces will find this guide quite useful. So too will those young men who may be considering a career in the military, and who might be wondering if they have "what it takes" to qualify for a Special Forces unit.

How This Book Is Organized

This guide is divided into six parts.

Part 1, "Special Forces in History," provides a short history of special warfare units from ancient times to our modern times. This part also explores the role of special operations units in American history, beginning with the War for Independence and continuing on through World War II—which many military historians regard as the golden age of special operations.

Part 2, "The Green Berets," concentrates on the origin and history of the largest and most active special warfare group in America's arsenal, the U.S. Army Special Forces—the legendary "Green Berets." This part will study the origin of the Green Berets during the Kennedy Administration, as well as their performance during the war in Vietnam, and its aftermath.

Part 3, "The U.S. Army Special Forces," guides you through Special Forces training and missions, as they exist today. We will also explore how the command structure of America's elite special warfare units have been transformed over the last decade and a half by the creation of the joint U.S. Special Operations Command. This part ends with a look at the elite 75th Ranger Regiment, their training, their history, and their traditions.

Part 4, "The U.S. Navy SEALs," provides an introduction to the Navy's ultra-elite Sea, Air, Land Teams (SEALs), a look at their rigorous Basic Underwater Demolition (BUD/S) training, and an examination of a typical SEAL operation during wartime.

Part 5, "U.S. Air Force Special Operations," provides a basic tour of the most "high-tech" of America's Special Operations Command, their history, their aircraft and equipment, as well as their training, missions, and deployment.

Part 6, "The First Special Operational Detachment—Delta," provides a glimpse into the operations of the most secretive and elite of all of America's special warfare units. Though the Army consistently denies that Delta even exists, this tiny unit is America's first line of defense against international terrorism.

Finally, you'll find additional useful information in the appendixes, including a detailed breakdown of Special Forces ordinance, a list of books and films that focus on various aspects of the Special Forces, a guide to military acronyms, and a comprehensive glossary of military terminology.

Extras

In addition to the main text, you will find a series of sidebars to add some interesting facts, figures, and trivia to the basic history of America's elite Special Operations Forces. These facts will be divided into the following categories:

Special Ops Jargon

Look here for definitions of military terms and the deciphering of military acronyms. Turning complex armed services jargon into plain English is a tough job, but this box will do it. You may also find descriptions of particular weapons or devices used by special operations under this banner.

FUBARs

Not quite literally "Fouled Up Beyond All Recognition." Slang for a classic military blunder. Anyone near a FUBAR is in for a world of hurt because things are going cork-screw in a hurry.

Straight Shooting

This box conveys the plain-spoken truth about an organization, historical event, operation, campaign, military philosophy, or political movement pertaining to military and/or special forces units around the world.

Shop Talk

Here you will find interesting facts, or formerly classified anecdotes about particular special operations missions, often featuring the unorthodox techniques employed by the members of special warfare units to achieve their objectives.

Acknowledgments

Too many people and too many sources were used in the creation of this work for me to thank everyone adequately, but here it goes: I would like to thank Gary Goldstein at Alpha Books. It was Gary who conceived this volume and guided me through the process of creating it, and he deserves more thanks than I can offer here. I would also like to thank Michael Koch, who put up with a lot in the editing of this text and my sometimes slow responses to his suggestions; technical editors Sean Naylor and William Christie for making sure I didn't say anything too stupid; Krista Hansing for working hard at making certain that my rambling narrative generally adhered to the rules of the English language; production editor Billy Fields, who did a phenomenal job in a short time; Capt. Michael Harris, of the New York National Guard, for making valuable suggestions and providing the line illustrations that grace these pages; my agent John Talbot for getting me this gig and then giving me a wide berth while I did the work; and my twin literary mentors, Robert E. Howard and Tom Clancy (who both helped more than they could possibly know).

I would especially like to thank my wife, Alice Alfonsi, for putting up with a postponed vacation, cancelled holiday celebrations, and delayed birthday dinners while I completed this challenging and difficult manuscript.

Finally, I must thank the men of America's Special Operations Forces, wherever they are—on land, sea, or in the air. It is only through your sacrifices that our freedom and our way of life is possible. Thanks, guys!

Special Thanks to the Technical Reviewers

The Complete Idiot's Guide to the U.S. Special Ops Forces was reviewed by two experts who double-checked the accuracy of what you'll learn here, to help us ensure that this book gives you everything you need to know about the U.S. special operations forces. Special thanks are extended to Sean Naylor for reviewing Chapters 1–13 and William Christie for reviewing Chapters 14–20.

Trademarks

All terms mentioned in this book that are known to be or are suspected of being trademarks or service marks have been appropriately capitalized. Alpha Books and Pearson Education, Inc., cannot attest to the accuracy of this information. Use of a term in this book should not be regarded as affecting the validity of any trademark or service mark.

Part 1

Special Forces in History

Though the notion of "special forces" may seem modern, specially selected, trained, and equipped units have fought alongside conventional military forces since ancient times. America's special operations forces also have a long tradition, with roots back to the unconventional warfare tactics the colonials employed to defeat the British in the War for Independence.

In this part I will introduce you to the special forces throughout history. I will also examine the origins of our modern unconventional warfare units, beginning with the German "storm troopers" of World War I, the British Special Air Service commandos, and U.S. Army "special warfare" groups of World War II.

Chapter 1

A Force to Reckon With

In This Chapter

- ◆ An introduction to special forces units
- ◆ Rogers's Rangers: America's first special forces unit
- ◆ The fighting Rangers of the American Revolution
- ◆ Special operations in the Civil War
- ◆ The coming of the storm trooper

Any specially selected, specially trained, and specially equipped military unit established to conduct special missions is, by definition, a special forces unit. Such units have been a part of military history since ancient times. In America, special forces units fought with distinction during the War for Independence and the Civil War. However, the high-tech, modern concept of special forces troops took shape in Europe, on the bloody battlefields of France, near the end of World War I.

Special forces have existed since warfare and armies began. Kings, princes, warlords, and even queens have singled out a unit, a regiment, or a guard for special favor. In ancient Greece, the Spartans became the military leaders of all the Greek states. Steeped in martial tradition, Spartans were admonished to win the battle or come home dead on their shields. So formidable were these warriors that a mere 300 of them saved Western civilization from Asian encroachment when they fought the elite troops of Persia's King Xerxes, the Immortals, to a standstill at Thermopylae.

The tradition of creating elite (and sometimes pampered) fighting forces continued throughout history: The Roman Ceasars had the Praetorian Guard, King Henry had his archers, Hitler had Maj. Gen. Otto Skorzeny and his Special Troops, Winston Churchill had the British commandos, and John F. Kennedy had his Green Berets. But what are these elite forces? What's so special about special forces? In this chapter, I'll define the term "special forces," explore the unconventional warfare tradition in America, from the Rangers who fought in the French and Indian War, to the reborn Rangers groups of World War II. I will also examine the first modern special operations unit ever created—the German Storm Troopers of World War I.

What's so Special About Special Forces?

Since ancient times, wars have been fought by large standing armies organized and equipped by nation-states to defend their interests, borders, and national sovereignty. These conventional armed forces are the product of rigorous discipline, martial training, and technological innovation. Conventional armies are controlled by a rigid command structure and are identified by their distinctive uniforms, weapons, and tactics. Soldiers operating in conventional armies are taught to respond to enemy action with formalized strategies and tactics designed to outflank, outmaneuver, and defeat their adversary on the field of battle.

Special Ops Jargon

The word **guerrilla** comes from Spanish and literally means "little war."

But there is a hidden side to modern warfare—an informal, clandestine style of *guerrilla* combat waged by small, highly trained, highly specialized units. These units are sometimes pitted against larger, traditional forces. More often they are sent into battle against guerrilla bands, narco-criminals, or terrorists. These units operate covertly and often employ unconventional weapons, strategies, and tactics.

In the modern world, this type of clandestine warfare is waged by "special forces" troops who are specially selected, specially trained, and specially equipped to fight a shadow war. Special forces troops possess talents and capabilities that far exceed the abilities of the average, front-line "grunts." Special forces are very different from conventional combat units. They are not organized, equipped, or trained to conduct sustained combat operations. Their missions are of short duration and limited goals.

Special forces do not usually fight on the front lines. Most are trained to operate deep within enemy territory. They do not rely on overwhelming force to defeat their adversary, but they prefer stealth, speed, and the element of surprise to achieve their goals. They do not annihilate, but they *undermine* the enemy. Some special forces never see combat. Psychological operations units wage war from a distance, through propaganda and misinformation.

Special forces units are usually small, though size does not matter—look at the holding action of the 300 Spartans at Thermopylae, or the performance of King Henry's longbowmen at the Battle of Agincourt to understand just what an elite force led by a competent commander can accomplish.

Special forces are different from conventional forces in another way. Elite forces are expensive to build and maintain. Special forces units might be small—because the pool of talented, patriotic, intelligent, self-motivated soldiers who meet the rigorous physical standards of the special forces is quite limited—but they receive a disproportionate share of military funding and support. This resource gap causes friction between special units and "regular" military personnel. Elite units are regarded as "teacher's pets" who rob precious funding and material resources from conventional military units. And when special forces fail to perform to expectations, many of their rivals in the traditional forces never hesitate to crow about it. Some military commanders tend to distrust the special forces, whom they regard as reckless, unruly, and undisciplined. One reason is that special forces units are something of a meritocracy, where rank and seniority often counts for less than real leadership skills and job performance. There are no "influence" or "political" appointments in a special unit.

 **FUBARs**

Gen. H. Norman Schwartzkopf did not want special forces units involved in Operation Desert Storm because he recalled their erratic and ineffectual performance in Vietnam. Even special forces veterans from the Vietnam era admit that some mavericks within their ranks damaged the reputation of them all.

America's First Special Forces Unit

In America, the concept of "special forces" is not new. As early as 1676, woodsmen skilled in Indian-style fighting scouted for colonial armies and British regulars during the French and Indian War. In 1756, a backwoodsman named Robert Rogers took command of four companies of frontiersmen culled from the wilds of New Hampshire and Massachusetts. These rugged frontier settlers were assigned to guard the rivers and lakes of the Hudson River Valley, which were crucial to the movement of the British army in America.

Despite their unruly and undisciplined temperaments, these "irregulars" became crucial to the success of British military operations in the colonies. They also were unreliable and hard to control, and they did what they pleased (fighting, drinking, carousing) when they were off-duty.

To help establish some measure of discipline within his units—at least when they were in the field—Major Rogers devised a list of "Standing Orders" to guide the actions of his troops. These 19 "do's and don'ts" became America's first special forces operations manual.

Robert Rogers's Standing Orders

1. Don't forget nothing.

2. Have your muskets clean and your hatchets scoured, and be ready to march at a minute's warning.

3. When you're on the march, act the way you would if you were stalking a deer. See the enemy first.

4. Tell the truth about what you see and what you do.

5. Don't ever take a chance you don't have to.

6. March single file, far enough apart so one shot can't go through two men.

7. In swamps or soft ground, march abreast so it's hard to track us.

8. Keep moving till dark, so as to give the enemy the least possible chance at us.

9. When we camp, half the party stays awake while the other half sleeps.

10. Keep prisoners separate so they can't cook up a story between them.

11. Don't ever march home the same way. Take a different route so you won't get ambushed.

12. Keep a scout 20 yards ahead, 20 yards on each flank, and 20 yards to the rear so the main body can't be surprised and wiped out.

13. Every night you'll be told where to meet if surrounded by a superior force.

14. Don't eat without posting sentries.

15. Don't sleep beyond dawn. Dawn's when the French and Indians attack.

16. Don't cross a river by a regular ford.

17. If somebody's trailing you, make a circle and ambush the folks who aim to ambush you.

18. Don't stand up when the enemy's coming—kneel down, lie down, hide behind a tree.

19. Let the enemy come till he's almost close enough to touch. Then let him have it and finish him up with your hatchet.

There was always tension between the regular army and the irregulars. British officers—gentlemen, all!—quickly discovered that these backwoodsmen were difficult to handle, rioted when subjected to camp discipline, and did not necessarily transfer their loyalties to a new commander unless they respected his abilities and leadership style. However, despite their volatility, Rogers's Rangers proved their worth in several violent and prolonged campaigns.

FUBARs

In 1760, Rogers was ordered to attack the Abenaki Indians who had been murdering settlers. Rogers's Rangers crossed 200 miles of wilderness, losing a quarter of their strength to disease. When they finally attacked, 200 Abenaki and 2 Rangers were killed in a pitched battle. It would have gone down in history as a great victory, but on their return trip, Rogers's "Standing Orders" were not obeyed and a third of his force was lost in Abenaki reprisal raids.

Throughout the French and Indian War, Rogers's Rangers served as scouts (on reconnaissance missions), advance troops, and guerrilla fighters. The following list shows the typical operations equipment at the time.

Special Operations Equipment, circa 1757

◆ Musket (sawed short for better performance in the field)

◆ Sixty shots of gunpowder and musket balls, supplemented with buckshot

◆ Bayonet

◆ Tomahawk (scoured clean)

◆ Scalping knife

◆ Mittens (attached to sleeves or tied around neck)

◆ Snowshoes

◆ Toboggan (for dragging food and supplies)

◆ Whiskey

In March of 1759, Rogers's Rangers carried out the most successful raid of their operational history—a long-range reconnaissance patrol of the French-controlled region around Fort Ticonderoga, New York. They returned with valuable intelligence, several prisoners, a brace of French and Indian scalps (that's what those scalping knives were for!), and a detailed sketch of the French-controlled Fort Carillon and the terrain around it.

Rangers of the American Revolution

Both the British and the Colonists used "irregulars" in America's War for Independence. British Rangers infiltrated New York and Pennsylvania through Canada, to join with their Indian allies to harass American settlements deep in rebel territory. The British ravished the countryside, burning homes and barns and destroying mills and farm fields in an effort to interdict vital supplies coming from the Mohawk Valley.

Shop Talk

During the Revolutionary War, Daniel Morgan's Rangers conducted long-range reconnaissance and raids against the British. Morgan was a typical frontier Ranger. Between conflicts he drank, brawled, took a common-law wife, and fathered two illegitimate daughters. After the Revolutionary War, Morgan helped quell the Whiskey Rebellion in western Pennsylvania.

East Florida and the Georgia border were also scenes of constant guerrilla conflict during America's fight for freedom. In 1777, British Loyalists formed the East Florida Rangers, a force comprised of British citizens and Creek Indians led by Thomas Brown. Although the efforts of the British Rangers and Brown's Loyalists were effective, the British ultimately lost the war. The British Rangers in America were disbanded, but Thomas Brown's regiment remained intact. They fled to Barbados after their cause was lost.

On the Colonials' side, in early 1776 Gen. George Washington gave Col. Thomas Knowlton permission to form a Ranger unit to perform delicate and hazardous duties such as scouting and foraging. Assembling 120 New Englanders, Knowlton was based on Manhattan Island near the East River, right above Harlem. During the campaign for control of New York City, Knowlton's unit was cut off from the main American army and was surrounded. Colonel Knowlton was killed in a bloody clash, and his Rangers surrendered to the British on November 16, 1776.

Although the American Rangers failed to stop the British advance, they had the satisfaction of siding with the winner. The survivors of Knowlton's Rangers were freed by the British at the end of hostilities.

Francis Marion, the Swamp Fox

America's first true guerrilla leader was Col. Francis Marion, who led an army of "irregulars" against the British forces stationed in the South during America's War for Independence. A wealthy planter from the Carolinas, Marian was also a patriot committed to the cause of liberty. In 1780, he accepted a commission in the Continental Army. His mission was to direct the partisan activities around Williamsburg.

American Gen. Horatio Gates subsequently ordered Marion to disrupt supplies coming down from Camden, South Carolina, to the army of British Gen. Charles, Lord Cornwallis. Colonel Marion's interdiction activities were so successful that Col. Banastre Tarleton was assigned the task of running down Marion and his men. It was Tarleton who dubbed Francis Marion the "Swamp Fox" because the rebel leader cleverly eluded capture, even when his force seemed to be cornered.

Unfortunately for Colonel Tarleton, Marion and his men were all veteran smugglers. They knew the swamps and forests of South Carolina like the backs of their hands. By 1780 they were staging lightning-fast guerrilla raids against British forces and their Tory allies. After each attack, they melted back into the forest.

The legendary Swamp Fox commanded fierce guerrilla fighters who held a grudge against all things British. Marion's men loaded their muskets with buckshot and etched grooves into their musket balls so that the projectiles would break apart upon impact and cause more grievous wounds.

The British never captured the Swamp Fox, and Marion's harassment of the British supply lines kept Cornwallis bogged down in the South far longer than he intended to be there. By keeping the British pinned in the Carolinas, Marion bought General Washington's Continental Army precious time to regroup.

In 1782, after the War for Independence had ended, Marion's brigade was officially disbanded by the Continental Congress. Marion's men returned to their farms and plantations, to vanish from the pages of history.

This cycle of military buildup during conflict and quick dismantling of those same forces after hostilities are over is an American tradition and was repeated in each of our wars.

> **Shop Talk**
>
> The British were never able to find Marion's unit because they operated from a secret base close to Lynch Creek, deep in the Great Pee Dee Swamp.

> **Straight Shooting**
>
> The Revolutionary War epic *The Patriot* (2000), starring Mel Gibson, was loosely based on the exploits of Francis Marion. Screenwriter Robert Rodat and director Roland Emmerich changed the name of their protagonist to Benjamin Martin because they discovered that the real Francis Marion was a slave owner who mistreated his "property."

The Rangers Live On

On January 2, 1812, Congress created six companies of Rangers to protect settlers on the frontier from Indian raids. These Ranger units were comprised of frontiersmen and backwoodsmen who enlisted for 12 months of service. They equipped and provided for themselves and their horses through an allowance of $1 a day, making these units very expensive for America's young government to maintain.

But despite the cost, the Rangers proved their worth. By 1814, there were over a thousand Rangers patrolling the American frontier, from Michigan to Louisiana.

In 1818, Gen. Andrew Jackson became the first president to have served with the "special forces" when this hard-fighting hero of the Battle for New Orleans took command of several Ranger units in the Florida panhandle and actively led them on several campaigns.

Though effective, the Rangers were regarded as an extravagance by the U.S. government and as undisciplined, ill-mannered louts by the officers and enlisted men serving in the regular army. By 1832, Secretary of War Lewis Cass had moved to disband the Rangers and replace them with European-style mounted Dragoons.

Even after most U.S. Ranger units were disbanded, they continued to patrol remote frontiers that were not technically part of the United States. In the 1820s and '30s, Rangers were the only force that maintained order in the regions of northern Mexico colonized by English-speaking, Protestant settlers. By 1832, these "Texas Rangers" had become an institution.

Rangers were also utilized as scouts by Gen. Zachary Taylor in the Mexican War. Although they proved effective, like all traditional military commanders, General Taylor disliked and distrusted them.

Special Forces in the Civil War

During the American Civil War, there was an explosion of special forces units. As many as 400 groups were officially or unofficially known as "Rangers." There were also traditional military units that performed many of the same missions and tasks that the modern special forces are charged with today.

The Confederate States led the way in the creation of Ranger units. In April 1862, Confederate President Jefferson Davis approved an act to form Rangers, both infantry and cavalry. Although there were many soldiers among the ranks of Confederate Rangers who truly sympathized with the Southern cause, most were soldiers of fortune who fought for profit. That was because all captured goods and equipment were considered "the spoils of war," and the act that created the Confederate Rangers stipulated that these units should be paid "full value" for the goods they captured or confiscated. This practice naturally led to abuse and corruption. Some Confederate Rangers became outright bandits. Soon the Rangers were as much of a threat to honest citizens of the South as they were to the enemy. By 1864, the Southern leadership had had enough of the Confederate Rangers. Gen. Robert E. Lee declared them "a terror to the citizens and an infamy to the cause." Most Confederate Ranger units were abolished that same year.

Shop Talk
One Ranger unit was praised by Robert E. Lee: Mosby's Rangers, led by Virginia lawyer John S. Mosby. Farmers by day and guerrillas by night, they killed, wounded, or captured a thousand soldiers. Mosby's men were so despised by the Union that General Grant ordered any who were captured to be hung without trial.

Ranger units were also organized by the Union Army, usually to counter the activities of Confederate Rangers.

Col. Benjamin Grierson's mounted Rangers ravaged parts of Mississippi, wrecking more than 50 miles of railroad track and several vital supply bases. His small-unit campaign was so effective that the Confederates had to pull some of elements of the regular army away from the defense of Vicksburg in a vain attempt to halt Grierson's attacks.

One of the most spectacular special forces operations of the Civil War was mounted by James J. Andrews, a Union spy from Kentucky. This secret mission, known as The Great Locomotive Chase, was carried out by 20 volunteers from the Union Army—all of them former railroad workers who knew how to repair and operate locomotives.

At 4:00 A.M. on April 12, 1862, Andrews's Raiders boarded a train at Marietta, Georgia, mingling with other passengers. When the train made a daybreak stop at Big Shanty, the Raiders stole the locomotive—called The General—along with several boxcars. Their plan was to burn all the railroad bridges in Georgia.

Although Andrews's Raiders managed to cut telegraph lines and uproot miles of track, their main objective was thwarted because they were pursued by an angry conductor named William Fuller. It was Fuller's locomotive that the Raiders had snatched, and the Southern conductor took the theft as a personal affront. Fuller chased the Raiders in a handcar and then another locomotive that he managed to commandeer. Along the way, Fuller gathered volunteers to help him hunt down the Union saboteurs. Soon, the Confederate Army was alerted and troops gathered at the end of the rail line to capture the Union raiders. Unable to accomplish their mission of burning the Georgia bridges, Andrews's Raiders abandoned The General and melted into the wilderness to continue their guerrilla campaign.

> **Shop Talk**
>
> Disguised as a Confederate sympathizer and a smuggler of quinine, James Andrews gained the trust of local Confederate leaders in Georgia. With each trip to the South, Andrews infiltrated his "Raiders" into Confederate-controlled territory, one or two at a time.

> **CAUTION**
>
> **FUBARs**
>
> Buster Keaton starred in *The General*, a silent film about The Great Locomotive Chase. Today it's regarded as one of the finest comedies Hollywood ever produced. Keaton did not portray heroic Union leader James Andrews, but a character based on William Fuller, the Confederate railroad conductor who thwarted the mission.

Over the next few weeks, the Raiders were captured and tried for espionage. James Andrews and seven of his Army volunteers were hanged. Eight others were condemned to death but escaped from captivity before their sentences could be carried out. The Union volunteers who participated in Andrews's failed raid and later escaped hanging, were the first American soldiers to be awarded the Medal of Honor, America's highest award for valor.

Special Forces Come of Age

The first use of special forces troops in the twentieth century came near the end of World War I. In 1918, after four years of constant warfare, Germany was handed a reprieve of sorts. Russia, an ally of England and France, had collapsed into anarchy. Czar Nicholas and his family were prisoners of Bolshevik revolutionaries. The Russian army mutinied and melted away. The Soviet Union would soon emerge from this chaos, but for now, one enemy of Germany had been eliminated.

With the threat from the east neutralized, German High Command transferred large numbers of troops, artillery, and equipment to the Western Front. This bounty arrived in the nick of time—the United States, which had remained neutral for three years, was about to enter the war against them. Reinforced by large numbers of fresh troops from America, the French and English were poised to annihilate the German army through sheer numbers. Gen. Erich Ludendorff, the commander-in-chief of the German army, planned to mount a general offensive in the spring of 1918, before American troops could enter the war in effective numbers.

However, General Ludendorff had a problem. After years of static trench warfare, his army lacked the training, experience, and fighting spirit necessary to wage an offensive campaign. Ludendorff knew he would have to create a new, elite fighting force within the German army to spearhead his spring offensive. In the autumn of 1917, he initiated an ambitious retraining program that would transform the face of modern warfare. He transferred his most effective officers and enlisted men from the front, along with the most promising new conscripts from boot camp, to newly established special warfare schools where they were taught aggressive new tactics and instilled with a determination and fighting spirit.

These training schools stressed individual and small unit initiative and mobility. Troops were taught hand-to-hand combat and new assault techniques. The process took many months and was accomplished in absolute secrecy.

Small units of these highly trained officers and men, called *Stosstruppen* (shock troops), assaulted enemy positions through *infiltration* rather than in massed formations because traditional large unit attacks were vulnerable to machine gun and artillery fire (naturally, because the enemy saw them coming!). Shock troops moved under cover of darkness and were trained to strike before the enemy knew they were even there.

Special Ops Jargon

In 1918, General Ludendorff's visionary strategy did not have a name. Twenty years later, with the addition of dive bombers and armored columns, his tactics would become the basis for the Nazi **blitzkrieg** (lightning war) that Adolf Hitler used to conquer Poland, Belgium, Holland, France, and Scandinavia.

Ludendorff's *Sturmtruppen* (storm troopers) traveled light, relying on mobility rather than overwhelming numbers to neutralize enemy emplacements. Speed was the key to their success. Lightly armed with rifles, light machine guns, and hand grenades, storm troopers hit the French and British lines fast and hard. These advance shock troops led their assaults with hand grenades and then quickly punched a hole through the Allies' lines. They were adept at disrupting communications, disorganizing defense efforts, and crushing enemy resistance before reinforcements had time to arrive. In an effort to enhance their mobility, Ludendorff's storm troopers were trained to bypass pockets of heavy resistance, which were isolated and neutralized by follow-up support units armed with heavy machine guns, trench mortars, flamethrowers, mobile artillery, and tanks.

When General Ludendorff's offensive was finally launched in June 1918, the shock troops and their close support units performed magnificently. The Allies were so stunned by these new tactics that their defenses crumbled. Within a few hours, the French and British armies were in full retreat. For the first time since 1914, Paris itself was threatened by the German advance.

The Germans were finally stopped on June 6, 1918, at Belleau Wood. The shock troopers were defeated by the closest thing the United States had to "special forces" in 1918—the fighting men of the United States Marine Corps. In the thick forest of Belleau Wood, using the small-team assault tactics they had perfected while fighting bandits in the jungles of Haiti, the Dominican Republic, and the Philippines, the Marines of the American Expeditionary Force stymied the German advance. Fighting hand to hand, or against entrenched German machine gunners, the Marines delayed the enemy offensive long enough for Allied reinforcements to reach the front.

After the Battle of Belleau Wood, the U.S. Marines were hailed as heroes by the French people and the American press—to the eternal chagrin of the U.S. Army. Twenty-three years later, the Army—fearing it would be upstaged yet again—barred the Marines from participating in the European theater of World War II.

> **Straight Shooting**
>
> The Marines paid a terrible price to stop the German advance at Belleau Wood. Five thousand Marines fell on June 6, 1918, the bloodiest day in the history of the Corps up to that time.

The Least You Need to Know

- Elite, specially trained military units are called "special forces."
- Special forces have been part of military history since ancient times.
- America's first special forces units fought in the War of Independence and the Civil War.
- The first modern special forces units were the German storm troopers of World War I.

Chapter 2

The Special Forces of World War II

In This Chapter

- ◆ In Europe with the 1st Ranger Battalion
- ◆ The origin of the First Special Services Force unit
- ◆ Into the jungle with America's new elite units
- ◆ Underwater demolition teams swing into action

Special operations forces are elite military units trained and equipped to conduct an unconventional combat campaign behind enemy lines. Although they're an essential component of modern warfare, such units were not always a part of America's military arsenal. Today's highly trained and highly skilled Airborne Rangers, U.S. Army Green Berets, and the Navy SEALs can all trace their origins to the elite fighting units established during World War II. Every nation that participated in that global conflict created elite fighting forces to call their own. Sometimes these units sprang out of necessity. Often they were created to enhance national pride. Great Britain and Germany led the way, creating impressive special forces and elite units, many of which performed with great success.

These special forces units were perfect for difficult and dangerous assignments behind enemy lines. Some elite units, such as the Army Rangers, the Waffen SS, Germany's "Special Troops," and the British commandos, served as valuable propaganda tools as well.

During World War II, special forces units from different services and nations sometimes worked in concert. Along the way they borrowed tactics and swapped trade secrets, evolving them to fit the mission profiles.

In this chapter, you'll find a brief history of the various special forces groups created by the United States military during the World War II.

The 1st Ranger Battalion

After mixed results in the Civil War, the U.S. military didn't deploy Rangers again until World War II. Gen. George C. Marshall, Brig. Gen. Lucian Truscott Jr., and Gen. Dwight D. Eisenhower all admired the capabilities of the British *commando* units in the army and the Royal Navy. With help from the British, they decided to train a new generation of American troops in commando-style tactics.

 Special Ops Jargon

The term **commando** was revived by the British army in 1940 to denote special selected and trained amphibious forces. *Commando,* however, is a word of Portuguese origin, first used in the nineteenth century to describe the military system of the Boer Republics, Britain's adversary in the Boer Wars of Africa. Because the term *commando* was closely associated with the British, General Truscott chose to designate U.S. special forces units as *Rangers* because of the rich history of such groups in America.

America's premier Special Forces unit was the 1st Ranger Battalion, which began training at Carrickfergus, Northern Ireland, in June 1942. Guidelines for recruiting were stringent. Both officers and enlisted men had to demonstrate leadership skills, with an emphasis on individual initiative and common sense. Recruits also had to display better than average skills in self-defense, weaponry, scouting, mountaineering, and even seamanship. Individuals with a working knowledge of mechanics, aviation, demolitions, and engineering; or those who worked on railroad engines, with public utilities, power plants, or radio stations, were actively recruited. Such skills would be required in the highly specialized missions the Rangers would be asked to perform.

Ranger volunteers were trained to scale mountains, to speed-march, to fight in urban settings, and to solve tactical problems. They lived, trained, and worked together in pairs. Each Ranger relied on his "buddy" to watch his back. As training progressed, British commandos used live ammunition to simulate enemy attacks. It wasn't long before these first Rangers became legends. Americans on the home front, hungry for good news about the war, eagerly devoured newspaper accounts about these elite new "glory boys." Soon Hollywood jumped on the bandwagon, turning the factual exploits of Darby's Rangers and Merrill's Marauders into celluloid fable to boost the morale on the home front.

It was during and after World War II that the myth of the special forces trooper as a steely and invulnerable super-soldier began.

Straight Shooting

By the end of hostilities in 1945, there were seven Ranger battalions. The 1st, 3rd, and 4th Battalions fought in North Africa and Italy. The 2nd and 5th went ashore on D-Day. The 6th Ranger Battalion and Merrill's Marauders fought the Japanese in the Pacific.

Operation Torch

The first test of America's Rangers came in November 1942 during Operation Torch, the Allied landings in North Africa. Under the command of Col. William O. Darby, units of the 1st Ranger Battalion came ashore at Arzew, on the Algerian coast, in advance of the main landings.

The Rangers successfully neutralized the enemy's shore defenses and secured the beachhead in advance of the landing force. Because of their quick and decisive action, the Allies maintained the element of surprise during the naval landings, overwhelming and obliterating the defenders.

Darby's Rangers

The 1st Ranger Battalion—now popularly known as "Darby's Rangers"—scored another success in February 1943 when it staged a daring nighttime raid on Italian front-line positions. The Rangers killed 70 enemy soldiers, destroyed an antitank gun, and eliminated several machine gun emplacements. American losses were light: One Ranger killed and twenty wounded.

Under the overall command of Gen. George S. Patton, the Rangers assisted in the attack on Gafsa, Tunisia. They made contact with the enemy, determined the identity and strength of opposing units, and actually entered the town and made contact with the enemy.

FUBARs

Special forces do not fare well when they perform the duties of conventional troops. After the disastrous defeat of American forces at the Kasserine Pass in Tunisia, Rangers were utilized as regular infantry troops. Their casualty rate nearly doubled.

The Pass at Djel Jel Ank

Following their actions at Gafsa, Darby's Rangers were ordered to infiltrate the Italian lines and assault the Djel Jel Ank Pass from the rear, while conventional forces attacked from the front.

Colonel Darby personally carried out a risky daylight reconnaissance of the pass and the surrounding terrain. This action was followed by a series of night reconnaissance patrols. In the end, the Rangers devised a winding, 10-mile trail that led to an unguarded plateau overlooking the Italian positions.

When the attack came, Darby's Rangers overwhelmed the Italians, mopped up stubborn pockets of resistance, and moved forward to take the high ground overlooking the Pass.

The Invasion of Sicily

Although the 1st Ranger Battalion participated in the landings in North Africa and in several campaigns, its first real test came during the invasion of Sicily.

When Patton's 7th Army stormed the beachhead on July 10, 1943, the 1st, 3rd, and 4th Ranger Infantry Battalions were among the lead elements. In hard and sustained fighting, the Rangers captured the town of Gela and held it against a determined counterattack.

Shop Talk
As Rangers approached the town of Porto Empedocle, they ambushed and annihilated an Italian motorized company. The Americans captured so many prisoners that they did not have enough men to guard them. The Rangers were forced to march their prisoners back to the 7th Army's lines.

After that, the Rangers were sent forward to spearhead the assault of Porto Empedocle. The town was heavily defended, and American units moved through areas that were crawling with Italian defenders. On July 18, the Rangers secured Porto Empedocle and moved forward to Messina.

Rangers in Italy

During the invasion of Italy, the Rangers landed west of Salerno, destroyed coastal defenses, and then quick-marched 20 miles and captured the city. By the afternoon of the first day, all their objectives had been met.

The Rangers then moved forward to Chiunzi Pass and attacked the enemy's rear. Casualties were light. But when the invasion got bogged down, the Rangers were ordered to perform regular infantry duties. During these actions, 70 Rangers were killed or injured, again demonstrating that special forces do not fare well when fighting as conventional troops.

Eventually, the Rangers pulled back to integrate replacements and train for the pending amphibious assault at Anzio. Unfortunately, new replacements were not as proficient in the arts of war as the first wave of volunteers. During practice amphibious landings conducted near Naples, these replacements got lost, made too much noise, established themselves in indefensible positions, neglected to post sentries, and failed to scout ahead. Any one of these mistakes could easily result in annihilation in actual combat. Unfortunately, this deterioration in training quality would be repeated during the Vietnam era and would damage the reputation of another special operations unit—the Green Berets.

Anzio and Disaster

For the Rangers fighting in Europe, the glory days ended at Anzio. The 1st, 3rd, and 4th Ranger Infantry Battalions hit the beaches on January 22, 1944. They held their position at the front until January 30, when they were ordered to capture the town of Cisterna di Lattoria.

The 1st and 3rd Battalions moved toward the outskirts of town through a shallow ditch. The units became separated, and then the 3rd became disoriented and moved in the wrong direction for a period of time. Suddenly radio contact between the 1st and 3rd Battalions was interrupted.

Soon the Americans discovered that the Germans had infiltrated the area and occupied the town. The Rangers had been advancing through the middle of the enemy lines all along. Now the Americans were surrounded and the fighting heated up. The Rangers inflicted heavy casualties on the Germans as they fought their way into Cisterna—only to find more Germans and more tanks garrisoned in the town. Some Rangers took cover in the Pantano ditch, where German tanks rolled up to the edge, lowered their guns, and fired into the American ranks. The slaughter was so horrible that the Germans actually dragged some Rangers to safety—only to use them as human shields during their subsequent advance.

Shop Talk
Despite suffering horrendous losses at Cisterna, the Rangers inflicted far more casualties than they took. Less than a thousand Americans fell. German losses were a staggering 5,500, and the Germans were forced to postpone their advance to deal with the Rangers, buying the American Army precious time to regroup.

Meanwhile, the 4th Ranger Battalion began its advance in support of the 1st and 3rd. It was supposed to rescue the advance units, but it ended up going head to head with the Germans. Fighting was furious, and the 4th stalled.

Cut off and surrounded, the 1st and 3rd Battalions were slaughtered. Out of the 800 Rangers who reached Cisterna, only 6 returned. The rest were either killed or captured. The survivors of Cisterna were incorporated into the First Special Services Force (FSSF), a joint American and Canadian Airborne unit. Veterans of this outfit would sow the seeds for the modern Army Special Forces and elite Airborne Rangers to come.

The Birth of the First Special Services Force

The First Special Services Force (FSSF) was a joint venture—a marriage of U.S. and Canadian airborne units created at the insistence of British Prime Minister Winston Churchill. Trained in deep reconnaissance and close combat at Fort William Henry Harrison in Montana beginning in 1942, the brigade was created to take part in the airborne raid into Norway, an operation that was ultimately cancelled.

Special Ops Jargon

Menton Day, December 5, is celebrated by every branch of America's Special Forces. On this date, the First Special Services Force was stood down in the French village of Menton near the close of World War II.

Rerouted to combat operations in Italy and France, the unit came to be known as "the Devil's Brigade" due to the ferocity of its fighting. The Devil's Brigade was a well-honed weapon of battle, often defeating enemy forces much larger than its own. Participating in five grueling European campaigns, by the time the war ended, the FSSF was nearly decimated.

Today, the United States Army Special Forces trace their history back to their roots in the FSSF. Each Special Forces group celebrates that history every December 5—the date on which the original Devil's Brigade was stood down in the French village of *Menton*.

Into the Jungle with America's New Elite

Physically fit American volunteers fighting in the South Pacific—some of them veterans of the Battle for Guadalcanal—along with fresh-faced volunteers from the United States were sent to India for additional training before they were called "Rangers." Under the command of Gen. Frank D. Merrill, they became Merrill's Marauders.

Merrill's Marauders

Compared to the rigorous survival and wilderness training that the guys fighting in the Pacific had to endure, the Rangers in Europe had it easy. What Merrill's Marauders experienced during their training in Burma more resembles the merciless physical tribulations that the Army Special Forces volunteers endure today.

The Marauders were trained far from civilization, deep in the wilderness. Conditions were appalling, but trainees were forced to endure them for at least two months. During that time there were long marches (with full packs), punishing rounds of calisthenics, and other endurance tests.

The Marauders learned long-range penetrations tactics, map reading, advanced weapons and marksmanship skills, forward reconnaissance tactics, and the basics of jungle fighting. Small-unit tactics were stressed. Platoon leaders and noncommissioned officers (NCOs) learned how to direct mortar fire and learned the rudiments of jungle navigation. Rear echelon troops included "kick-out" units, to deliver supplies to Marauders by low-flying aircraft. This was not an easy task! Pilots had to be specially trained for low-level drops in tiny jungle clearings, and the kick-out guys in the back of the plane had to place the goods on target every single time.

> **Shop Talk**
>
> Direct communication with one another and with headquarters was vital to the success of Merrill's Marauders. General Merrill was in constant contact with forward units using long- and short-wave radios. Long-range radios were carried by mule. Small units carried SCR-300 walkie-talkies with a 3- to 5-mile range.

The new volunteers became proficient warriors and capable leaders under this harsh regimen of training. The veterans became even harder and more battle-ready than they were before volunteering for Ranger duty.

Codename: Galahad

In January 1944, the Marauders were sent to Burma. Under the command of Gen. Joseph Stillwell, they were known as the 5307 Composite Unit, code-named Galahad.

Burma was a rugged region of broken hills, tall mountains, and deep, fog-shrouded valleys gouged out by rapidly flowing rivers. The jungle was dense and forbidding. There were no roads, bridges, or even trails. Rivers were filled with leeches, and the jungles teemed with clouds of predatory mosquitoes, mites, and ticks.

As with most jungle climates, there was a dry season and a wet season. But in Burma the dry season was quite humid, and the wet season is better known as the *monsoon* season. During the monsoon rains, valleys are flooded and low-lying areas are swamped. Hillsides and mountain paths become muddy slopes. Everywhere men and mules became mired in knee-deep muck.

Despite this inhospitable terrain, Galahad earned a reputation for rapid movement through seemingly impassible wilderness. Its reconnaissance platoon could be relied upon to provide accurate and on-the-spot information from as far away as 7 miles in advance of the main force.

The men of Galahad cut Japanese supply lines, blocked trails, harassed the enemy, and gathered intelligence. They operated with many Allied forces, including native guerrilla fighters, and Chinese troops. They developed many innovative tactics while fighting in

Burma. In an era before helicopters, they succeeded in extracting their wounded by air. Light aircraft piloted by specially trained aviators made hazardous landings on makeshift runways, including dry riverbeds, jungle clearings, and rice paddies, to pick up Galahad's casualties and deliver them to aid stations dozens of miles away.

Galahad had many successes. In one lightning-fast, daylight attack, the men captured Myitkyina airfield, striking before the Japanese knew they were there. Galahad also suffered costly defeats. During operations with the Chinese, a Galahad unit was trapped at Nhpum Ga, and many died from combat wounds, disease, and malnutrition.

The rigors of climate and combat eventually took their toll. Within a few months, the original 3,000 Marauders had shrunk to a force of less than a thousand. Most of the casualties came from disease or exhaustion. Hunger—especially with units trapped at Nhpum Ga—also took a heavy toll on Galahad's combat readiness.

Unfortunately, Galahad units were in demand, and General Stillwell did not have much sympathy for their plight. General Merrill tried to intervene on his men's behalf, but he was in poor health with an ailing heart and had to be evacuated himself.

Straight Shooting

While elements of Galahad were trapped at Nhpum Ga, food became scarce. Chocolate bars were divided in elaborate rituals watched by all. Chocolate was served with dry, stale, moldy biscuits. Hungry Galahad members swore that if chewed together, this "feast" tasted just like chocolate cake!

General Stillwell demanded constant action from Galahad despite the fact that these units were under-strength and on the point of exhaustion. It got so bad that Stillwell ordered hospitalized members of Galahad back to the front. Soon the entire unit suffered from morale problems. Most suffered from malaria and chronic psychological complaints. Finally the men of Galahad mutinied. After their brutal stint in Burma, those serving in Galahad units were evaluated by their commanders. Most were declared unfit for further service and were sent home.

Guerrilla Fighters of the Pacific

Several "independent" units were created by forward-thinking officers in the U.S. military during World War II. Most of these units performed what we now call "special operations."

In the Pacific theater, Lieut. Gen. Walter Krueger established a small elite unit called the Alamo Scouts, in honor of the general's home town of San Antonio. Never exceeding 60 or 70 in number, the Scouts earned 44 Silver Stars and 33 Bronze Stars by the end of the war. Although they performed nearly a hundred missions, the Alamo Scouts never lost a man in action.

A number of U.S. Army officers conducted guerrilla campaigns against the Japanese in the Philippines. One of the most famous was Col. Russell Volckman. During the war, Volckman eluded capture to form a Filipino guerrilla band in Luzon. By 1945, when the war ended, his force consisted of five regiments.

Maj. Windell Fertig, a U.S. Army reservist, raised his own guerrilla force from scratch in the Philippines. By the end of hostilities, his army of irregulars numbered over 20,000 men bearing nearly 40,000 small arms.

After World War II the Ranger units serving in Europe and the Pacific were disbanded. Though quite successful in operations for which they were trained, Rangers often failed to perform when overused or when dispatched to perform combat tasks for which they were not trained or equipped. When used in place of conventional troops, special forces lose much of what makes them "special"—speed, surprise, and mobility, to name a few. Fighting side by side with conventional troops, special forces unit losses increased three to five times.

> **Shop Talk**
>
> In what was to be the unit's greatest accomplishment, Lieut. Gen. Krueger's Alamo Scouts led U.S. Rangers and Filipino guerrillas in an attack on the Japanese prison camp at Cabantuan, liberating over 500 Allied prisoners of war.

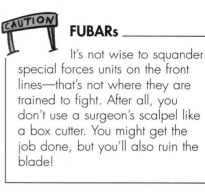

FUBARs

It's not wise to squander special forces units on the front lines—that's not where they are trained to fight. After all, you don't use a surgeon's scalpel like a box cutter. You might get the job done, but you'll also ruin the blade!

In the cycle of buildup and teardown that proceeded and followed every American war, the Rangers and other units like them were considered expendable. In the next war, the American military would pay for this lack of foresight.

Underwater Units and Amphibious Invasions

The technological advances of the 1920s and 1930s led to the emergence of many new weapons systems in World War II. One of those innovations was scuba-diving gear. Through the use of an air tank and a diving mask, a swimmer could remain underwater—and undetected—for up to an hour.

The invention of *scuba* gear led to the creation of two types of special forces—the underwater commando and the manned torpedo operator.

Italian Underwater Demolition Units

It was the Italian navy in World War II that pioneered the use of underwater commandos. The *Decima Flottiglia Mas* (10th Light Flotilla) was a combat swimming unit that specialized in the use of explosives, motor boats, manned torpedoes, and limpet mines. Transported close to an enemy port by small boat or submarine, these Italian underwater commandos would swim to an enemy vessel, plant explosives on its hull, and make their escape undetected.

Shop Talk
The Italian navy also pioneered the use of underwater motorcycles—two-man miniature submarines operated by scuba divers. These subs were called *Maielli* ("pigs"). Using Maielli, the Italians sank two British battleships moored at Alexandria harbor. The British Royal Navy tested an underwater vehicle of its own, called the Chariot.

Italian operations were particularly successful near the port of Gibraltar. An Italian merchant vessel interned at the Spanish dock across the Bay of Algeciras, and a luxurious hillside villa were secretly transformed into underwater commando staging areas. Scuba teams entered the water through a hidden airlock at the bottom of the merchant ship, swam across to the British side of the bay, and planted mines on the hulls of warships.

Italian divers were also effective at Alexandria, where underwater commandos severely damaged two British battleships and gave the Italian navy local superiority for a time. Unfortunately, because the British vessels sank on an even keel, Italian air reconnaissance photographs did not detect that they were disabled, and the Italians never exploited this tactical advantage. Sometimes the Italian divers timed their explosives to detonate when the ships were far out to sea, further confounding the British. The existence of these secret staging areas were not revealed until Italian fascism was stamped out and Italy joined the Allies.

"Scuba-Do" U.S. Naval Combat Demolition Units

While the Army experimented with elite forces, the U.S. Navy created a special operations force of its own. Although the Navy began to experiment with underwater teams in 1942, these units did not appear in combat until much later in the war.

Special Ops Jargon

The word **scuba** is really an acronym for self-contained underwater breathing apparatus.

In May 1942, the Naval Combat Demolition Unit (NCDU) was formed at Fort Pierce, Florida. Snatching volunteers from Naval Construction Battalions (because of their engineering and demolitions skills) and the Navy/Marine Corps Scouts and Raiders (for their reconnaissance and combat abilities), the men came into the program with lots of swim experience and plenty of physical stamina.

Most volunteers in the NCDUs came to the unit possessing nautical and navigation skills. Some had been commercial divers or professional salvage workers before the war. Others were just passable swimmers but were *very* good with explosives, or they possessed special engineering skills required in the mission profile.

For NCDU volunteers, class never ended. The training was 24 × 7 and full of surprises. They trained on the beaches, in the ocean, and in the swamps of Florida. They worked among the alligators and mosquitoes, sometimes neck-deep in murky water.

Unlike the Italian and British underwater commandos (and despite the name), U.S. NCDUs were not used for combat. They were trained for forward reconnaissance and demolitions work against enemy shore defenses.

The first NCDUs were trained to support large-scale, long-range Marine Corps amphibious operations against the Japanese-held islands of the Pacific. Tragically, they were not deployed soon enough to prevent a disaster.

> **Shop Talk**
>
> If someone had told NCDU volunteers that they were part of an elite unit, they would have chuckled. Yet their training was deliberately intense, and the stress level was high. Their brutal regimen resembled the rigorous curriculum of today's Navy SEALs.

The Disaster at "Bloody Tarawa"

Guadalcanal, the first amphibious landing by the Marine Corps in the Pacific, was easy compared to later combat landings. There was no Japanese resistance on the beaches. The Marines simply walked ashore. The tough fighting came later, in the jungles around the hotly contended airfield and on Bloody Ridge. Unfortunately, Guadalcanal gave the Americans the false hope that future amphibious landings would be just as easy.

The Navy and the Marine Corps didn't have much time to plan for the invasion of Tarawa. They also lacked resources to dispatch reconnaissance units to explore the barrier reefs, beaches, and enemy defenses prior to the attack. Tragically, the Marines would pay for this mistake in blood.

On D-Day, November 10, 1943, as Marine Corps amphibious troop carriers—the "Alligators" and "Buffaloes"—attempted to land on the beaches, they got tangled up on the reefs surrounding the island. The Marines were forced to debark into heavy machine-gun fire. As they struggled across the reef to the beach, hundreds were gunned down. Advancing across the sandy beaches, Marines stumbled into mine fields or were cut to pieces by Japanese machine guns that they didn't know were there.

Not all of the casualties at Tarawa were caused by enemy action. Some Marines plunged through holes in the reef, to drown under the weight of their equipment. Landing boats were sunk by antiship artillery as they fruitlessly searched for a channel through the barrier reef that practically surrounded Tarawa.

Straight Shooting

Ironically, advance reconnaissance of Tarawa wouldn't have changed history. The high tide that was supposed to float the Marines over the reefs never arrived that day. A rare lunar phenomena called an apogean neap tide prevented it. This phenomena occurred only twice in 1943—one of those times was the day of the Marine Corps' amphibious landings.

After the disaster at Tarawa came the realization that amphibious landings in the Pacific were risky business and that better reconnaissance and advance preparations were required if they were to succeed. Both the Navy and the Marine Corps concluded that good reconnaissance could have prevented some of the mistakes that were made at Tarawa and would have saved many lives.

NCDUs were used in future amphibious operations to counter four hazards to the landing force: enemy defensive fortifications on shore, enemy-built obstacles such as concrete blocks and ironworks placed in the water, natural obstacles such as coral reefs, and the time, depth, and range of the local tides.

As with all special forces, teams were organized in small units, with six enlisted men and one officer per Navy Combat Demolition Team (NCDTs). Ironically, their first action came on June 6, 1944, not in the Pacific, but on the coast of France.

The Longest Day

The Naval Combat Demolition Teams were among the first American troops to hit the beaches at Normandy. They provided advance reconnaissance and cleared German-made obstacles along the French coast.

FUBARs

In the chaos of D-Day, many soldiers in the first wave took shelter behind obstacles that had been wired to blow by demolition teams. Some were detonated anyway, killing Americans. Others were spared destruction because they were surrounded by friendly troops. These unharmed obstacles often delayed the follow-up landings.

In the predawn hours before the invasion, NCDTs swam to the Normandy beaches through chilly water to place their explosive charges. By dawn, as the invasion fleet approached Fortress Europe, many of the obstacles still had not been cleared. But now the Germans could see the demolition teams at work and began picking them off.

Losses were enormous. Forty percent of all NCDT members did not survive D-Day. At Utah Beach, one in three perished. At Omaha Beach, one in three *survived*.

After the success of NCDTs in Europe, this strategy was adopted for the island-hopping campaigns of the Pacific. There the units were called Underwater Demolition Teams (UDTs), and they played a vital role in future Navy and Marine Corps operations.

The Frogs of War

The UDTs were the brainchild of Lieut. Comm. Draper L. Kaufman, who organized the first teams in 1943. The first UDTs were tested in the invasion of Sicily in July 1943 and at Normandy. But after the tragedy at Tarawa, they were rushed to the Pacific Theater. UDTs were organized in platoons, with 3 officers and 15 enlisted men.

In the assault on Kwajalein, UDTs without scuba gear braved the cold; the dark, deadly riptides; and the enemy to clear the sea lanes of mines and man-made obstacles. Before the invasion of Guam, UDTs cleared away antiboat mines and underwater obstacles. At Peleliu, UDTs did a better job of softening up the beach for the Marine landings than the U.S. Navy's ineffectual bombardment of the island. During the fight for Okinawa, UDT swimmers brought food, ammunition, and supplies to the Marines who captured the town of Nago.

> ### Shop Talk
>
> "Welcome Marines" read the sign left behind by UDTs who cleared the sea lanes for the amphibious invasion of Guam. The message faced seaward along the reef, where only the oncoming American troops could see it.

Near the end of World War II, the UDTs began to practice for their toughest job yet—clearing the mines, obstacles, and shore defenses for Operation Olympic, the invasion of the Japanese Home Islands.

When the war ended, the UDTs, like the Ranger units, were disbanded. American military planners believed that the era of amphibious operations was over. Why storm a fortified beachhead and capture an occupied island when a single atomic bomb could destroy the entire land mass and everything on it?

Of course, such thinking is always short-sighted. In this case, a major amphibious invasion would be mounted again, much sooner than anyone expected!

On to Korea

After the communist North Koreans invaded the marginally democratic south in the summer of 1950, the United Nations forces sent to rescue the Korean people found themselves on the ropes. Pushed into a shrinking perimeter on the southern tip of the Korean Peninsula, and surrounded by the enemy, the Allies faced a disastrous, Dunkirk-style evacuation unless they were somehow saved from annihilation.

U.S. Army Gen. Douglas MacArthur devised a brilliant end-run operation to flank the North Korean army and cut off its escape route. The plan called for a Marine Corps amphibious invasion of the port city of Inchon, near the occupied capital of South Korea, Seoul.

Straight Shooting

The tides posed the biggest problem at Inchon. High tide came twice a day, so the invasion had to be divided. The first wave neutralized the enemy defenses at Wolmi-Do. Twelve hours later, the second wave came in with the next tide to attack the city.

Inchon was difficult to take. The approach from the Yellow Sea required 13 miles of precision navigation through the narrow and hazardous Flying Fish Channel. Once through the strait, the port itself was surrounded by shallows and mudflats that could easily strand an amphibious landing craft.

The Navy's UDTs performed spectacularly at Inchon. They provided detailed information about the tides, the docks, and the enemy defenses on the docks and on the island of Wolmi-Do that guarded the mouth of the harbor.

After the successful invasion at Inchon, the UDTs remained active. They destroyed bridges and tunnels, and they sabotaged railway lines far from the beaches. This dual role demonstrated the units' flexibility, and the concept and role of underwater demolition teams soon was expanded.

In 1962, the UDTs began to be replaced by a brand-new, highly trained, elite special force called the Naval Special Warfare units, better known today as the Navy SEALs.

The Least You Need to Know

- The seeds of America's modern special forces groups were sown in World War II.
- The U.S. Army Rangers were America's premier special forces unit, and they fought with distinction in Africa and Italy.
- The U.S. Navy's Underwater Demolition Teams of World War II paved the way for major Allied amphibious invasions.
- The U.S. Navy's Underwater Demolition Teams were the forerunners of the modern Navy SEALs.

Covert Operations in World War II

In This Chapter

- ◆ Special operator: Lieut. Col. Earl Ellis, USMC
- ◆ "Wild Bill" Donovan, America's spy
- ◆ America's secret agents: the Office of Strategic Services
- ◆ The birth of the Central Intelligence Agency

So far, I've discussed the origin of the combat component of the modern special forces as they took shape during World War I. However, combat proficiency, though necessary, is only one aspect of modern special warfare operations.

To get a complete picture, you have to look at the history of U.S. espionage and covert activities during war and peace—another important aspect of America's unconventional warfare activity today.

Tough as they are, U.S. Army Special Forces personnel are not mere super-soldiers. That's because they do a lot more than just fight. Today's Special Forces are also required to perform the duties of spies, counterinsurgents, and covert operatives. They must be able to speak at least one language other than their own (and most speak more than one) and possess a working knowledge of many diverse cultures and societies. They must be educated and well versed in current events, and they must be a good judge of the character, strengths, and weaknesses of others.

That means that members of the Special Forces must possess leadership skills, interpersonal skills, and a certain amount of entrepreneurial spirit. Although these qualities are not easily defined, a few years in the military tend to reveal those individuals who possess them.

Because their duties are so varied, the men of the Special Forces must be well versed in intelligence gathering, covert operations, antiterrorism, counterinsurgency, unconventional warfare (more on that later), and combat search and rescue. They may be asked to assume the role of counternarcotics agents or to provide humanitarian assistance. In the past, American special forces groups have performed countermine activities, peacekeeping, security, psychological operations, and direct action (a euphemism for combat raids).

Both soldiers and spies, the men of the Army Special Forces must be, by definition, the master of many skills. But when were these skills "married"? And who performed the "ceremony"? In this chapter, I'll explore the origins of America's espionage community, and how the evolution of the Central Intelligence Agency from its roots in the Office of Strategic Services impacted the development of the U.S. Army Special Forces.

Lieut. Col. Pete Ellis and Operation Plan 712

Before World War II, intelligence gathering and covert operations (spying) were left to the principal arms of U.S. foreign policy: the State Department and the various intelligence branches of America's armed services. Attachés and diplomats based in foreign nations collected intelligence and passed it along to their superiors in Washington. Businessmen and academics living and working in foreign countries sometimes provided information.

Shop Talk

In 1921, Lieutenant Colonel Ellis published a study titled *Advanced Base Operations in Micronesia, 1921*. Adopted by the Marine Corps as Operation Plan 712, this document not only predicted the coming Pacific war, but it also detailed the strategies and tactics that would be employed by the United States to defeat Japan.

At times, military personnel based in or visiting foreign lands observed enemy or potential enemy activity and reported what they saw to their superior officers. One of the most influential military practitioners of this pseudo-espionage activity was Lieut. Col. Earl "Pete" Ellis of the U.S. Marine Corps. Ellis first saw combat in France during World War I, where he earned a Distinguished Service Cross and caught the eye of the Commandant of the Marine Corps, Gen. John Lejeune.

Lieutenant Colonel Ellis was a tactical genius and something of a visionary. He sensed that Japan would soon clash with American interests in the Pacific, and he planned accordingly. Ellis learned to read and write

Japanese after World War I, and he studied American and Japanese deployment in the Pacific region. Ellis prophesized in 1921 that America would fight a war in the Pacific against the Japanese, a war that did not erupt until two decades later, in 1941.

Pete Ellis, Spy!

In 1921, Ellis took a "leave of absence" from the Marine Corps to travel through the Pacific Rim and observe Japanese activities in the region. Disguised as a commercial traveler, Ellis mingled with European and American businessmen, prowled around Japanese military installations, and observed their military maneuvers. The Japanese authorities suspected that Ellis was spying but could not prove it. Police and military officers in civilian clothes shadowed his every move and made it very difficult for him to make reports to his superiors. Little is known of the full extent of Lieutenant Colonel Ellis's activities, but one thing is certain: In 1922, Ellis was hospitalized in Yokohama for "acute alcohol poisoning."

Ellis (who was always on active duty, never on leave) was ordered home by his commanding officer but decided to complete his mission by penetrating several Japanese-controlled islands to study their defenses. He literally walked out of the Yokohama Naval Hospital on the night of October 6 and vanished. Weeks later, Ellis turned up in the Marshall Islands, where he boarded a Japanese commercial ship bound for the island of Koror in the Palaus. There he lived with a native girl, drank heavily, prowled around Japanese military installations, and was followed closely by undercover Japanese officials.

The Mysterious Death of Lieutenant Colonel Ellis

One morning in 1922, while in Japanese territory, Ellis went "crazy drunk," according to a Koror native who knew him. By that afternoon, Lieut. Col. Earl "Pete" Ellis was dead. The official cause of death was listed by Japanese authorities as "acute alcohol poisoning." Today most believe that Ellis was murdered—probably poisoned—by his reluctant Japanese "hosts."

Whatever the truth of his end is, Lieutenant Colonel Ellis made a difference. Without formal training in covert operations or espionage, this heroic Marine Corps officer managed to observe the military activities of a potential adversary, warn his government of the danger, and propose a strategy to counter the enemy's aggression. Not bad for an amateur! Despite his alcohol problem (which may have been part of Ellis's cover—after all, who suspects a drunk of espionage?), he possessed many of the skills and traits required by U.S. Special Forces units today.

"Wild Bill" Donovan, Coordinator of Information

Unfortunately, visionary thinkers such as Lieutenant Colonel Ellis were few and far between. But as the threat of war loomed in the 1930s, the armed services of the United States needed visionaries more than ever. America's meager intelligence communities, which included the Office of Naval Intelligence (ONI) and the War Department's Military Intelligence Division (better known as G-2) were primitive, bureaucratized, overextended, and understaffed.

Vital information—sometimes gathered at great monetary or personal cost—was seldom passed along in a timely fashion to those with the "need to know." Only the White House staff attempted to collate and access the information acquired by these other agencies because little information was shared across departmental lines or among the separate branches of the armed services. President Franklin Delano Roosevelt knew that something more would be required if America was forced into the war.

In the spring of 1941, Roosevelt created a brand-new organization to coordinate the various governmental and military intelligence arms. On July 11, 1941, FDR appointed New York lawyer William J. Donovan as the nation's first Coordinator of Information (COI), a new civilian office attached to the White House.

Straight Shooting

In 1941, FDR created the office of Coordinator of Information (COI) to "collect and analyze all information and data, which may bear upon national security ... and to make such information and data available to the President." Today the Central Intelligence Agency (CIA), the National Reconnaissance Office, the Defense Intelligence Agency, and the National Security Agency (NSA) fulfill this function.

Donovan was born in Buffalo, New York, on January 1, 1883. He earned a law degree from Columbia University and, during World War I, joined the U.S. Army's 165th Infantry Division (also known as "The Fighting 69th" from its glory days in the American Civil War). During the Meuse-Argonne Offensive, Donovan earned the Medal of Honor as a battalion commander. Donovan's official Medal of Honor citation states that the young lieutenant colonel "personally led the assaulting wave in an attack upon a very strongly organized position .... When he was wounded in the leg by machine-gun bullets, he refused to be evacuated and continued with his unit."

After the war, Donovan traveled through Europe and visited Siberia and Japan, and he served as the assistant attorney general in Calvin Coolidge's administration, where he supervised a young J. Edgar Hoover and his new Federal Bureau of Investigation (FBI). A staunch Republican, Donovan lost the 1932 election for Governor of New York and became a private citizen. As the first COI, Donovan inherited the espionage arms of the ONI and the G-2. More important, Donovan was given the authority to utilize *unvouchered funds* from the president's emergency budget. Donovan's signature was all that was required to access this funding.

Wild Bill Donovan energetically went about recruiting what he regarded as America's "best and brightest"—citizens who traveled abroad or who studied world affairs at Ivy League universities such as Harvard, Yale, and Princeton. He also tapped a large pool of business leaders, academics, and lawyers to fill the ranks of this new organization.

By the autumn of 1941, Donovan's COI was submitting its first intelligence reports to the president. These reports were focused on Nazi activity in Europe—Donovan still didn't have the resources or expertise needed to gather intelligence on Japanese activities. Two months later, the Japanese attacked Pearl Harbor, and America entered World War II.

> **Special Ops Jargon**
> **Unvouchered funds** are vital for clandestine operations. Money granted by Congress and spent at the personal responsibility of the president, these funds are not audited in detail. Unvouchered funds and the espionage authority granted to Wild Bill Donovan paved the way for the creation of today's Central Intelligence Agency (CIA).

The Office of Strategic Services

On June 13, 1942, the COI became the Office of Strategic Services (OSS). Under the leadership of Wild Bill Donovan, the OSS would go on to coordinate intelligence gathering and clandestine operations for the rest of the war.

Mirroring the rivalries that plagued special operations through the 1980s, the Department of State and the various military intelligence agencies banned the OSS from acquiring intercepted radio traffic between the Axis powers. Without translated intercepts from Germany (code-named MAGIC) or Japan (code-named ULTRA), the operations of the OSS were hamstrung in the early part of the war. Adding insult to injury, the FBI, the G-2, and the ONI made sure that the OSS could not operate domestically to root out enemy spies and saboteurs.

When Donovan could not get support from his own countrymen, he turned to the British. Although British intelligence initially distrusted the Americans, it also envied the rich resources available to the OSS. In time, the two intelligence agencies learned to work together quite effectively.

> **FUBARs**
> Although the OSS learned much from its dealings with British intelligence, the Brits inside the intelligence community considered Americans interlopers and treated them like junior partners for much of the war. The OSS was even denied a role in the covert operations in France before the D-Day landings in Normandy.

As another response to the bureaucratic hostility that the OSS faced, Donovan created the X-2 branch. The X-2 managed clandestine operations abroad, and Wild Bill sent his operatives to every theater of war, beginning with North Africa. By the middle of 1942, the OSS had established intelligence-gathering networks in several North African ports. Working covertly, OSS operatives acquired vital information that was important to the success of Operation Torch, the Allied landings in North Africa in November 1942.

Operation Torch brought the OSS widespread bureaucratic and military acceptance in the European theater and in Washington. However, Douglas MacArthur in the South Pacific and Adm. Chester Nimitz in the Central Pacific, stubbornly resisted OSS incursion into their territories. Despite this resistance, the OSS began to fashion worldwide clandestine and intelligence-gathering capabilities, and its power and prestige grew. By 1944 the OSS employed 13,000 men and women—about the same as an Army infantry division. Two thirds came from the Army, civilians made up another quarter, and the rest were from the Navy, Marines, and Coast Guard. Over 7,500 OSS employees, including 900 women, served overseas.

Behind Enemy Lines with the Special Operations Branch

The Special Operations Branch of the OSS organized and ran guerrilla campaigns in Europe and Asia. Working in conjunction with the British Special Operations Executive (SOE), the Special Operations Branch (or SO—the B was dropped for obvious reasons) created the legendary Jedburgh Teams.

> **Shop Talk**
>
> Perhaps the most famous SO operative was Virginia Hall, an American woman who helped organize partisan activity in German-occupied France under the code name Diane. Born of wealthy parents in Baltimore, Hall was awarded the Distinguished Service Cross— the only one presented to a civilian woman in World War II.

The Jedburgh Teams were a select special warfare unit of about 300 volunteers from Britain, France, and America. They parachuted into France in small, three-man teams to train and arm partisan resistance fighters. Between Operation Overlord (D-Day) and VE Day, the Jedburghs mounted over a hundred missions in the European Theater. Some members of the Jedburghs were dispatched to Burma to continue their activities against the Japanese after hostilities in Europe ended. Jedburgh Teams airdropped into occupied Europe were comprised of two officers and an enlisted radio man. The senior officer was British, the second was an American, and the enlisted man was a member of the Free French Forces loyal to General Charles de Gaulle.

Jedburgh Teams were trained at Milton Hall in the English countryside. The force was comprised of French patriots who escaped the Occupation, soldiers of fortune, adventurers, and enlisted men. Other members of the Jedburgh Teams were future business and political leaders from America and Britain.

When their training was completed, the teams were parachuted into France and, hopefully, into the waiting arms of the French Resistance. At its peak, there were 93 Jedburgh Teams operating in Europe.

At Milton Hall, officers trained alongside enlisted men, and Americans and British trained alongside French, Belgian, and Canadian volunteers to create camaraderie. Once on the ground, rank would become secondary to knowledge, ability, leadership skills, and raw courage. It is with these Jedburgh Teams that we find the origin of today's small-unit Army Special Forces Operational Detachment Teams (ODTs).

> **Shop Talk**
>
> Accomplished former members of Jedburgh Teams include author Stewart Alsop and the late William Colby, former Director of the Central Intelligence Agency.

In France, Jedburgh Teams coordinated arms and supply airdrops, trained and guided partisans on hit-and-run attacks and sabotage, and assisted the advancing Allied armies.

Walking a Political Minefield in the Pacific

Except for the activities of Detachment 101 (discussed shortly), the OSS was kept out of the Pacific Theater because U.S. Army Gen. Douglas MacArthur and U.S. Navy Adm. Chester Nimitz wanted it that way. By the last year of the war, the OSS had made significant inroads into Asia, far from the territories controlled by MacArthur or Nimitz. However, to operate in the remote China-Burma-India theater, the OSS still had to negotiate a hazardous political minefield.

The Nationalist Chinese (NC) regime in Chungking, America's ally in the Pacific, was a government in name only. Led by Gen. Chiang Kai-shek, the NC was fighting a war on two fronts—one against the Japanese, the other against the communists led by Mao Zedong.

Chiang Kai-shek's intelligence chief, Tai Li, tried to keep the OSS out. Even more daunting for the OSS was the fact that a half dozen other intelligence units were operating in China. They didn't want the Americans around, either. Nevertheless, in 1943, Bill Donovan personally informed Tai Li that the OSS was on Chinese soil, whether he liked it or not. By the end of the war, the OSS was among the most effective covert organizations active in the region.

 **Straight Shooting**

OSS operatives in China provided vital targeting information to Claire Chennault's legendary Flying Tigers through an Air and Ground Forces Resources Technical Staff.

In August 1945, OSS Maj. Paul Cyr and a team of Chinese guerrillas, dubbed Team Hound, accomplished the impossible when they infiltrated Japanese-occupied territory to destroy a railroad bridge that spanned the Yellow River near Kaifeng. The bridge was blown up just as a Japanese troop train was crossing it, causing maximum damage to enemy forces. Unfortunately, this action is virtually forgotten today because it occurred on August 9, 1945, the same day that the second atomic bomb was dropped on Nagasaki.

The OSS also operated out of Thailand—despite the fact that the Thai government had declared war against the United States after Pearl Harbor. Washington simply ignored the declaration of war because many members of the Thai ruling elite were secretly opposed to the Japanese.

> **FUBARs**
>
> OSS Col. Peter Dewey, stationed in Saigon, became the first American killed in Indochina when his vehicle was ambushed by Communist guerrillas in September 1945.

Ironically, the OSS operating in Indochina actually assisted communist leader Ho Chi Minh in his struggle against the Japanese. Twenty years later, the OSS had evolved into the Central Intelligence Agency, which actively opposed Ho Chi Minh's guerrillas during the Vietnam War.

In the Jungles of Burma with Detachment 101

OSS operations in Burma during World War II more closely paralleled our modern concept of a special forces operation. Detachment 101 was established in Japanese-occupied Burma to provide strategic support to more traditional combat operations in the Pacific Theater. With fewer than 120 volunteers, Col. Carl Eifer's Detachment 101 managed to recruit and train 11,000 native Kachin tribesmen to fight the Japanese in less than a year.

> **Straight Shooting**
>
> Detachment 101 received the Presidential Distinguished Unit Citation for its service during the 1945 campaign to liberate Rangoon.

When the Allies invaded Burma in 1944, Detachment 101 teams scouted ahead of the regular army, gathering intelligence, sabotaging Japanese installations, rescuing downed Allied pilots, and destroying isolated Japanese bases.

Changing Attitudes: The Morale Operations Branch

One of the earliest examples of psychological operations (psyops) came out of the Morale Operations Branch (MO) of the OSS. The MO created "black" propaganda—that is, propaganda that appeared to originate from Germans or Japanese citizens disgusted with the war or their impending defeat at the hands of the Allies. Its purpose was to demoralize Axis military personnel and inflame civilian resistance to their repressive governments.

MO operatives spread rumors about Adolf Hitler's health or sanity and the incompetence of the leaders of the Third Reich. They distributed subversive leaflets and posters, created fake German newspapers and radio broadcasts, and produced anti-Nazi slogans and stickers.

By the end of World War II, the Morale Operations Branch had proved the value of psychological warfare to America's military and political leaders.

> **Shop Talk**
>
> A series of fake radio broadcasts supposedly coming out of Nazi Germany (but created by the MO) featured the now-famous rendition of the song "Lilli Marlene," sung by Hollywood star Marlene Dietrich.

Super-Secret Clearance: X-2

The best intelligence of World War II came from the intercepted and deciphered Axis messages. But the OSS was denied access to MAGIC and ULTRA by the U.S. Joint Chiefs. The British were willing to provide the OSS with some intelligence, but only if the Americans adopted the stringent security measures practiced by the Brits. The result was X-2, an elite force within OSS.

Headed by attorney James Murphy, X-2 operatives filtered information to the Special Operations Branch, but only when they deemed it safe to do so. X-2 held the ultimate power within the OSS. Operatives could deny information or veto an operation without explanation. Needless to say, this ultimate authority frustrated and angered some OSS field operatives, but it also attracted some of the best and the brightest that the OSS had to offer into the ranks of X-2.

Traitors and Double Agents

The FBI and the G-2 had long suspected that Donovan's maverick agency could not be trusted. In fact, the OSS office in Washington, D.C., was practically riddled with spies and double agents. These were not agents spying for the Axis powers, but they were highly educated Americans who were willing to funnel information to the Soviet Union. Although the Soviets were technically America's ally, American sympathizers to the communist cause were rightly regarded as traitors. Yet the OSS employed some operatives precisely because they were communists. Donovan needed their help in dealing with European partisans and was willing to overlook their leftist tendencies. The FBI and the G-2,

> **CAUTION**
>
> **FUBARs**
>
> Some OSS operatives who were not communists or even sympathizers funneled classified information to Moscow for their own personal reasons, giving credence to critics of Donovan's outfit who believed that the OSS was made up of a bunch of maverick oddballs.

however, were not so inclined. The situation was even worse in Asia, where OSS operations were penetrated by Chinese communist agents working as clerical staff at training camps or even as cooks and housekeepers.

Because Bill Donovan had to build his organization from scratch, he was forced to cut corners. Sometimes he neglected to run security clearances for members of his staff. In the end, this misguided policy sullied the reputation of the OSS and was perhaps its greatest failure.

Allen W. Dulles and the Secret Intelligence Branch

William Donovan never intended his organization to run espionage operations in foreign countries. He wanted the OSS to gather information and support military operations in the field through the dissemination of intelligence and propaganda. But with access to MAGIC and ULTRA all but denied to him, it didn't take Wild Bill long to find a way to gather intelligence on his own. In 1942, the OSS established the Secret Intelligence Branch (SI), a branch of the organization created to open field stations, train case officers, run agent operations, and process intelligence reports—in other words, to spy.

> **Straight Shooting**
>
> Switzerland, a neutral country open to travelers from all nations, was the ideal location for the Secret Intelligence Branch to set up shop. On the door-steps of France, Austria, and Germany, Switzerland became a focal point for espionage activities in Europe.

In November 1942, Allen W. Dulles came to the American Legation in Bern, Switzerland, to establish the first active SI branch in Europe. Dulles was destined for government service at an early age. The nephew of one Secretary of State and the grandson of another, he joined the Foreign Service during World War I, fresh out of Princeton. When the war ended, Dulles attended the Paris peace talks at Versailles, followed by more diplomatic postings in Berlin and Constantinople. He also headed the State Department's Division of Near Eastern Affairs before resigning from government service in 1926 to practice law in New York.

As a junior diplomat, Dulles was involved in prewar espionage activity in Vienna. After America joined the war, Dulles worked briefly as the head of COI's New York Office. He interviewed refugees fleeing the Axis powers and also spoke with American businessmen, journalists, and government bureaucrats with ties to Germany and Italy. In late 1942, Dulles was dispatched to Bern to oversee espionage operations for secret intelligence in Europe.

Allen Dulles was the perfect man to head SI operations. Long a foe of Adolph Hitler, Dulles persuaded his law firm to close its Berlin office in 1935, after the Nazis took power. He had many connections in Europe and worked well with America's allies.

In Switzerland, Dulles tried to reassemble what was left of the French military intelligence service after the fall of France. These former covert agents provided the SI with intelligence about German deployments inside occupied France. German citizens opposed to Hitler also brought him information, and soon Dulles had a vast network of German émigrés, resistance fighters, anti-Nazi intellectuals, and intelligence officers to provide him with information.

During the war, Dulles provided Washington with information about the development of the German V-1 and V-2 rockets. He assisted the British efforts to uncover the German spy Cicero, who did much damage to the Allied cause before being revealed. By the end of World War II, Dulles was so connected with covert, anti-Nazi activities in Germany that the plotters who tried to assassinate Hitler on July 20, 1944, provided him with regular reports on their progress.

By 1945, agents of the SI actually penetrated Nazi Germany and eluded the Gestapo. Some of these agents were former German prisoners of war, convinced to switch sides by William J. Casey, future head of the CIA. Two hundred of these turncoat agents were dropped into Nazi Germany to gather intelligence about German industrial capabilities and potential Allied bombing targets.

In the spring of 1945, as the Third Reich was tottering, Allen Dulles pulled off the espionage feat of the war. Although an "unconditional surrender" policy was in force, Dulles secretly met with SS Gen. Karl Wolff, who offered to broker the surrender of all German military forces still fighting in Italy. Negotiating with members of the Nazi high command was risky. Washington subscribed to the Allies' "unconditional surrender" policy, Gen. Dwight D. Eisenhower hated all Germans, and Josef Stalin would have pulled Russia out of the war if he had learned that American or British diplomats were "sleeping with the enemy." Yet this operation, called Sunrise, ultimately succeeded, resulting in an early end to the Italian campaign. Through his tireless efforts, Dulles saved thousands of American, British, Italian, and German lives.

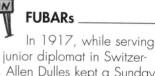

FUBARs

In 1917, while serving as a junior diplomat in Switzerland, Allen Dulles kept a Sunday morning tennis date with a beautiful woman—and lost his only chance to meet with a Russian revolutionary named Lenin. After that mistake, Dulles vowed that he would never throw away such an opportunity again!

Straight Shooting

German prisoners of war were "turned" by agents of the OSS Morale Operations Branch. They were trained in espionage; provided with documentation, clothing, and equipment; and parachuted into the Third Reich. Although 36 of them were killed or captured, these turncoat agents collected invaluable data that helped shorten the war.

Pack Up and Get Out!

Victory in Europe and the untimely death of President Franklin Delano Roosevelt dealt twin blows to the OSS. With few active operations or operatives in the East, the transition to the Pacific Theater was difficult. And with the death of FDR, William Donovan's dream of a peacetime agency to mirror the activities of the OSS seemed to perish as well.

Incoming President Harry S. Truman pretty much hated all things military, and he openly disliked William J. Donovan and distrusted Donovan's organization. Within days of Japan's surrender, Wild Bill was ordered to close up shop. The OSS was not even given enough time to preserve its most valuable assets.

FUBARs

President Truman eagerly signed an order dissolving the OSS on September 20, 1945. Donovan protested, but his pleas fell on deaf ears. Executive Order 9621 eliminated funding for the OSS as of October 1. Wild Bill had only 10 days to dismantle his outfit.

Fortunately, the Assistant Secretary of War, John J. McCloy, managed to save the Secret Intelligence and X-2 branches of the OSS from extinction. These elements of the former OSS formed the nucleus of a peacetime intelligence-gathering service. McCloy, a friend of Donovan, bent Truman's restrictive rules to create the Strategic Services Unit (SSU) under Brig. Gen. John Magruder, former Deputy Director of the OSS under Donovan.

Two years later, under the leadership of Col. William W. Quinn, the assets of the SSU were moved to a new organization. The Central Intelligence Group (CIG) functioned until the National Security Act of 1947 transformed the CIG into today's Central Intelligence Agency (CIA).

The U.S. Special Operations Command

In 1987, the U.S. government created the U.S. Special Operations Command (USSOCOM). Using the Office of Strategic Services as a model for interservice cooperation in unconventional warfare, the Pentagon created the USSOCOM as a vital component of America's combat doctrine and an important supplement to regular combat planning and operations.

The USSOCOM is a fulfillment of Bill Donovan's vision for the OSS. Today USSOCOM personnel wear a shoulder patch with a gold lance head set against a field of black, a patch that is modeled after the ones worn (unofficially) by OSS members in World War II. (For more details on the USSOCOM, see Chapter 10, "The Coming of the U.S. Special Operations Command.")

> ### Shop Talk
>
> Many of the CIA's best and brightest were trained in their craft by William J. Donovan. The ranks of former OSS members include four future directors of the Central Intelligence Agency: Allen Dulles, Richard Helms, William Colby, and William Casey. Donovan himself was never offered a position in the CIA.

Because of the tireless efforts of William J. Donovan and his agents in the OSS, centralized intelligence gathering and unconventional warfare capabilities are now vital components of our nation's security force.

The Least You Need to Know

◆ Espionage and covert activities are vital to the success of America's modern special forces units.

◆ The visionary activities of Lieut. Col. Earl Ellis, USMC, and William "Wild Bill" Donovan helped to establish an American intelligence community in the early days of World War II.

◆ The Office of Strategic Services, America's first intelligence agency, was established by William Donovan.

◆ The OSS performed brilliantly in the European theater and was instrumental in the defeat of Nazi Germany.

◆ The Central Intelligence Agency is a direct descendant of the OSS.

Chapter 4

America's Models: Foreign Special Forces

In This Chapter

- ◆ Winston Churchill's Special Operations Executive
- ◆ The Special Air Service
- ◆ The German special forces of World War II
- ◆ Foreign special forces after World War II

During World War II, the United States modeled its few special forces units on those of other nations—most notably Great Britain's. But England wasn't the only country to create elite fighting units during World War II. The Italian navy created the world's first underwater demolitions unit, and the Germans fielded so many special operations units that by the end of the war they were tripping over themselves as they vied for recruits, supplies, and missions.

In this chapter, I will examine the special warfare units created by Great Britain and Nazi Germany during World War II, provide a brief history of their operations, and explain how these units' tactics and traditions impacted their U.S. counterparts.

Winston Churchill's Special Operations Executive

After the fall of France and the British retreat from Dunkirk, there was little the British could do to fight the Nazis. However, rather than batten down the hatches and wait for the Battle of Britain to begin, Prime Minister Winston Churchill wanted to strike back at Germany and Japan any way he could. Churchill believed that much of the credit for the Axis victories belonged to the German special operations and infiltration forces, and he wanted to create this kind of force to fight for Britain.

The result was the Special Operations Executive (SOE), established in 1940. Its activities encompassed intelligence, subversion, sabotage, and the creation of armed "resistance movements" inside the borders of German- and Japanese-occupied countries. Almost immediately, the SOE found itself in competition with MI5 (British security) and MI6 (secret intelligence). Yet, by flaunting regulations and ignoring "regular channels," the SOE managed to achieve success; by the end of hostilities, the organization had grown to include 10,000 personnel, many of them women. Enthusiastically supporting irregular operations and special warfare, the SOE recruited linguists, radio operators, and saboteurs, and dispatched them to foreign nations for clandestine activities.

> ### CAUTION
>
> **FUBARs**
>
> SOE operations in Holland ended in disaster. The German *Abwehr* (literally, "defense"—here, "counterintelligence") infiltrated British cells and killed many resistance leaders. The operation was so compromised that British controllers ignored signals from all radio operators in Holland, costing more agents and sympathizers their lives.

Several SOE-trained resistance cells operated inside France and made valuable contributions to the Normandy landings. In Greece, Italy, and Yugoslavia, the SOE managed to convince various anti-Nazi groups with very different political outlooks to work together. SOE operatives were also instrumental in the destruction of Nazi heavy-water facilities in Norway, preventing Adolf Hitler from obtaining a nuclear weapon.

The SOE was disbanded in 1946, but historians still debate the effectiveness of this maverick organization. Many contend that the resources that the SOS devoured could have been better spent on conventional forces. However, others believe that the SOE made a significant contribution to the war effort.

David Stirling's Special Air Service

As you have seen, America's special forces in World War II and beyond sprang from a long, mostly British tradition. Though "king and country" have been replaced by "the People and the Constitution" among America's special operations units, there is no denying the important role that the British model had in the creation of the U.S. elite fighting forces.

The premier British special operations force was and remains the Special Air Service (SAS). Established in World War II, the SAS remains one of the finest special forces in the world. It is hard to imagine that this elite group began as the "crazy scheme" of a single individual. As Capt. David Stirling, a British commando, lay in a hospital bed recovering from a parachute accident, he had a vision. Why not create small, highly trained, and extremely motivated, 4- or 5-man special operations teams out of the larger, 50-man commando units then in service? These smaller teams would be easier to equip and support, and they could be parachuted behind enemy lines or infiltrated by jeep or small boat.

Stirling knew that 50 commandos stomping around the countryside certainly did a lot of damage. But they also made a lot of noise and demanded a considerable amount of support. Small units, on the other hand, are harder for the enemy to locate, and small-unit assaults are somewhat easier (and certainly less costly) to mount. Captain Stirling placed a lot of faith in his brigade of trained commandos, but he also believed that, if buried deep enough behind enemy lines, smaller commando teams could inflict as much damage on the enemy as a much larger force.

Captain Stirling took his idea to Gen. Sir Claude Auchinleck, commander-in-chief, Middle East Command, who gave him the green light to begin training—provided that Captain Stirling could find the equipment he needed at hand. Stirling "borrowed" tons of weapons and equipment from the New Zealand army and set to work creating a legend.

> ### Shop Talk
>
> "The boy Stirling is quite mad, quite, quite mad. However, in a war there is often a place for mad people," said Field Marsh. Bernard Law Montgomery, commander of all British forces in World War II, about Capt. David Stirling and his vision of the SAS.

Jock Lewis Builds a Bomb

Stirling visualized a force that would consist almost entirely of trained and blooded commandos, specially educated in additional skills. He gave his recruits training in endurance, seamanship, unconventional weapons skills, and the use of a brand-new explosive invented for his commandos by one of their own—the Lewis Bomb. The Lewis Bomb was named after Jock Lewis, the SAS commando who devised the formula. The SAS required a "blow and burn" bomb, something that was both explosive and incendiary. Experts claimed that such a solution was impossible, but Lewis's mixture of plastic explosives, oil, and thermite proved more than adequate—and illustrated the ingenuity of Britain's brand-new special forces unit.

This unit-in-training was called L detachment, and it began work at Kabrit, near the Suez Canal. The selection process was rigorous, and airborne training was mandatory. Unfortunately, Captain Stirling didn't have the time or the resources to build a jump tower for his paratroopers, so "jump practice" consisted of learning how to jump off a truck moving at 30 miles per hour! After weeks in the Egyptian desert, Stirling's teams were divided into smaller units, with individual members rounding out the strengths and weaknesses of teammates. Despite their extensive training and warrior skills, the first mission performed by Stirling's commando teams was a disaster. Only 22 men from a force of 66 survived. Stirling came to the realization that more training was required if his vision was to survive.

The Long Range Desert Group

Captain Stirling learned some hard lessons after his debacle, and with his next set of recruits the training was intensified. Stirling brought in desert-warfare experts from the Long Range Desert Group (LRDG) to instruct the men in how to conduct combat operations in the desert. The LRDG taught Stirling's commandos hundreds of simple tricks to make themselves and their equipment "desert-worthy." Stirling's commandos learned how to keep sand out of their weapons, locate and purify water, built a sun compass, and rig their vehicles with condensers for more efficient operation in desert conditions.

The second of Stirling's raids—mounted in December 1941 by a dozen commandos in conjunction with the LRDG—was an unqualified success. The raiders infiltrated 350 miles of occupied desert to destroy 24 *Luftwaffe* (literally, "air force") aircraft and a German fuel dump. The commandos were doing so well that they ran out of explosives in the middle of their raid and had to destroy the last few planes with their bare hands! The next morning, a four-man team from this same unit went out on its own and managed to destroy 37 German planes at a base near Agedabia. Within 15 days, Stirling's commandos had destroyed nearly 100 enemy aircraft—without suffering a single casualty.

As this triumphant campaign drew to a close, and after several subsequent assaults on Benghazi Harbor, the Special Air Service was officially activated. The unit's symbol became a winged dagger, to symbolize the Sword of Damocles. The members were given white berets (later changed to dun) and a distinctive "wings" patch worn on the right arm—the patch was earned by each commando after he completed seven combat jumps. Although SAS is an acronym for "Special Air Service," members of this elite unit like to say that SAS really means "Speed, Aggression, and Surprise."

Fifty Free French paratroopers joined the SAS a few weeks later. The unit was also strengthened by the addition of jeeps with twin Vickers Browning .50-caliber machine guns mounted on the back. The SAS used these jeeps to roll out of the desert, quick-strike the enemy, and vanish back into the arid waste before the Germans had time to mount a response. Using 18 of

FUBARs

Jeeps sporting machine guns, charging German half-tracks across a desert landscape, were a familiar sight to American television viewers in 1966–1968. Though supposedly based on the exploits of the Long Range Desert Group, the characters and situations on ABC television's *The Rat Patrol* bore little resemblance to the real-life LRDG.

these armed attack jeeps, the SAS struck the German airfield at Sidi Haneish. The raid was a stunning success. Although three jeeps and several commandos were lost, the German base was not operational for weeks after the attack. In all, the SAS destroyed over 400 German aircraft while operating in North Africa.

Greeks Bearing Gifts

Official regimental status was given to the SAS in the autumn of 1942, with the addition of the Greek Sacred Squadron and the Special Boat Section. Working with the Greeks, several secret missions were carried out in the Aegean Sea, behind enemy lines.

Tragedy struck the SAS at Tobruk. Due to a lack of foresight and planning, SAS units were squandered performing the work of conventional troops. Too many commandos were involved in the raid on Tobruk to keep it a secret. The Germans knew the Brits were coming and met them head-on.

Despite their failure at Tubruk, by October 1942, British commandos had so disrupted the activities of the Third Reich that Hitler issued his infamous Commando Order, which mandated that any Allied commandos captured by the Germans should be treated as spies and executed.

Straight Shooting

The exploits of the Greek Sacred Squadron and the Special Boat Section inspired author Alistair Maclean to write his epic war novel, *The Guns of Navarone.* An international bestseller, Maclean's book was later adapted into the classic film starring Gregory Peck, Anthony Quinn, Anthony Quayle, and David Niven.

Bad luck continued to dog the commandos. In February 1943, Captain Stirling was captured by the Germans while hiding in a cave. Overall command of the SAS was turned over to Captain Paddy Mayne. In April 1943, the Special Boat Service was formed by a marriage of the SAS D Squadron and the Commando Special Boat Section, and made into an independent unit under the leadership of Maj. Earl Jellicoe, a former SAS commander.

The SAS was active in Africa, Sicily, Italy, Norway, France, the Greek Isles, and Belgium. In France, the SAS worked behind the lines with members of the French Resistance to destroy rail lines, bridges, and command stations and to provide advance reconnaissance to the advancing Allied armies. Although the SAS members always wore their uniforms (which made them combatants, not spies, according to the Geneva Convention) even when operating

Shop Talk

Although SAS troops operating behind enemy lines in France wore uniforms, if they were captured by the Germans they were usually executed, in accordance with Adolph Hitler's infamous Commando Order. Some of those Nazi executioners were later tracked down and brought to justice by units of the Special Air Service.

behind enemy lines, the Germans still considered them to be spies and saboteurs and treated them accordingly. They were tortured and shot or hanged after interrogation. Of the roughly 2,000 SAS members who served in World War II, 300 were killed by the end of hostilities. Those numbers include Jock Lewis, the devilishly clever inventor of the Lewis Bomb, who was killed by a German rifle grenade fired from an airplane.

The SAS Today

Unlike the U.S. military, the British recognized the value of the SAS and kept the unit active after World War II ended. Since the 1940s, the SAS has operated in Malaysia, Borneo, and Oman. In January 1976, a full squadron of SAS soldiers was deployed in Ulster, where they monitored Irish Republican Army activities and protected IRA targets for assassination.

During the Gulf War, the SAS was inserted deep into Iraq to search out SCUD missile launching sites. One unit, BRAVO 2-0, suffered bad luck. The men were given the wrong frequencies for their radios, experienced some of the worst weather in Iraq in 30 years, and were eventually surrounded by Iraqi soldiers. Only one member of this eight-man team made it to safety. Four were captured and three were killed. Today the SAS is head-quartered in Hereford, England.

The British Special Boat Squadron

The Special Boat Squadron (SBS) was formed by a marriage between the SAS D Squadron and the Commando Special Boat Section. Headed by Maj. Earl Jellicoe, an early member of David Stirling's SAS, the SBS conducted combat operations in the Aegean, in the Mediterranean, and in the Adriatic seas.

When the SBS broke away from the SAS, it took most of members of the Greek Sacred Squadron with it. During operations on and around the Aegean Isles, the Special Boat Squadron harassed German ships, raided remote bases, and provided advance reconnais-sance. The members' lightning-quick surprise assaults kept the Germans on their toes and effectively kept over 18,000 German troops tied down in the region. The SBS accomplished this amazing feat with less than 250 active members—truly a mouse that roared!

The SBS was an unorthodox unit. The members had little respect for parade-ground dis-cipline. They wore whatever uniforms were available, and they acted with a reckless disre-gard for their own safety. Members of the SBS also favored the weapons of their enemies over those manufactured by their own countrymen, simply because it was easier for them to capture ammunition from the Germans than it was to wait for British-made stuff to be shipped out through normal supply channels. For boats, the SBS members used whatever they could get their hands on. Rubber rafts (dinghies), rowboats, dories, folboats, rafts, and motor launches were all utilized on SBS missions. A large, rusty schooner—the *Tewfit*, which sailed out of Port Said—served as their depot ship.

The SBS's primary area of operation was in the Aegean Sea. A favorite haunt was the Greek island of Simi, which the SAS had raided and even occupied several times before being driven off again. Eventually the Greek Sacred Squadron assumed all SBS duties in the Greek isles, and the British commandos moved on to Italy and Albania. Unfortunately, the SBS was disbanded after the war, but much of the members' training and many of their duties are now performed by the SBS of the Royal Marines.

Straight Shooting

The word *dashing* could describe many British special forces units. But few were as dashing as SBS officer David Clark, who landed on a German-occupied island, walked into the officer's mess, waved his pistol and said, "It would be all so much easier if you would just raise your hands."

The Royal Naval Commandos in Action

Early amphibious raids alerted the British Royal Navy to the need for better intelligence and control on the beaches. During Operation Ironclad—the capture of the port of Diego Suarez on the northern tip of Madagascar in May 1942—the British tried sending in advance "beach parties" to pave the way for the landing forces. Beach parties proved so effective that the Royal Naval Commandos—sometimes known as "Beachhead Commandos"—were formed.

The missions of the Royal Naval Commandos were highly specialized and anticipated the operations of the U.S. Navy's Underwater Demolitions Teams (UDTs) operating in the Pacific Theater in 1944–1945. Royal Naval Commandos came ashore with or ahead of the landing force to clear beaches, consolidate the beachhead, remove mines or underwater obstructions, establish ammunition and supply dumps, gather intelligence on enemy strength and deployment, and help evacuate the wounded after the landings.

The first Royal Naval Commandos were formed in the spring of 1942. Each unit consisted of a commander, three sections with two officers commanding each section, a petty officer and 15 to 20 men of various ranks and specialties.

In August 1942, the Royal Naval (RN) Commandos participated in Operation Jubilee, the unsuccessful raid on Dieppe, France. Of the 5,000 Canadian troops who landed on the coast of France with the RN Commandos, over 3,500 were lost. The Royal Navy decided that its commandos required much additional training, so a special school was established in Scotland.

Straight Shooting

Although the duties of the Royal Naval Commandos mirrored those of America's UDTs, there was one important difference. Beyond their training in underwater demolitions, amphibious landings, and shore reconnaissance, the Brits were also highly trained commandos who could wage war on land as well as on the beaches.

The commando school at Ardentinny could train up to 600 commandos at a time. There the officers lived and worked in the same quarters as the enlisted men—a practice previously shunned by the British military, but very effective for building unit cohesiveness.

At Ardentinny and nearby Loch Long, the Royal Naval Commandos practiced amphibious landing drills, field survival, and shore reconnaissance. Training included the use of explosives, special weapons, rock climbing, and the operation of various types of landing craft. Graduates of the training school at Ardentinny moved on to receive additional training at Achnacarry, where they were put through their paces by British Army Commando officers. At Achnacarry, the motto for the Royal Naval Commandos was established: *Imprimo Exulto* ("First in, last out"). Additional training was carried out at Kabritt, near the Suez Canal, for those units serving in the Middle East. Some Royal Naval Commandos were sent to the Jungle Battle School at Chittagong for duties in southeast Asia; still others were sent to parachute training courses and would wear the wings of the SAS/SBS.

Shop Talk
Royal Naval Commandos who specialized in jungle warfare at the school at Chittagong were active in Malaya all through 1945. Their actions prevented the Japanese from carrying the war into India.

Operation Neptune

By the end of 1943, 22 units of the Royal Naval Commandos (RNC) had been formed. Over 400 of them participated in Operation Torch, in which they landed on the beaches of Algeria with the first wave. For the Royal Naval Commandos, the landings at Elba were a disaster. Coastal defenses were so heavy and the defenders were so spirited that enemy gunners were killed by their own guns, which blew up from overuse. The RNC lost 6 officers and 32 commandos—over 50 percent of its force.

During Operation Husky, the invasion of Sicily, the commandos assisted with the landings and captured the island of Monte Cristo, where the enemy had established a radio station and observation post. Commandos also participated in the landings at Salerno and Anzio. The commandos faced a fierce new foe—men conscripted into the army from German-occupied countries. These men had nothing to lose: If they failed to fight, they would be shot by their German masters. If they were captured, they would be repatriated to their native country to be shot as traitors for siding with the enemy. Caught in the middle, they had no choice but to fight to the death. During the Italian Campaign, some Royal Naval Commandos crossed into Yugoslavia or moved into the Aegean with the Special Boat Squadrons.

The largest Royal Naval Commando operation of the war was Neptune, the naval component of Operation Overlord, the D-Day invasion of Normandy. It was the largest amphibious operation of the war and would prove to be a complex exercise in logistics.

Commandos came in with the first wave to determine whether the beaches were safe for the next wave. Casualties were heavy, and sometimes the commandos had to dig in and fight off counterattacks, side by side with regular troops. Needless to say, their commando training made them very effective in this regard.

After Normandy, the Royal Naval Commandos participated in the crossings on the Rhine. In the East, they trained for the pending invasion of Japan, which was cancelled after Hiroshima and Nagasaki were bombed and Japan surrendered. At the end of World War II, the Royal Naval Commandos were disbanded.

> **Shop Talk**
>
> The commandos lived up to their motto at Normandy. They were the first in—arriving in the very first wave—and the last out, remaining on the beaches for six weeks after the landings. They helped salvage sunken landing craft, established supply routes, and evacuated the wounded.

The *Führer*'s Secret Warriors

Like the British, the Germans were good at forming special forces units for a variety of missions and tasks. But even the regular German army employed many of the skills used by special forces as it overran Europe. Using fast-attack *blitzkrieg* tactics, the German military struck quickly and hard; like commandos, mobility was the key to their success.

But the German High Command discovered early that if its *blitzkrieg* tactics were to succeed, it would need to establish special forces units to penetrate enemy territory in advance of the armies. Attacking fast and hard was fine, but the German army needed to find intact bridges, tunnels, and rail junctions at the end of its quick march if it was to conquer the enemy. German special forces units were established to move forward, in advance of the main army, to secure such structures for use by the follow-up forces.

> **CAUTION**
>
> **FUBARs**
>
> Adolf Hitler was mad—about special forces! Inspired by World War I General Ludendorff's *Sturmtruppen*, Hitler created so many special operations units that they were practically tripping over themselves as they vied for missions and funding, proving that you *can* have too much of a good thing.

Adm. Wilhelm Franz Canaris and the Brandenburg Division

The story of the Brandenburg Division began at the end of World War I. In the chaos after the armistice, political action committees called *Industrieschutz Oberschlesien* were created to prevent Polish insurgents from gaining power in Silesia—a part of Poland with a large German-speaking population. In 1938, these political units were redesignated the *Deutsche Kompanie* and moved into the Sudetenland, a part of Czechoslovakia with a large German population. They successfully rallied popular support for that region's eventual absorption by Germany.

As the German army began to rebuild in the 1930s, High Command recognized the need for a more formal special forces organization controlled by the military. Adm. Wilhelm Franz Canaris was chosen to lead German intelligence, which included the Brandenburg Division. A former captain of a destroyer sunk during World War I, Admiral Canaris fled to Argentina after the war, only to return secretly to Germany to help his nation rearm. Admiral Canaris was staunch anti-Nazi, yet he became the head of the *Abwehr*, the German intelligence and counterintelligence service. The *Abwehr* was a powerful organization and remained active from 1920 until Germany's defeat in 1945.

Shop Talk

German intelligence and counter-intelligence was divided into three components. *Abwehr I* dealt with espionage and intelligence. *Abwehr II* established and controlled special operations units. *Abwher III* dealt with counterintelligence. The Brandenburg Divisions were the responsibility of *Abwehr II*.

FUBARs

Abwehr III, which was responsible for German counterintelligence in World War II, succeeded in infiltrating the Soviet espionage ring known as Red Orchestra. Unfortunately for the Nazis, *Abwehr I*, the espionage branch, failed to penetrate British intelligence or control even one reliable agent in America or Britain.

Admiral Canaris had performed intelligence work during World War I and had a gift for languages. Many historians suspect that Canaris assumed command of the Brandenburgs with an eye toward overthrowing Adolph Hitler. Although Hitler long suspected Canaris of disloyalty, he did not move against the admiral until after the July Bomb Plot against him failed. Hitler then had Admiral Canaris arrested, tried for treason, and hanged.

The first Brandenburg unit was formed in 1939. The volunteers who filled its ranks were men from Silesia and the Sudatentland who knew local customs and were familiar with Polish government documents such as passports and identity cards. Training was quite realistic, and live ammunition was used. Brandenburg units were trained in partisan tactics in forests and street-fighting techniques in urban settings. Survival, tracking, and navigation skills were stressed, and members were taught how to manufacture and use a variety of explosives.

As their training progressed, Brandenburgs learned parachuting, seamanship, and skiing for winter combat. The result of this extensive training was warriors who were self-reliant and who could fight in any setting. But what the Brandenburgs did best was foment unrest. Through subversion tactics taught to all volunteers in *Abwehr* II, Brandenburg units engineered the pro-Nazi uprisings that were an essential component in the annexations of Austria and Czechoslovakia and in the invasion of Poland.

Prior to Hitler's invasion of Poland in September 1939, Brandenburg units were deployed to cause chaos and unrest and to ensure the safe capture of the Polish factories in Silesia, which were essential for the Nazi war effort. In 1940, the Brandenburg units were expanded to include three companies, all based at Brandenburg-am-Havel (where the name "Brandenburg" originated). Eventually, the Brandenburg units were expanded into a division, and the units saw action in Denmark, Norway, Holland, and Belgium.

Trained Brandenburg units were sent to the field in small, tightly knit units. Loyalty to the team was encouraged, and recruits were urged to shake hands instead of saluting to enhance unit cohesiveness and loyalty. Brandenburg recruits were sometimes handed bizarre assignments during training. One unit was ordered to get the local police chief's fingerprints without being discovered. Another unit was ordered to capture five regular German army officers and deliver them to their instructors.

As usual, traditional army commanders disliked the Brandenburgs, and many in the German army questioned the concept of "special forces." These units proved their worth in time—before Hitler's invasion of Russia, Brandenburg units recruited Ukrainian volunteers to help fight the Soviets and were instrumental in the capture of the bridge across the San River. But these Ukrainian recruits proved to be unreliable and were disbanded in a few months.

As Russian partisans resisted the advance of the German army in Russia, Russian volunteers were accepted into the Brandenburgs for counterinsurgency work. They had only limited success in stemming the Russian tide. Brandenburg units also fought in Italy and Yugoslavia before being absorbed into the regular army in 1944.

> **CAUTION**
>
> **FUBARs**
>
> Ukrainian volunteers in the Brandenburg Divisions formed the Nightingale Unit. Most had an ulterior motive for siding with the Nazis—they wanted to free their homeland from Soviet domination. During the invasion of the Ukraine, the Nightingales seized a radio station and proclaimed an independent Ukrainian state, only to be rounded up and punished by the Nazis.

Maj. Gen. Otto Skorzeny: "The Most Dangerous Man in Europe"

In April 1943, the Waffen SS formed its own special forces unit. Based north of Berlin at Friedenthal, it was known as the Friedenthal Special Duties Battalion, commanded by *Obersturmbandführer* Otto Skorzeny. Initially volunteers came only from the ranks of the SS, but in 1944 2,000 members of the Brandenburg unit joined Otto Skorzeny's *Jagdkommando* Division. Air support for these special forces came from *Kampfgeschwader* 200, the Special Operations Squadron of the *Luftwaffe*.

Shop Talk

In 1943 the German navy formed its own special forces units, the "K Companies." All highly trained combat swimmers, K units were experts in the use of small craft, explosive motor boats, manned torpedoes, explosives, and antishipping mines. Other German special forces units of World War II include the SS *Fallschirmjäger* Battalion 500/600, comprised primarily of disgraced Waffen SS personnel and assorted German officers who were given a second chance to redeem themselves. The 7th SS *Freiwilligen* "Prinz Eugen" Division was composed of ethnic Germans who volunteered or were conscripted from the occupied countries of the Balkans.

Maj. Gen. Otto Skorzeny was probably the most effective special forces commander of World War II. An officer in the Waffen SS and the commando leader of the Friedenthal Special Duties Battalion, Skorzeny is best known for his daring rescue of dictator Benito Mussolini in September 1944. Although this operation was an amazing success, it was but one of the accomplishments of this colorful and charismatic special forces commander.

Skorzeny was born on June 12, 1908, to a middle-class Viennese family. After World War I and the coming of the Great Depression, the Skorzeny family fell into poverty, but Otto managed to gain admittance to the University of Vienna, where he studied engineering. While at the university, Skorzeny joined a *schlagende Verbindung*, a dueling society, where he received the prominent scar that ran from his chin to his eye. Skorzeny wore this wound, called a *Schmisse* ("honor scar"), with pride, as a visible example of personal courage and fearlessness. Skorzeny joined the Nazi Party in the 1920s and later volunteered for the SS (*Schutzstaffel*, or "Defense Unit"). An impressive figure with a powerful physique, Skorzeny fit Hitler's image of the Aryan superman. As a soldier with the *Waffen SS*, Skorzeny quickly moved up the ranks. As a junior officer, he participated in the invasions of Holland, France, and the Balkans. During the invasion of Russia, Skorzeny was wounded and sent back to Germany to recover.

Shop Talk

The *Waffen SS* was the fighting arm of the SS. It began as a security force to guard Hitler's life, but by 1942, the Waffen SS became an elite special combat branch of the German army. Other SS organizations included the infamous "death's head" units that operated the concentration camps.

After several successful raids by British commandos, Hitler decided that he wanted a special force of his own. Skorzeny, who was still recuperating from his wounds, was made Chief of Special Troops and promoted to the rank of captain. Within six months, he had created a formidable commando force—and just in time. In September 1943, Captain Skorzeny was ordered to pull off the most improbable mission of the war.

Skorzeny's Stratagem: The Great Mussolini Rescue

When southern Italy was invaded by the Allies in 1943, Fascist dictator Benito Mussolini was toppled from power. Once Hitler's staunchest ally, Italy was now making peace with the British and Americans. Italian authorities held Mussolini prisoner in a secret location, using the fascist dictator as a bargaining chip in the tense negotiations.

Hitler wanted to establish a puppet government in northern Italy and hoped to place Mussolini in charge. But they had to snatch him away from his captors first.

Skorzeny tracked Mussolini across half of Italy for six weeks before he finally located him. On September 8, the *Abwehr* intercepted a coded radio message confirming that Mussolini was being held prisoner at the Hotle Campo, a resort high in the Gran Sasso mountains of the Abruzzi region of Italy. At any time Mussolini could be transferred to another facility, so Skorzeny had to move fast.

Fearing the use of powered aircraft because their engines might be heard, Skorzeny commandeered 12 gliders and packed them with 10 commandos each. The force took off at 6:00 A.M. on the morning of September 12. Several gliders never got off the ground, and others became lost during the journey over the foggy mountains. One aircraft crashed, killing most of its passengers, as Skorzeny watched from a distance. At 2:00 P.M., the gliders passed over the meadow where they were supposed to land, only to discover that what they had thought was flat farmland was really a steep hillside.

Skorzeny ordered the gliders to crash-land on the rocky slopes right outside of the Campo resort. They did, and the German commandos came charging out to storm the hotel, shouting, *"Mani in alto!"* (Hands up!). The Italians were taken completely by surprise and Mussolini was rescued. *Il Duce* was loaded into an airplane and flown to Vienna. Skorzeny accompanied the fascist dictator and received a hero's welcome and a Knight's Cross from a grateful Hitler.

More amazing exploits quickly followed. In 1944, Skorzeny kidnapped the son of the Hungarian Regent and occupied the Citadel of Budapest, a move that prevented Hungary from surrendering to the Russians and spared a million encircled German troops from annihilation. After the July Bomb Plot, Skorzeny used his commandos to restore order in Berlin and round up the plotters.

> ### Shop Talk
>
> The DFS 230 gliders that Skorzeny and his commandos used to rescue Mussolini were primitive affairs. Skorzeny described them as "a few steel members covered with canvas." DFS 230s had to be dragged into the air by other aircraft. They boasted wooden seats and cellophane windows, and they were "unpleasantly hot and stuffy."

Skorzeny's Infamous American Brigades

During the Battle of the Bulge, Otto Skorzeny created the American Brigades. These units were made up of English-speaking German soldiers disguised as American troops and using captured American weapons, vehicles, and equipment.

The American Brigades wrecked havoc behind Allied lines. Gen. Dwight D. Eisenhower, the commander-in-chief of the Allied forces in Europe, was a prisoner in his own headquarters for a week due to fears for his personal safety caused by the infiltrators.

Near the end of the war, Otto Skorzeny was named "the most dangerous man in Europe" by the Allied prosecutor of war criminals. Ten days after Germany's collapse, Skorzeny surrendered to the Americans, who tried him for the crime of "fighting in enemy uniform"—a capital offense.

During the trial, Skorzeny's lawyer called a surprise witness—British war hero Forrest Yeo-Thomas, who revealed that the British operative had worn German uniforms behind enemy lines as a matter of course. Skorzeny was acquitted and quickly fled to South America.

 FUBARs

> After he was acquitted of war crimes, Skorzeny became a target for assassination. Russian agents and Jewish organizations hunted him all over Europe, but Skorzeny was already gone. In Argentina he became close to Juan and Eva Peron, who protected him in exchange for Nazi gold. Skorzeny was believed to be the brains behind the formation of Odessa, a secret organization that was established to save former Nazis from Jewish groups and Allied war crime tribunals.

In Argentina, Otto Skorzeny briefly became Eva Peron's bodyguard and foiled at least one attempt on her life. He also served as a military advisor to Egyptian dictator Gamal Nasser. Skorzeny returned to Europe (Spain) in the 1950s and became an engineering consultant. His last years were spent rescuing over 500 former SS members from vengeful Jewish groups. Otto Skorzeny died of natural causes in July 1975 in Madrid. Skorzeny has sometimes been regarded as one of the fathers of our modern special operations forces. It's a title that makes many members of today's elite units squirm, for Skorzeny is a dark father indeed.

Foreign Special Forces Since World War II

After World War II, many countries downsized or eliminated their special forces units, only to regret it later. Today special forces have been retained in the orders of battle of most armed services. The Special Air Service (SAS) and the Royal Marines Special Boat Service (SBS) have seen action in almost all post–World War II conflicts that Great Britain has been involved in.

While America's special forces were expanding during the Vietnam era, the Australian SAS Regiment, the New Zealand SAS Squadron, and the special forces units of the Republic of Korea all saw action in South Vietnam. Today South Korea maintains seven special forces brigades, and Thailand maintains a special forces division comprising of four regiments.

The Union of Soviet Socialist Republics placed great emphasis on special forces. With its Warsaw Pact allies, the Soviet Union created an indeterminate (but quite large) number of *Spetsnaz* forces. Many of these units have disappeared since the collapse of the Eastern bloc, but there are still eight active Russian brigades, each specializing in operations in specific areas of the world.

French special forces units include the *Regiment de Dragons Parachutiste*, the *Regiment de Parachutistes d'Infanterie de Marine*, and the Commando Hubert combat swimmer unit. Israel has the Sayeret Matkal General Staff Reconnaissance Unit, the Sayeret Shaldag Long-Range Reconnaissance Patrol Unit, the Sayeret Hadruzum Druze Muslim Reconnaissance Unit, and Flotilla 13 (a naval special operations unit).

> ### Shop Talk
>
> "It is not big armies that win battles; it is the good ones."
>
> —Maurice de Saxe (1696–1750)

The Least You Need to Know

- American special forces units established during World War II were modeled after the special forces groups of Great Britain.
- The British and Germans led the way in creating special forces units in World War II.
- The British Army's Special Air Service was one of the first special warfare groups created in World War II.
- The most dramatic special warfare operation of World War II was the rescue of Mussolini by Otto Skorzeny, the dark father of the modern special forces.

Part 2

The Green Berets

After World War II, as the European powers attempted to reclaim their colonial territories, they often faced stiff resistance from their former subjects. Fierce insurgency wars erupted in Asia, Africa, the Caribbean, and the Middle East. To defeat these communist-inspired revolutionary movements, a new philosophy—counterinsurgency—and a new type of warrior were needed.

U.S. President John F. Kennedy believed that an American counterinsurgency force would be required to defeat insurgency, and the U.S. Army Special Forces was born. In this part I will introduce the history of "the Green Berets" from their humble beginnings, through the war in Vietnam and its aftermath to the rebirth and reorganization of the U.S. Army Special Forces that took place during the 1980s and 1990s.

When Counterinsurgency Was All the Rage

In This Chapter

- ◆ Harry Truman and the American military machine
- ◆ Britain and the Malayan emergency
- ◆ Col. Aaron Bank, father of America's special forces
- ◆ The birth of America's special forces
- ◆ The CIA and the Bay of Pigs fiasco

Counterinsurgency is defined in the *Oxford Essential Dictionary of the U.S. Military* as "the military, paramilitary, political, psychological, and civil actions taken by a government to defeat insurgency." It was upon the philosophy of counterinsurgency that America's special operations forces were created.

The rise of communism caused worldwide unrest, as the Soviet Union willingly sponsored popular uprisings in many developing nations. To prevent the wave of communism from smothering human rights in emerging nations, the United States, led by President John F. Kennedy, began to create special warfare groups to counter proletariat uprisings that threatened to destabilize America's allies in the Third World.

In this chapter, I'll trace the rise of communist insurgencies following World War II, and how the British and French reacted to the unrest in their former colonial possessions. This tension between communist nations and the Western democracies would ultimately lead to the creation of America's modern special operations forces.

Harry Truman's Postwar Purge

As soon as World War II ended, President Harry Truman began to dismantle the formidable American military machine that had liberated Europe and the Pacific. Either unconcerned or oblivious to Soviet moves in eastern Europe and the activities of Chairman Mao's communist minions on mainland China, Truman systematically reduced the size and scope of every branch of the armed service.

The intelligence community—what there was of it—was not immune to the chopping block. America's sole espionage arm, the Office of Special Services (OSS), was disbanded. Truman gleefully signed Director "Wild Bill" Donovan's walking papers and gave the OSS director less than two weeks to vacate the premises—not nearly long enough to preserve the precious intelligence resources that Donovan had developed to help win the war.

FUBARs

Harry Truman tried to abolish the Marine Corps under the absurd notion that nuclear weapons made amphibious warfare obsolete! "Give 'em Hell, Harry" learned the error of his ways when the communist takeover of Korea was thwarted by a U.S. Marine Corps amphibious assault on Inchon.

Blindly adhering to America's military cycle of "build up, then tear down," the Truman administration acted under the misguided belief that the development of nuclear weapons had rendered large, conventional armed forces and conventional warfare obsolete.

Meanwhile, America watched as a century of colonial stability was wiped away in the 1940s and '50s, in numerous "wars of liberation" that sprang up like weeds all over the emerging world. In Korea, Cuba, Vietnam, the Belgian Congo, and Latin America, guerrilla armies backed by communist China or the Soviet Union attempted to establish—through violent revolution—socialist puppet regimes that effectively abolished individual freedom, property rights, and religious liberty.

Fortunately, even in the post–World War II era, there were those who resisted Truman's "urge to purge," believing that common sense dictated that there would always be a need for conventional ground troops, no matter what forms future warfare might take. There were also military strategists and policy wonks who cautioned against an overreliance on an all-nuclear deterrence at the expense of conventional forces.

A small number of political and military leaders landed between these two extremes, in essence rejecting both the concept of a total nuclear deterrence *and* the traditional reliance on conventional armed forces. Men such as Gen. Maxwell Taylor argued that small guerrilla wars would most likely be the only kind of wars waged in the nuclear age. Impressed with the SAS's success in Malaya, officers such as Col. John McCuen urged America's military to explore new methods of counterinsurgency as a possible means to defeat communist-inspired insurrections. In *The Art of Counter-Revolutionary War: The Strategy of Counterinsurgency*, Colonel McCuen argued that it was possible to "apply revolutionary strategies and principles in reverse" and, by "outbidding" insurgent promises and propaganda with a better deal, the colonel cogently argued that the loyalty of the populace could be "bought."

Straight Shooting

In his 1959 book *The Uncertain Trumpet*, Gen. Maxwell D. Taylor argued against a dependence on nuclear deterrence, insisting that America should develop its own limited-war capability, including the ability to battle insurgencies. President John F. Kennedy appointed General Taylor to the Joint Chiefs of Staff in 1960.

The military, like any human institution, will ultimately respond to the whims of its leaders and the political and cultural trends of the day. Because of the British success in putting down communist guerrillas during the Malayan Emergency, by the time John F. Kennedy was elected president in 1960, counterinsurgency was all the rage among the leaders of the Western democracies.

Trouble in the East: The Malayan Emergency

In 1948, the Malayan Communist Party (MCP) began an insurgency movement in an attempt to end colonial rule in Malaysia. Guerrilla forces disrupted the country's economy, overran small towns and villages, and declared huge areas of Malaysia "liberated" zones. The British military was unprepared for such an uprising, and the communists enjoyed initial success.

The Malayan People's Liberation Army sprang from the Malayan Races Liberation Army, which had been formed by the British in the 1940s to defeat the Japanese. Though officially demobilized in 1945, a hard-core group of nationalists and socialists inside the army refused to lay down their arms. By 1948, they had renamed themselves the Malayan People's Liberation Army, and their ranks began to swell. Composed of 8,000 ethnic Chinese living inside Malaya, the communist insurgents had close ties to the Chinese farmers and rural villagers in Malaya, and they relied on their support to prosecute the war.

The British were unprepared for this war. They had a paltry military presence in the region. What few troops they had in the region were wasting their time chasing through the jungle after insurgents, responding to guerrilla activity instead of curtailing it. After several waves of violent attacks and political assassinations, the British military changed tactics: Instead of chasing the guerrillas across the countryside or blowing up wooden huts with high-performance aircraft, they stepped up their political and propaganda activities. Beefed-up intelligence (through the Special Branch) and the arrival of Special Air Service units helped the government take control of the heavily populated areas, pushing the communists into the sparsely populated rural zones, where there was no food or local sympathizers to feed the guerrillas or support their cause.

Britain Takes Drastic Action

Because 90 percent of the insurgents were Chinese, the British resettled a half million ethnic Chinese peasant farmers living in Malaya, moving them to 500 villages, hamlets, and camps that were under the complete control of the Malayan police and the British military. To obtain food, supplies, and intelligence, the guerrillas were forced to approach these resettlement villages. When they did, the guerrillas were eliminated through aggressive military action.

The resettlement system worked, and Malaya was kept out of the communist sphere of influence. By 1960, the Malayans had formed their own democratically elected government and had become independent. The ruling elite still have close ties to the British government today.

The British operating inside of Malaya were fortunate in one respect: Unlike the insurgents in Vietnam, the Malayan guerrillas received no assistance beyond the borders of their own country. Had the Soviets or the Chinese chosen to support the communist guerrillas with heavy weapons, ammunition, and supplies (as they did in Vietnam), the outcome in Malaya might have been very different. As it turned out, however, no one could deny that the British counterinsurgency efforts in Malaya were successful beyond anyone's dreams.

During the Malayan Emergency, British counterinsurgency expert Sir Robert Grainger Ker Thompson (1916–1992) was instrumental in suppressing the revolutionaries. Drawing on his experiences, Sir Robert devised five rules for successfully defeating an insurgency movement.

Straight Shooting

Of course, Thompson's rules don't *always* apply. Despite vigorous use of counterinsurgency techniques in Vietnam, the French failed to halt communist aggression. The United States also failed, in part because the North Vietnamese were receiving heavy weapons, aircraft, ammunition, and supplies from the Soviet Union.

Sir Robert Thompson's Five Cardinal Rules for Defeating Insurgency Movements

1. The goal must always be the establishment of a democratic, economically stable state.
2. The establishment of such a state must be done within the law rather than outside of it, to avoid state-sponsored brutality or a dictatorship.
3. There must be a coherent plan.
4. The first priority must be the defeat of opposing political *operatives* rather than the guerrilla army in the field.
5. Creating base areas and making them secure must be the first priority.

Sir Robert Thompson Goes to Vietnam

At the request of the U.S. government, Sir Robert Thompson went to Vietnam in 1961 as the head of the British Advisory Mission. A vocal opponent of large conventional military operations, which he felt only served to alienate the general population, Sir Robert advocated native police, social, cultural, and military programs to bolster political support in the Vietnamese countryside.

Needless to say, despite his active intervention between 1961 and 1965, U.S. policymakers in Washington and Vietnam failed to obey even one of Sir Robert Thompson's five cardinal rules, with disastrous results.

Col. Aaron Bank and the U.S. Special Forces

If Otto Skorzeny is the dark father of our modern special forces, then Col. Aaron Bank of the United States Army is its visionary light. After World War II ended and the OSS was disbanded, Bank remained in the military. Working side by side with Col. Russell Volckmann (another OSS veteran), Bank was relentless in trying to convince the Army to adopt its own unconventional, guerrilla-style special forces group—forces that could operate behind the Iron Curtain in eastern Europe, where these units could create a guerrilla army to counter the Soviet oppressor.

Their ally in this struggle was Brig. Gen. Robert A. McClure, who headed the Army's psychological warfare operations at the Pentagon. Colonel Bank especially wanted to establish a small number of American soldiers who could sow a large amount of trouble for the enemy behind their own lines. This new type of unit was dubbed Special Forces, a name derived from the OSS, whose operational units in the field were given that same name in 1944.

> **Shop Talk**
>
> American Special Forces units were a long time coming. Brig. Gen. Robert A. McClure, chief of the Office of Psychological Warfare, advocated the creation of U.S. Special Forces units before the outbreak of the Korean War in 1950.

When the first U.S. Army Special Forces units were formed in the early 1950s, it was Col. Aaron Bank who trained them.

The Birth of the U.S. Special Forces

In response to Chinese and Soviet aggression and expansion throughout the Third World, Congress passed Public Law 597, popularly known as the Lodge Bill, in June 1952. The Lodge Bill mandated the formation of specialized units that were capable of conducting unconventional warfare operations (mostly counterinsurgency missions) behind enemy lines. Adopted as the U.S. Army Special Regulation 600-160-10, the tenets of the Lodge Bill were implemented on April 25, 1952. Two months later, on June 20, 1952, the first permanent unconventional warfare unit in America since the end of World War II was formed at Fort Bragg, North Carolina, under the command of Col. Aaron Bank.

Colonel Bank was allocated 2,300 personnel slots for his special unit. The first recruits to the 10th Special Forces Group (SFP) were immigrant soldiers from eastern European nations, almost all of whom were fluent in Russian, and all with extensive military experience. Bank wanted the best troops in the Army, and he generally got them—former OSS operatives, airborne troops, ex-Rangers, and combat veterans of World War II and Korea. Colonel Bank sought out mature, experienced noncommissioned officers (NCOs) and officers, most of them in their early 30s and most with foreign language skills. An all-volunteer force, recruits had to be willing to operate behind enemy lines—in civilian clothes, if necessary. That meant that, if captured, Bank's men could be summarily shot as spies.

Their training was extensive and stressed behind-the-lines, guerrilla warfare tactics, infiltration, land navigation, and the use of parachutes and small boats, along with specialized cross-training in sabotage, intelligence gathering, first aid, communications, foreign languages, and weaponry. Those recruits who successfully completed the rigorous training were assigned directly to the growing ranks of the U.S. Special Forces (USSF).

> **Shop Talk**
>
> In the spring of 1952, Colonel Bank went to Fort Bragg to find a suitable location for his Special Warfare Center. He chose a remote area of the post called Smoke Bomb Hill. Within a decade, this sleepy location would become one of the busiest placed in the U.S. Army!

On June 19, 1952, Colonel Bank's unit was finally activated. On the day of activation, total unit strength was just 10 men—Colonel Bank, a warrant officer, and eight enlisted men. But within months, the volunteers numbered in the hundreds. When the 10th Group became large enough, Colonel Banks began to train the men in the most advanced techniques of unconventional warfare.

Some of the graduates of airborne training and Ranger school were surprised at Bank's curriculum. What they learned was not simply a rehash of Ranger techniques. Rangers and airborne units were "shock troops" designed to hit the enemy hard and fast and then get out—usually to be replaced by larger, more conventional units. Colonel Bank was training his men to spend weeks, months—perhaps even years—deep within hostile territory. Bank wanted his men to be self-sustaining, which meant that they would have to speak the language of the indigenous population and know how to survive and conduct combat operations without outside help or resupply.

After 18 months, Colonel Bank had proved to the Army that his men had what it took to conduct guerrilla-style combat operations. On November 11, 1953, after an aborted labor uprising in communist East Germany, half of the 10th Special Forces Group was permanently deployed to Bad Tolz, West Germany. The other half remained at Fort Bragg, to be rechristened the 77th Special Forces Group.

The Evil Empire Strikes Back

Although there was some initial enthusiasm for Special Forces among the Army brass, there was overwhelming resistance to the formation of such units, too—most of it coming from inside the highest ranks of America's military establishment.

Though America had a "special forces tradition" dating back to the War for Independence and the Civil War, since the eighteenth century, the American military has rejected the concept of elite units. "Special forces" were perceived to be decadent, European-style conceits that ran counter to our populist notions of a common defense composed of citizen soldiers. Like ribbons, medals, pretentious titles, and other pseudo-military trappings, elite units were perceived to be downright undemocratic within the ranks of the U.S. military.

Of course, traditionally minded military leaders had other reasons to resent the formation of special forces. They also knew from sometimes bitter experience that special forces soldiers tended to lack sufficient respect for rank and often thought and acted "out of the box"— always a threat to conventional (hidebound) military thinking. These critics also spoke about the dangers of unauthorized operations and out-of-control operatives, fears that were to prove valid in the decades to come.

When John F. Kennedy became President of the United States in 1960, he recognized that the focus of communist expansion had shifted away from Europe to the Third World, threatening America's own interests in Asia and Latin America.

> **CAUTION**
>
> **FUBARs**
>
> Nikita Khrushchev unwittingly helped America refine the role of its Special Forces when on January 5, 1961, the Soviet premier stated that the USSR would recognize and support "just wars of liberation and popular uprisings." President John F. Kennedy created new special forces units to counter the communist threat.

In 1959, the sudden collapse of the Battista government in Cuba brought communism to America's doorstep. Young and energetic, and riding a wave of popular support, newly elected President John F. Kennedy decided to take a stand against the communist menace. Unfortunately, he turned to the U.S. intelligence community to help him resolve the crisis in Cuba—with disastrous results, as it turned out.

Fade to Black: The Central Intelligence Agency

When Truman abolished Bill Donovan's Office of Strategic Services in 1945, some intelligence-gathering functions were transferred to the State Department and others to the various military intelligence services. But some resources were also transferred to the new Central Intelligence Agency, created in January 1946. Within its first year, the CIA expanded its role in national security to include covert operations.

The CIA was established by Congress and operated under the National Security Council, a presidential advisory board created after World War II. In its charter, the CIA was given legal access to the intelligence information of all other civilian and military agencies.

This overarching power over others led to a long bureaucratic struggle over jurisdiction and resources with a dozen other military and civilian agencies. In the end, the Federal Bureau of Investigation (FBI) retained control of domestic counterintelligence activities, and each branch of the military was allowed to continue its own covert and intelligence-gathering activities. In this respect, the "Central" Intelligence Agency never achieved the "centrality" its directors sought.

The National Security Act of 1947 authorized the CIA to collect, correlate, and evaluate intelligence relating to national security matters. It was also authorized to perform "other functions and duties related to intelligence affecting national security." Nowhere were the words *espionage* or *covert operations* mentioned, but this broad language became the justification for future CIA expansion in these areas.

In 1949, Congress gave its tacit approval for the CIA's espionage activities by funding it through a secret budget. With a "black budget"—as secret funding is called—the CIA was granted extraordinary authority to spend money with accountability to no one. Despite these expanded perks, the Central Intelligence Agency didn't always perform to the high expectations of Congress or the president.

Straight Shooting

Fear of establishing an all-powerful secret police force spying on all Americans led Congress to prohibit the CIA from "police, subpoena, and law enforcement powers or internal-security." All domestic counterintelligence remained in the hands of the Federal Bureau of Investigation.

FUBARs

In 1950, the CIA had its credibility badly damaged when it failed to anticipate the North Korean invasion of the South. Although "The Company" mounted several major covert operations during the Korean War, every single one of them failed.

Growing Pains

When Dwight D. Eisenhower became president in 1953, he immediately expanded the authority of the CIA, making covert operations a major component of his foreign policy. Eisenhower appointed Allen Welsh Dulles as the CIA's first civilian director. Under Dulles, covert operations expanded exponentially, and the CIA successfully toppled unfriendly governments in Iran and Guatemala. By the end of the Eisenhower administration in 1960, clandestine operation accounted for 54 percent of the CIA's total budget. By contrast, covert activities account for just 15 percent of the CIA's current budget, with the responsibility for most covert actions shifting to "other agencies."

Despite its failed attempt to overthrow the government of Indonesia, it looked as if the CIA had gotten its act together by the time John F. Kennedy assumed office in 1961. With a string of success stories under the CIA's belt, it was perfectly understandable that the newly elected president would turn to "The Company" when he wanted to foment a clandestine war to overthrow Fidel Castro's communist dictatorship in Cuba.

Disaster at the Bay of Pigs

Even before Kennedy took office in January 1961, President Eisenhower had broken off diplomatic relations with Cuba. Seven months before that, in May 1960, the CIA began training anti-Castro Cuban exiles in Guatemala for a possible covert operation. The CIA planned to gradually build up anticommunist forces within Cuba to create a cohesive political and military unit capable of toppling Castro. But when Kennedy took office, he intensified the pressure on the CIA, demanding quick action to overthrow Fidel Castro. Kennedy feared that a flood of Russian "military advisors" and a few Soviet bases would appear in Cuba, dangerously close to America's shores. Under the new president's urging, the slow, cautious operation planned by the CIA quickly escalated into a full-scale invasion campaign—with its budget jumping from $4 million to $46 million!

FUBARs _____

Most Americans had never even heard of the Central Intelligence Agency until 1961, when an American U-2 spy plane was shot down by a Russian MIG fighter over the Soviet Union and the pilot, Francis Gary Powers, confessed to being a CIA operative.

Straight Shooting _____

The CIA trained the Cuban exiles in Guatemala because they had a lot of power in that nation. In June 1954, The Company helped to overthrow the leftist government of Jacobo Arbenz after the newly elected president of Guatemala nationalized land owned by the United Fruit Company. The CIA-inspired invasion of Cuba was code-named Operation Zapata. (*Zapata* is the Spanish word for "shoe.")

In Guatemala, U.S. Army Special Forces units set up shop at Helvetia, a 5,000-acre plantation in the Sierra Madre mountains near the town of San Felipe. The land was owned by Roberto Alejos, who was the brother of the Guatemalan ambassador to the United States. Nearly 1,500 Cuban exiles were based on that plantation. Supplied with American weapons and vehicles, the exiles completed basic combat training, and then some were selected for extra training in clandestine operations, courtesy of the Army Special Forces.

Secrecy abounded, which verged on the paranoid side. The CIA's Directorate of Operations was so fixated on secrecy that it did not consult the Agency's own Directorate of Intelligence. If it had, the intelligence bureau could have told the spooks in operations that there was almost no chance that the Cuban people would rise up to support the invasion—which was an essential component of the campaign. Although there were a number of anti-Castro forces in the hills of Cuba, Castro's hold on the urban areas was complete—anyone in the cities who wanted to fight Castro had already been arrested by his secret police. Ironically, although most members of the CIA were in the dark about the planned invasion, the information soon leaked to the rest of the world. Even *The New York Times* found out about the "secret" operation but agreed to bury the story.

Too Many Mistakes

President Kennedy's own actions, both before and after the invasion, also hamstrung the CIA's chances for success. For instance, Kennedy insisted that the U.S. government should not be seen as helping the invasion—which was completely absurd. The exiles were carrying American weapons and equipment, were using American-style tactics, and were supposed to be supported by American air strikes and ships. Under such conditions, "plausible deniability" was impossible. How could the U.S. government realistically deny its role in such an operation?

Far too much was done to booster the cause of "deniability." To further hide American involvement, President Kennedy insisted that the invasion be launched neither from the U.S. mainland nor from any of America's territories, including Puerto Rico (which was the CIA's planned staging point). Finally, as the operation began, President Kennedy vacillated and finally suspended American air strikes against Cuban air fields, which effectively ended any chance the Cuban exiles may have had for success.

The Invasion Begins

On April 17, 1961, between 1,300 and 1,500 Cuban exiles armed with U.S. weapons landed in La Bahia de Conchinos (the Bay of Pigs) on Cuba's southern coast. The assault began at 2:00 A.M. with a team of divers going ashore to establish a beachhead and set up equipment. Between 2:20 and 3:00 A.M., two battalions of the Brigada Asalto 2506 came ashore at Playa Giron, while a third battalion landed at Playa Larga.

Unfortunately, some anti-Castro groups meant to link up with the invaders came down from the hills too early. Many were killed; others were captured and interrogated. By the time the main force landed on the beach, Castro knew they were coming and was ready for them. Over 20,000 Cubans converged on the Bay of Pigs, encircling the invaders. Meanwhile, Castro's fighters took to the skies and beat back the exiles' meager air support, shooting down the vintage B-26 bombers given to the anti-Castro forces to attack Cuba military bases. With no American fighters to stop them, Castro's air force went on to sink the U.S. command vessel *Marsopa* and the supply ship *Houston*. Without the ammunition and supplies off these ships, the exile army was doomed.

FUBARs

Kennedy's special assistant, Arthur Schlesinger Jr., urged the president not to participate in the invasion coverup. "When lies must be told, they should be told by subordinate officials. At no point should the President be asked to lend himself to the cover operations." This is the essence of "plausible deniability."

Fidel Castro took personal command of the communist counterattack. Although the Cuban exiles fought hard, they were outnumbered and outgunned, and they were running out of ammunition. Within a few days, almost all the members of the exile army were either killed or captured. When the shooting stopped, 114 members of the Brigada Asalto 2506 were dead and 1,189 had been captured.

"Plausible Deniability"

Despite all evidence to the contrary, the Kennedy administration labored to maintain the absurd fiction that the Cuban exiles were acting on their own for many days after the invasion. U.S. Ambassador Adlai Stevenson even stood before the United Nations General Assembly and repeated the CIA-invented cover story that Cuban planes and Cuban troops, taking off from Cuban bases, had began the "insurrection" against Castro on their own.

A basic truth in modern, post-Nixon, post-Clinton politics—that the coverup is almost always worse than the crime—was never more true than after the Bay of Pigs fiasco. To support Kennedy's assertions that America was not involved, the CIA unleashed its veteran propaganda specialists to influence international opinion about the invasion. The CIA issued pro-exile, anti-Castro press releases—supposedly generated by a Cuban exile group—through Lem Jones Associates, Inc., a small, CIA-hired public relations firm in New York City.

Straight Shooting

Many of the press releases issued by Lem Jones in the name of the exiled "Cuban Revolutionary Council" were actually written by E. Howard Hunt, who would later come to the attention of the American public as one of the prime co-conspirators in the Watergate burglary scandal and coverup.

The CIA coverup went to absurd lengths. The Agency actually staged supposed "defections" from Castro's air force. CIA-owned B-26 bombers, painted with Cuban markings, landed at a Florida airport. The pilots (Cuban exiles working for the CIA) claimed that they were part of Castro's military who had decided to defect. These pilots denounced Castro and declared that they had bombed Cuba with their own planes before fleeing to America. Unfortunately, this complex and unlikely cover story disintegrated under intense press scrutiny, further eroding the CIA's credibility at home and abroad.

Straight Shooting

Operation Mongoose was the name of the Miami-based CIA campaign to assassinate Fidel Castro. The operation was personally supervised by then–Attorney General Robert Kennedy.

In Washington, the president's "plausible deniability" evaporated, and Kennedy was forced to acknowledge American involvement in the operation. Unrepentant, President Kennedy also stated that the U.S. efforts to oust Castro had been restrained and warned that future U.S. action against the Cuban government might be more extreme.

Killing Castro

Unfortunately, subsequent CIA moves against Castro were more desperate and comical than they were effective. A 1967 CIA Inspector General's report recounts many of the bungled attempts to assassinate or embarrass Fidel Castro. One plan called for spraying the radio station where Castro made his broadcast with hallucinogenic drugs or lacing his cigars with a chemical that would induce "temporary personality disorientation." One CIA plan even involved placing thallium salts into Castro's shoes so that his beard would fall out, in an absurd effort to destroy the dictator's "public image."

Shop Talk

Because of the highly publicized assassination attempts against Castro, President Gerald Ford signed Executive Order 11905, which states that no government employee can participate in assassination attempts against foreign leaders. President Ronald Reagan's Executive Order 12333, which governs the CIA's activities today, expanded the strictures against the assassination of political figures.

CIA operatives also proposed detonating fireworks off the coast of Cuba that would portray the image of Jesus Christ in the sky, in an effort to prove to the Cuban people that their leader was in disfavor with God! The CIA even enlisted the aid of the Mafia to kill Castro. Crime boss Salvator Giancana agreed to help the CIA and asked the agency to provide a lethal poison to lace Castro's food. The CIA passed Giancana the toxin, but the organized crime chief failed to assassinate the Cuban dictator as promised.

The fallout of the Bay of Pigs fiasco effectively ended the CIA's "golden age" and marked the beginning of its decline. Since the Bay of Pigs and subsequent operations in Vietnam, The Company has slowly transformed itself from an instrument of covert actions to an intelligence-gathering organization.

Although the failure of the Bay of Pigs disaster was due in large part to President Kennedy's indecisiveness, it should also be noted that members of the CIA convinced JFK that an invasion had a good chance of success, even though better intelligence would have determined otherwise.

The Bay of Pigs fiasco was no way to run a special forces operation, to say the least! After its very public bungling of the Cuban invasion and its failed attempts to assassinate Castro, it is no wonder that Kennedy turned away from the CIA and toward the U.S. Army Special Forces to deal with the crisis in southeast Asia.

The Least You Need to Know

- ◆ The war changed in the second half of the twentieth century, when counterinsurgency replaced full-scale superpower conflict.
- ◆ The CIA succeeded the OSS.
- ◆ The administration of President John F. Kennedy relied on the Central Intelligence Agency to wage war against international communism.
- ◆ After the CIA-inspired invasion at the Bay of Pigs failed to overthrow Castro, John F. Kennedy turned to the U.S. Army Special Forces to contain communism in Vietnam.

Chapter 6

The Green Berets at Their Finest Hour

In This Chapter

- ◆ A crisis in southeast Asia
- ◆ John F. Kennedy and the Green Berets
- ◆ Robin Moore joins the Army Special Forces
- ◆ Sgt. Sadler sings "The Ballad of the Green Berets"

Turning his back on the CIA after the Bay of Pigs fiasco, John F. Kennedy searched for a new way to fight the rising tide of insurgencies sweeping the emerging world. Heeding his advisors, JFK began to enhance or establish special operations forces within the military. The first of those units was the United States Army Special Forces, better known today as the Green Berets.

But there was much resistance to JFK's plan within the military and inside government. It would take an informal public relations campaign mounted by a novelist and a songwriter for America's first modern Special Forces unit to gain acceptance. Meanwhile, as a new political crisis loomed in southeast Asia, the Green Berets began to train for their very first mission in Vietnam.

In this chapter, I'll explore the tumultuous early years of the Green Berets, their growing pains in the years before the Vietnam War, the origin of their distinctive headgear, and their sudden fame—courtesy of a poignant act honoring a slain president, a best-selling novel, and a popular ballad that reached the Top 40.

Trouble in Southeast Asia

According to the Geneva agreements of 1954, Vietnam was divided into North and South Vietnam, along the seventeenth parallel. In North Vietnam, the Vietminh (called the Viet Cong by American forces) under the control of the Vietnamese Lao Dong (Communist) Party consolidated its power. The French were finally driven out of southeast Asia in 1954, after the Battle of Dien Bien Phu. During that two-month siege, the communist forces in Vietnam defeated 2,200 French "Paras"—elite troops of the French Expeditionary Corps—and ended French colonial power in the region. Under the leadership of Ho Chi Minh, the new government collectivized agriculture and put down a bloody peasant uprising sparked by the economic changes in 1956.

South Vietnam, meanwhile, was controlled by Emperor Bao Dai under the French and then by President Ngo Dinh Diem after the emperor was deposed in 1955. Diem was a Catholic and a committed anticommunist, and he was backed by increasing economic and covert aid from the United States. By the late 1950s, the hard-pressed Vietminh forces still fighting the South begged Hanoi for military supplies and reinforcements.

At a meeting of the Lao Dong Party in May 1959, the communists agreed to support the armed revolution against Diem's government. Almost immediately, North Vietnamese troops began to travel down the Ho Chi Minh Trail into North Vietnam. In 1960, the National Liberation Front was established to oppose Diem's regime. By 1962, the communists had murdered thousands of Saigon's government employees and had begun to inflict defeats on the Army of the Republic of Vietnam (ARVN).

By the early 1960s, Diem was under enormous pressure and cracked down on all dissent, including the Buddhists, who resented Diem's Catholicism and were willing to set fire to themselves to protest Saigon's government. Although the Kennedy administration was disenchanted with Diem's regime and had over 15,000 American military "advisors" in Vietnam already, neither Kennedy nor his staff had a hand in the November 1963 *coup d'état* that ended with Diem's assassination and more political destabilization.

Meanwhile, Viet Cong activity in the South spread, and all of Vietnam was in danger of joining the communist bloc. If the *domino theory* was true, then Laos and Cambodia were also in danger.

Special Ops Jargon _____

The **domino theory** was predicated on the belief that if one country fell to communism, its neighbors would be threatened with a chain reaction of communist takeovers, falling like dominoes. Presidents John F. Kennedy and Lyndon Baines Johnson both subscribed to the domino theory.

John F. Kennedy watched the chaos in Vietnam with mounting trepidation. After the debacle in Cuba, he was determined to halt the spread of communism *somewhere*. Unfortunately, JFK chose to draw the line in Vietnam, with tragic consequences to the United States.

John F. Kennedy and the Green Berets

Burned by the intelligence community's bungling of the Cuban invasion (as well as his own timidity), Kennedy was looking for a new counterinsurgency force. He turned to the meager numbers of special forces units within the U.S. military, hoping that they would have better luck in Vietnam than the CIA had had in Cuba.

President Kennedy ordered a vast expansion of the unconventional warfare units in all branches of America's armed services. But Kennedy also paid special attention to the U.S. Army Special Forces, based in Fort Bragg, North Carolina. As the communist threat in southeast Asia intensified, Kennedy dispatched these units to fight the North Vietnamese forces of Ho Chi Minh and their Viet Cong allies fighting a guerrilla war in the South.

Whatever his other limitations were, President John F. Kennedy was an original thinker, and he was very well read compared to his predecessors in one important subject. At the urging of Roger Hilsman, Director of the State Department's Bureau of Intelligence and Research (and an OSS veteran), Kennedy studied the revolutionary writings of Mao Tse-tung, Che Guevara, and Vietnamese Gen. Vo Nguyen Giap. Kennedy realized that one major threat to national security came from communist clandestine and covert political and military aggression in small, underdeveloped countries.

What made this a threat was the fact that the guerrilla fighters supported by the Soviet Union and Red China were not vulnerable to attack by conventional military forces or traditional tactics. To defeat communist-inspired insurgency (and the utopia that it promised, though never delivered), Kennedy believed that the front line of defense had to be the "hearts and minds" of the endangered populace.

Shop Talk

John F. Kennedy embraced a "whole new kind of strategy, a wholly different kind of force, and, therefore, a wholly different kind of military training." That "new strategy" and "different" type of military training would become the purview of America's Special Forces.

Kennedy Faces Resistance

America's military high command did not agree with the president. They felt there was nothing special about the war in Vietnam or the irregular guerrilla force fighting it. Traditional military minds saw the Viet Cong as another in a long line of insurgency movements, one that could be easily quashed by the same conventional military strategies and tactics that had won all of America's previous conflicts of this kind.

"After all," argued some detractors of special forces, "what made Castro so different from Charlemagne Peralte in Haiti or Augusto C. Sandino in Nicaragua? It took only two quick-thinking Marines to stop Peralte and a thousand troops to bring down Sandino!" Few—even among Kennedy's own Joint Chiefs of Staff—agreed with the president's assertion that Ho Chi Minh's guerrilla army was somehow unique in the annals of warfare.

But Kennedy argued that waging a large-scale, conventional war in Vietnam—or anywhere else in the world—was a risky proposition in the post-nuclear age. With a thousand warheads pointed at American and Russian cities, there was a danger that any such conflict could escalate into a nuclear exchange. JFK knew better than anyone how close the world had come to nuclear extinction during the Cuban Missile Crisis.

There were political considerations as well. Although the Cold War was running hot in the early 1960s, the American public was in no mood for an all-out war over some Asian nation that most had never even heard of.

Running out of options, Kennedy decided to build the special forces as the first line of defense. Because of the promise of their motto, *De Oppresso Liber*, JFK insisted that America's special forces become proficient in guerrilla warfare and counterinsurgency, to block communist expansion and protect the indigenous peoples of the Third World from communist domination. Although President Kennedy met with initial resistance, he persisted until he finally got his way.

Special Ops Jargon

De Oppresso Liber (To Free the Oppressed) is the official motto of the U.S. Army Special Forces.

In pushing his agenda, JFK focused especially on the Army's Special Forces, known unofficially as the Green Berets. He admired their determination and *esprit de corps*; according to some sources, the charismatic young president was particularly fond of their stylish headgear.

The U.S. Special Forces crest and patch.

It's the Hats, Stupid

It was the 1950s, and Col. Edson F. Raff II, commanding officer of the 77th Special Forces group —at that time one of the very few active special operations force in the American military—had a dangerous morale problem on his hands. The high priority accorded to the special forces just a few years before was waning rapidly, along with their independence. No longer a high priority within the Army, the commanders of the XVIII Airborne Corps at Fort Bragg were attempting to exert control over the unit, sapping the unit's individuality and robbing them of their "specialness."

Colonel Raff suggested to his men that some type of distinctive headgear—perhaps a colored baseball hat—would substitute for the unit's waning importance. One officer, Capt. Miguel de la Pena, collected military berets from many armies and thought that an appropriately colored beret would bolster the unit's fighting spirit.

The first berets adopted by Colonel Raff were teal blue with gold piping around the sweat band. The beret's color was met with loud criticism, so a rifle-green beret was tried next. These berets, based on the hats worn by the British Royal Marine Commando units, also had some problems but were generally accepted. Soon they were sold for around $2 at the Fort Bragg exchange. A few weeks later, at a review for a retiring general, the crowd seemed impressed with the "foreign troops" who wore berets on the parade ground; after that, the use of the berets by the 77th was universal.

The first green berets sold at Fort Bragg "looked like man-sized Girl Scout berets complete with a half-inch pigtail sticking up out of the center of the crown." Special forces soldiers clipped off the pigtail with nail clippers before donning their berets.

High command was less enchanted with the special headgear and demanded to know who had authorized the wearing of berets. Of course, the answer was no one, but the members of the 77th stubbornly insisted on sporting their berets, despite regulations to the contrary. Meanwhile, the men of the 10th Special Forces Group stationed in Germany saw the berets and adopted them, without authorization. As their popularity grew, the berets were replaced by Canadian military berets, which sold for $6 at the local exchange. Now a highly prized badge of special forces qualification, these new berets were snapped up in record time.

When an Airborne division requested permission to wear red berets a few months later, the "crap hit the propeller." Instead of granting Airborne's request, the Army forbade *all* units from wearing berets of any color. This was a blow to the Special Forces, which maintained the tradition when possible, despite pressure from above. To gain sympathy for their plight, the 77th tried to present President Dwight D. Eisenhower with a green beret. He accepted the gift without comment, and it looked as if the green berets were heading for the scrap heap of history, although the 10th SFG continued to sport the now-familiar headgear in Germany.

President Kennedy Authorizes the Green Beret

Recognition—and authorization—for the green berets came a few years later. When President John F. Kennedy visited the Special Warfare School at Fort Bragg in October 12, 1961, the White House sent word to Gen. William P. Yarborough, requesting that all Special Forces soldiers wear their green berets as part of the event. A year later, in 1962, President Kennedy called the famous headpiece "a symbol of excellence, a badge of courage, a mark of distinction in the fight for freedom."

Shop Talk

During President John F. Kennedy's visit to the U.S. Army Special Warfare School, the members of the 77th Special Forces Group at Fort Bragg presented him with a green beret and a request for a presidential authorization to wear their own. Kennedy granted that request, and the legend of the "Green Berets" was born.

During JFK's visit to the U.S. Army's Special Warfare School, the 77th presented its commander-in-chief with a green beret and a request for permission for its members to wear their own. In due time, that request was granted.

Although it proved to be a real public relations coup, Kennedy's permission for the Army Special Forces units to wear green berets did not solve the main problem—lowered priority and a lack of funding. Both were the results of continued resistance against *special* troops within the military. That struggle would continue for two decades.

A little bit of that resistance ended at President Kennedy's funeral. Sgt. Maj. Francis J. Ruddy, a member of the graveside honor guard, stepped forward, removed his green beret, and laid it on his commander-in-chief's grave, giving back for all Army Special Forces soldiers the honor that Kennedy had bestowed on them. That poignant incident, seen by the entire nation on television and written about in newspapers, ensured that the green beret would be known and respected throughout the military from that moment on. On Memorial Day 1997, the John F. Kennedy Library created a place of honor in its museum to display the actual green beret left by Sergeant Major Ruddy at the Arlington National Cemetery gravesite of President Kennedy on November 25, 1963.

JFK placed great faith in his unconventional warfare groups. He saw them as the answer to America's Cold War dilemma—an unobtrusive, less costly force of specially trained warriors, capable of battling communist-inspired guerrillas in the Third World, a *force multiplier* capable of achieving substantial results with small numbers.

Special Ops Jargon

In unconventional warfare jargon, a **force multiplier** is a 10- to 12-man unit (such as a Special Forces A-Team) that is capable of training, fielding, and leading 300 to 500 indigenous warriors into combat.

During the Kennedy era, the Green Berets attained their greatest notoriety and their most rapid expansion. By 1963, the newly formed 8th Special Forces Group was operating in Latin America, the 5th Special Forces Group was in Vietnam, and the 3rd and 6th were being formed for future operations in the Middle East and Africa.

Because of John F. Kennedy's dedication to the Army Special Forces, his name will be forever linked to their glory. Few commanders-in-chiefs since Kennedy have put so much thought and effort into nurturing America's special operations forces.

It was because of JFK's dedication to their mission and faith in their prowess that Sgt. Maj. Francis Ruddy proposed that the Army's Special Warfare School be named after the assassinated president. Today The John F. Kennedy Special Warfare Center trains successive generations of Special Forces soldiers, each of them dedicated to living up to John F. Kennedy's vision.

Robin Moore Joins the Green Berets

After John F. Kennedy bestowed his blessings on the Army Special Forces and granted them permission to wear green berets, their headgear and their name became synonymous as a torrent of publicity came crashing down on them. Although some critics of the Special Forces thought that the Green Berets were waging a propaganda war of their own in order to garner more military funding, recognition, and respect, very little of the publicity originated from the Special Forces.

In fact, the next round of press coverage came courtesy of Attorney General Robert Kennedy, JFKs brother, and an old friend of his from Harvard University.

Robert Lowell Moore Jr. was born on October 31, 1925, in Boston, Massachusetts. Raised in Concord by affluent parents, Moore attended Belmont Hill School. After graduation, he joined the Army Air Corps and flew a tour of combat missions in the skies over Germany in the closing days of World War II. After the war, Moore attended Harvard, where he met classmate Robert (Bobby) Kennedy, also from Massachusetts. When Moore graduated in 1949, he moved to New York City to produce television shows.

In 1952, Moore returned to Boston to work for his daddy's business—the Sheraton Hotel Company, co-founded by Robert Lowell Moore Sr. Although he was competent at his job, Moore grew restless and began to write his first novel. Published under the penname Robin Moore, *Pitchman* was a scathing peek at the burgeoning television business in the mid-1950s. The novel failed to generate much excitement, so Moore continued to work for the Sheridan Hotel Company, moving to the Caribbean in an ongoing effort to establish new Sheraton Hotels in the region. While there, Robin Moore met Fidel Castro, a fateful meeting that led to his second book, *The Devil to Pay*.

Straight Shooting

Robin Moore's first nonfiction book was called *The Devil to Pay* and chronicled the history of Fidel Castro's Cuban guerrilla campaign.

Moore's third book was a novel that featured a thinly disguised peek inside his family's business. The shocking revelations in *Hotel Tomayne* effectively ended Robin Moore's future in hotel management, even as it launched his writing career.

"Author" Moore Trains for Action

In 1963, through the active intervention of Robert Kennedy, Robin Moore was granted permission to join the U.S. Army Special Forces as a civilian. Special Forces commander Lieut. Gen. William Yarborough allowed Robin Moore to join the group as a civilian, with the rank of Author. It was Yarborough who demanded that Moore spend at least a year with his troops in training and during combat operations in Vietnam.

For the next 11 months, civilian Moore, at age 40, attempted to keep up with the 30-something active-duty Army volunteers in Green Beret training. After a year, Moore shipped out to Vietnam with the Special Forces, living in the field and going out on dangerous combat missions.

As the result of this experience, Robin Moore wrote his third and most famous novel, *The Green Berets*, which was published in May 1965 to mostly mixed reviews and a wildly enthusiastic reading public.

Robin Moore's novel made the Green Berets a household name. More than the fancy hats or a martyred president's imprimatur, the novel focused America's attention on the Special Forces even as the war in Vietnam—and the American public's resistance to it—was heating up. Although *The Green Berets* was fiction, everything that Moore chronicled in his best-selling book was fundamentally true, and Americans who read it got their first glimpse into the secret world of special operations.

> **Shop Talk**
>
> *The Green Berets* was controversial from the moment it was published. Some critics called it propaganda; others felt it was the definitive novel of the Vietnam War. The book went on to become an international bestseller and introduced a new generation of young American males to Army's Special Forces.

The Green Berets Go Hollywood

The book spent months on the hard-cover and paperback bestseller lists, and Warner Brothers/Seven Arts snapped up the movie rights. In 1967, the motion picture adaptation starring John Wayne, Aldo Ray, Jim Hutton, and David Janssen began production, with Wayne as producer and co-director. President Lyndon Baines Johnson offered the Army's full cooperation for the production, including permission to film large-scale helicopter maneuvers at Fort Rucker, Alabama's Helicopter U.S. Army Aviation Center and School. A remote 250-square-acre area inside of the Army's post at Fort Benning, Georgia, doubled (unconvincingly) for the jungles of Vietnam. Elaborate sets were constructed, and hundreds of extras were brought in to shoot the epic battle scenes.

When filming was complete, the production company left the elaborate sets standing. They included two authentic-looking Montagnard villages, a Green Berets "strike camp," and four "typical" Vietnamese villages, constructed of lumber, bamboo, barbed wire, thatch, and rice bags stuffed with sawdust. The production company also donated mock Soviet-style weapons and thousands of rubber "pungi sticks" to simulate the lethal bamboo spikes used as man-trap weapons in Vietnam. Army recruits planned and executed many training raids on the "camps" built by the Hollywood filmmakers.

When *The Green Berets* was released in 1968, the film, like the novel it was based on, became the focal point of controversy. Seen as a jingoistic tool of American propaganda by most critics and antiwar activists, the film drew lovers of old-fashioned "gung-ho" war films to the

> **Shop Talk**
>
> Robin Moore returned to southeast Asia for the setting of the novel *The Country Team* about American diplomacy and Special Forces operations in the region. He also spent three years in Africa, observing American and European mercenaries fighting communist-inspired terrorism for his novel *The White Tribe*.

theater. Some who supported the war in Vietnam seemed to feel that it was their patriotic duty to attend a screening. The film, like the novel, became an international hit despite (or because of) the controversy attracted by its subject matter.

For his fourth book, Robin Moore rode with the New York police department and wrote about one of the most spectacular heroin busts in history. *The French Connection* went on to become a bestseller and then a highly acclaimed motion picture that launched the career of little-known character actor Gene Hackman, who won the Oscar for Best Actor for his riveting portrayal of crusader cop Popeye Doyle (real name Eddie Egan). The film also earned director William Friedkin an Academy Award.

The Ballad and the Balladeer

Barry Sadler—singer, songwriter, author, and Green Beret—was born in Carlsbad, New Mexico, on November 4, 1940. The second son of John Sadler and Bebe Littlefield—both originally from Phoenix, Arizona—Sadler was born into a troubled family. Within a few years, John and Bebe divorced. John remarried, only to die of a rare form of neuro-logical cancer at the age of 36.

After the divorce, Bebe led a freewheeling, sometimes hard-scrabble life. At age seven, Sadler and his older brother, Robert, journeyed through the seedy Southwest, with stops at Ruidoso, Hobbs, Santa Fe, Las Vegas, El Paso, Lubbock, and the rough-and-tumble oil town of Midland, Texas. When Sadler was 12, he spent the summer at a logging camp in Mora, New Mexico—just 17 miles from the nuclear testing ground at Los Alamos—where he listened to the men play country western and Mexican songs until late into the night and tuned in to a "Top 40" radio station broadcasting from Las Vegas. His intro-duction to music changed his life. Without a formal education, Sadler learned to play a flute, the harmonica, and the drums before focusing on mastering the guitar. That same summer, Sadler learned to shoot and camp in the wilderness. He hunted with a .22-caliber pistol and became a crack shot.

Shop Talk
Before Barry Sadler was 18 years old, he had become a U.S. Air Force radar specialist and was serving overseas in Japan. That was only the begin-ning of his short but intense career in the military.

Sadler dropped out of school in the tenth grade and hitchhiked across the country, working odd jobs, camp-ing out and sometimes living off the land. In June 1958, Sadler joined the Air Force. He was just 17 and needed his mother's permission to enlist. After training, Sadler was sent to Japan.

After a year in Japan, Sadler returned to the United States and left the Air Force. Unable to find real work, he went on the road with fellow musician Walter Lane. The pair traveled through the West in a 1953 Chevy, playing in bars, clubs, restaurants, and strip malls. On this odyssey, Sadler met an African-American piano man named Elmo, who gave him his first real music lessons. Lane and Sadler moved on, traveling through Colorado, Wyoming, Montana, Washington, and Oregon; they ended up in California, where they loaded fruit into railcars for a little over a dollar an hour.

Barry Sadler Joins the Green Berets

Tired of life on the road, Sadler enlisted in the Army, volunteering for airborne training. Sadler thrived in the military, facing and surmounting each challenge. He graduated jump school at Fort Benning, Georgia. Proud of this accomplishment, Sadler began to write a song about airborne school. Later, he told a music journalist, "I had no idea what (the song) would be, but I wanted it to include the line 'silver wings upon their chests.'"

Soon Sadler shipped out to Vietnam, where he made a name for himself singing in the clubs and in the field. While on a combat mission, Sadler was dragged out of the jungle and rushed to Saigon. Still covered in the "muck from the boonies" he was brought before a public information officer who offered Sadler two projects. The first was to write a song honoring Maj. Gen. Delk N. Oden, "The Flying General," who was in charge of the Army Support Command in Vietnam. The second was to film and tape himself singing his song, "The Ballad of the Green Berets," for an ABC film crew.

Returning to duty, Sadler participated in several combat missions in the Central Highlands of Vietnam. In May 1965, while leading a patrol in the tall grass southeast of Pleiku, Sgt. Sadler ran his knee into a Viet Cong pungi stick. The Cong placed pungi sticks all over the jungle and smeared the sharp wooden poles with human excrement, to cause wounds to fester.

Straight Shooting

Staff Sgt. Barry Sadler was filmed singing "The Ballad of the Green Berets" for ABC television in-country, directly in front an Army bunker in South Vietnam.

Because he had already been given powerful antibiotics to treat dysentery, and because the wound seemed superficial, Sadler put an adhesive bandage on it and continued with the patrol.

A Star Is Born

Neglecting his wound proved to be a mistake: A massive infection quickly set in, and doctors talked about amputating Sadler's leg. While lying in the hospital, Sadler heard Robert F. Kennedy's speech dedicating the new John F. Kennedy Special Warfare Center at Fort Bragg. Sadler vowed that if the doctors could save his leg, he would give away the rights to his "Ballad" just so that Americans could hear the song and realize the sacrifices made by the troops fighting in Vietnam.

On December 18, 1965, RCA provided Sadler—now a decorated combat veteran—with a 15-piece orchestra, a male chorus, and studio time to record his songs. Arriving in the studio that morning with less than an hour's sleep, Sadler recorded a dozen original songs for the album by 11:00 P.M. that night. Three weeks later, RCA released "The Ballad of the Green Berets" as a single. A week after that, Sadler's first album was released.

FUBARs

Although "The Ballad of the Green Berets" became the Special Forces anthem, there were "gallows humor" lyrics invented by the men serving in Vietnam, including: "Back at home a young wife waits, doing the Twist at Annex 8, ten thousand bucks she got today, 'cause Charlie greased her Green Beret."

"The Ballad" sold two million copies in five weeks. An instant celebrity, Sadler was featured in *Life Magazine*, *Time Magazine*, *Newsweek*, *Variety*, and *Billboard*. He sang his now-famous song on *The Ed Sullivan Show*, *The Jimmy Dean Show*, and ABC's *Hollywood Palace* show. He received two industry Gold Records, marking sales of one million on both the single and the album. In the bargain, Staff Sgt. Barry Sadler became the poster boy for the war in Vietnam. Ultimately, Sadler sold 11 million records. "The Ballad of the Green Berets" was the number-1 tune for 5 weeks in 1966 and ended up as the top-selling song for that year, eclipsing Nancy Sinatra's "These Boots Are Made for Walking." Sadler's ballad still ranks 21 on the Billboard Chart for the entire 1960–1969 decade.

Barry Sadler Becomes a Novelist

Barry Sadler never again achieved success as a musician. By the 1970s, he was broke and living in Nashville, hoping to revive his career. During that period, he wrote his first novel, *Casca, the Eternal Mercenary*. The book was a best-seller, and Sadler went on to write 21 sequels, selling over 2 million copies.

In the 1980s, Sadler moved to Guatemala, where he continued to write and lead a life of adventure that was tragically cut short. On September 8, 1989, Barry Allen Sadler was with a local woman in a taxi driving along the Antigua Highway when he was shot in the head. He had been drinking for many hours, and both the taxi driver and Sadler's female companion claim that his own .380 Pietro Barretta pistol had been drawn and fired.

Shop Talk

The plane that carried Barry Sadler's comatose body to Nashville was chartered by Bob Brown, editor-in-chief of *Soldier of Fortune* magazine.

Whether Sadler was a victim of assassination or robbery is unclear, but it was the beginning of the end of his checkered career. Lingering near death at Roosevelt Hospital in Guatemala City, Sadler was flown via a chartered flight to a Veterans Administration Hospital in Nashville. He clung to life for another 14 months before finally succumbing to his wounds.

There is still a lot of mystery surrounding Barry Sadler's untimely death, and Guatemalan authorities continue to list the case as unsolved even though the cab driver spent a year in prison for his involvement in the murder. But whatever happened on that lonely road that fateful night, it was an unhappy and ironic end to one of the key figures who had popularized—and glorified—the legend of the U.S. Army Special Forces during the Vietnam era.

The Least You Need to Know

- John F. Kennedy was the father of America's Special Forces. During the Kennedy era, the legend of the Green Berets was born.
- The first test of the U.S. Army Special Forces came during the Vietnam War.
- Author Robin Moore published a novel that helped to popularize the Green Berets.
- Green Beret Staff Sgt. Barry Sadler enhanced the legendary status of the Army Special Forces with his hit song "The Ballad of the Green Berets."

Chapter 7

The Green Berets in Vietnam

In This Chapter

- ◆ President Kennedy turns to the Special Forces
- ◆ The formation of the Civilian Irregular Defense Group
- ◆ Project Delta, Apache Force, and Eagle Scouts
- ◆ Projects Sigma and Omega
- ◆ Vietnam heats up: The Tonkin Gulf Resolution

After years of recruitment, training, and preparation, the U.S. Army Special Forces finally went to war. By 1963 there were over 1,500 Green Berets in southeast Asia, committed to the struggle against communism by President John F. Kennedy himself.

As you'll see in this chapter, U.S. Army Special Forces units in the Central Highlands region trained indigenous people called the Montagnards to resist communist expansion. Meanwhile, in hundreds of rural villages in South Vietnam, Green Beret civil action units were providing medical care and agricultural assistance to the most needy, in an effort to win the hearts and minds of the Vietnamese people.

Vietnam was the longest war in our nation's history—and America's first defeat on the battlefield. The undeclared war in southeast Asia was also the most divisive conflict since the American Civil War, pitting young Americans against their government, their military, and even their parents. The Army Special Forces spent 14 years in Vietnam, beginning in June 1956, when the original 16 members of the 14th Special Forces Operational Detachment entered the country to train a cadre of indigenous Vietnamese Special Forces teams.

The ground war in Vietnam was an ugly, brutal series of guerrilla campaigns fought against a ubiquitous enemy alongside a corrupt, unreliable ally. It didn't take long before Special Forces teams were on the ground, fighting side by side with—and sometimes leading— Vietnamese troops in battle. After all, Vietnam was the messy insurgency war that the Green Berets were created to fight.

Initially greeted with suspicion and hostility by the military hierarchy, the Green Berets expanded rapidly after 1961 at the insistence of President John F. Kennedy, who firmly believed that their formidable counterinsurgency skills would play an important role in future conflicts all over the globe. As the war in southeast Asia heated up, it was time for the Special Forces to deliver on their promise.

Kennedy Turns to the Special Forces

After a string of foreign policy disasters in Cuba, Kennedy turned eastward, toward the continued anarchy in Vietnam. It was there that he decided to draw another line against communism. By 1963, JFK had dispatched over 1,500 Green Berets from the 5th Special Forces Group to Vietnam. Some of these soldiers trained the South Vietnamese and other indigenous peoples in counterinsurgency tactics—in essence, giving them the means and the skills to defend themselves. The most prominent indigenous people to receive American assistance were the Montagnards. Their name comes from the French for "mountain people" because they dwelled exclusively in the Central Highlands and the rugged hills around the Red River Delta.

> **Shop Talk**
>
> The Special Forces were in Vietnam before anyone else. The first American to die was Capt. Harry G. Cramer of the 14th Special Forces Operational Detachment of the 77th Special Forces Group, killed on October 21, 1956. His name heads the list on the Vietnam Veterans Memorial in Washington, D.C.

Other Special Forces teams worked in the jungle, where A-Teams were assigned reconnaissance and sabotage missions, penetrating deep into communist-held territory. These small units operated independently, sometimes for weeks at a time.

For the most part, these strike-force operations consisted of patrols deep into communist-held territory. Hundreds of contacts with the enemy occurred, and many small engagements were fought. There were also a fair number of joint operations with regular Vietnam Army units, particularly as the war escalated in 1964. The Special Forces attempted to establish intelligence nets that would produce accurate information on the location and disposition of enemy forces, as well as the identities of Viet Cong political operatives.

Civil action and psychological operations were also conducted as part of the Special Forces mission. Their objective was to raise the living standard of the people and enlist their loyalty to the government in Saigon. Although emphasis is usually placed on the role the Special Forces played as warriors in Vietnam, they were also "community developers in uniform," providing vital humanitarian aid to the people they defended.

Straight Shooting

In 1954, Vietnam was partitioned along the 17th parallel, in much the same way that Korea was partitioned along the 38th parallel. The region north of the partition (North Vietnam) was under communist control, and the region to the south (The Republic of Vietnam) was nominally democratic.

The Face of the Enemy in Vietnam

The war in Vietnam involved combat with two distinct enemy forces. The *Viet Cong* (from the French *Viet Nam cong-sam*) were indigenous guerrillas who lurked undetected among the populace of South Vietnam, mingling with both the rural and the urban populations. They evolved from the Viet Minh, or *Vietnam Doc Lap Dong Minh Hoi* (Vietnam Independence Allied Committee), which was first organized to fight the French. Soldiers of the Viet Cong were sometimes farmers and tradesmen by day and guerrilla fighters by night. Because the Viet Cong hid among the general population, Vietnam was dubbed a "360° war" because the enemy lurked in every direction.

The conventional combat troops of the Democratic Republic of Vietnam (North Vietnamese communists controlled from their capital city, Hanoi) were the soldiers of the People's Army of Vietnam, or PAVN. At the time of the Vietnam war, the PAVN was a formidable force. PAVN troops wore regulation uniforms, fought with Soviet-supplied weapons, and used traditional military tactics. Though proficient at arms and quite numerous, PAVN troops fared poorly when facing similarly trained American troops, and the communists relied mostly on their guerrilla forces and their relentless propaganda machine to win their struggle. America's military ally in the Vietnam War was the Army of the Republic of (South) Vietnam, or ARVN. Its soldiers fought to defend the nominally democratic government based in Saigon.

Special Ops Jargon

The communist guerrillas in Vietnam were called **Viet Cong.** The People's Army of Vietnam (PAVN) was the name of the conventional North Vietnamese military. In American slang, the Viet Cong were dubbed "Charlie," while the regular troops of the PAVN were more formerly addressed as "Mr. Charles."

Competing Strategies in Vietnam

When JFK visited Fort Bragg in 1961, he gave the Special Forces troops in review (and proudly wearing their green berets) one of his signature speeches about battling communism, finishing his rousing words with the promise that the Green Berets would be on the front lines in the battle to come.

These were prophetic words, for the 5th Special Forces Group—activated on September 21, 1961—was swiftly dispatched to southeast Asia. The 3rd, 6th, and 8th Special Forces Groups followed in 1963. The rate of escalation during the Kennedy administration was astounding. In January 1961, when Kennedy took office, there were less than 700 American advisors in Vietnam. At the time of Kennedy's death in November 1963, there were 16,700 U.S. troops serving there, along with 300 aircraft and more than 100 helicopters.

The strategic thinking behind America's war in Vietnam was questionable from the start. Since the partition of Vietnam in 1954, the U.S. Army had created the large and unwieldy Military Advisory and Assistance Group (MAAG) in Vietnam. From the mid-1950s to the 1960s, MAAG helped create a conventional South Vietnamese army made up of large, unwieldy infantry and armored divisions. These organized infantry divisions and tanks were totally useless against communist insurgents roaming in the jungles, rice paddies, and mountains of Vietnam. The result was that, by 1964, the Army of the Republic of Vietnam (ARVN) was suffering losses of a battalion a week to communist insurgents. Unfortunately, when the United States committed large military forces of its own, American units all used the conventional military approach—the same erroneous strategy that had failed to achieve satisfactory results for the ARVN in more than two decades of fighting.

Shop Talk
The operations to train counterinsurgency tactics to the many indigenous groups in Vietnam were collectively known as the Civilian Irregular Defense Group (CIDG) program. The development of paramilitary forces among the minority groups became the primary mission of the U.S. Special Forces in Vietnam.

The U.S. Special Forces chose to fight a different kind of war. Where ARVN units (and later U.S. Army and Marine Corps units) maneuvered battalion-sized formations of 300 to 500 soldiers through the countryside, the Special Forces concentrated on small unit action, meeting the Viet Cong in quick hit-and-run engagements. Although such tactics did not produce large battles or decisive victories, they tended to keep the insurgents off balance and caused a slow but steady attrition of the enemy forces.

The Civilian Irregular Defense Group

To create the small units necessary to engage in guerrilla warfare, the Green Berets began to teach counterinsurgency tactics to the various tribes, religious factions, and ethnic minorities inside Vietnam under an ambitious program called the Civilian Irregular

Defense Group (CIDG). Within a few years, the Green Berets advisors in this program created indigenous units that could operate in the field, meeting Viet Cong guerrilla activity with guerrilla actions of their own, thereby returning the most enemy casualties with the least cost to the United States.

By 1966–1967, the indigenous units of the CIDG were so proficient that they transitioned from defensive to offensive operations, aggressively moving against the Viet Cong guerrillas operating in both the North and the South.

The Indigenous People of Vietnam

The history of Vietnam was complex, with wave after wave of new immigrants coming into the region over the centuries. Some of these groups attempted to supplant (or eradicate) the others. The ethnic Vietnamese tend to live in the lowlands, cities, or provincial towns, along with the Han Chinese, or "overseas" Chinese, who settled Vietnam in the last three centuries and now number in the millions. The Khmer, which number half a million, and the Cham (50,000 or more) are both descendants of peoples who occupied Central and South Vietnam prior to the Vietnamese conquest of the region. Although these groups coexisted, they lacked the cohesiveness necessary to defeat outside aggressors such as the North Vietnamese communists.

Perhaps the most diverse group falls under the name Montagnards, whom the ethnic Vietnamese majority referred to as *moi* ("savages"). The Montagnards are a tribal people who live almost exclusively in the hills around the Red River Delta and the mountains of the Central Highlands. At the time of the Vietnam War, these various Montagnard tribes were divided into approximately 50 different language and ethnic groups, including the Tho, the Tay, the Nung, the Muong, the Rhade, and the Jarai. These tribes made constant war on one another and on both the North and South Vietnamese.

Straight Shooting

The Vietnamese people were also divided by their religious beliefs. Buddhist groups such as the Hoa Hoa and Cao Dai were vehemently anticommunist, but did not get along with the government in Saigon because it was nominally Roman Catholic.

As the Special Forces began to establish base camps in every province of South Vietnam, feuding ethnic and tribal groups were often forced to live together in these encampments. They did not always get along, and mutinies were common. Before America's involvement in the war, the Montagnards had actually forged their own resistance movement to fight against encroachment by the governments of both North and South Vietnam—the *Front Unifie Pour La Libération Des Races Opprimées* (Unified Front for the Liberation of

Oppressed Peoples), or FULRO. During the war, FULRO rebellions erupted in the Special Forces camps. These rebellions began with the detainment of the U.S. forces followed by the killing of all the Vietnamese troops in the camp, after which the Americans were released to act as middlemen to restore order. Many of these rebellions made the nightly newscasts in America.

The Green Berets "Unify" South Vietnam

The U.S. Army Special Forces were faced with the nearly impossible task of training South Vietnamese peoples of *all* ethnic groups the fine arts of counterinsurgency and molding the many Montagnard tribes into a credible anticommunist threat. But the cultures were so diverse and their cultural differences were so ingrained that the only unifying force in the region became the men of the U.S. Special Forces themselves.

> **Shop Talk**
>
> Until the arrival of U.S. Special Forces teams, the South Vietnamese made no attempt to gain the support of the Montagnards and had actually antagonized them. In 1954, 80,000 refugees from the North flooded into the Central Highlands, displacing the Montagnards even as the Saigon government tried to disarm them.

Until the arrival of U.S. Special Forces teams, the South Vietnamese made absolutely no attempt to gain the support of the Montagnards. Instead, the South Vietnamese government actually *antagonized* them when, in 1954, 80,000 refugees fleeing communism in the North flooded into the Central Highlands, displacing the Montagnards. Instead of helping the Montagnards cope with the flood of refugees living among them, the Saigon government tried to disarm the tribes and put sanctions on their movements.

The Green Berets Employ the Practice of Cultural Diversity

To gain the trust and respect of the *indigs* they trained, the Green Berets were forced to learn and adapt to their customs. For instance, the Montagnards were primarily hunter-gatherers, so their U.S. Special Forces advisors learned to combine tribal hunting expeditions with combat and local security patrols, killing two birds with one stone.

 Special Ops Jargon

Indigs is a term for "indigenous peoples." In Vietnam, there were many waves of immigration over the centuries. The Chiam, aboriginal Muslims, were among the first inhabitants, followed by the Montagnards, the Malayo-Polynesians, the Han Chinese, the Cambodians, and the French. Every ethnic group harbored some grudge against the others, and the ethnic divide was quite deep. Vietnamese children were taught that the Montagnards were covered in body hair and had tails.

Like Lawrence of Arabia, some Special Forces political officers became adept at playing tribal politics and forged fruitful alliances with local chieftains. Sometimes American Special Forces soldiers were adopted by a Montagnard tribe, becoming a valued member of their warrior caste. It was a custom among the Montagnards to give trusted friends a brass bracelet. The presentation involved much ritual, including the sacrifice of a cow, pig, or water buffalo, and the consumption of rice wine blessed by the village shaman. Eventually, wearing a *Jarai* bracelet became a status symbol among the Special Forces troops serving in Vietnam.

The Achievements of Project Delta

In the area of combat development, the achievements of Project Delta must be mentioned. Project Delta was the name given to the first unit of indigenous Vietnamese specifically trained by U.S. Special Forces officers and NCOs to perform special operations. When Delta first became operational in December 1964, it consisted of six reconnaissance teams, each comprised of eight Vietnamese and two U.S. Special Forces men.

By 1967, Project Delta had expanded to 16 reconnaissance teams composed of 4 Vietnamese and 2 U.S. Special Forces members. Delta operations began with team infiltration into enemy territory—usually by helicopter at dusk or after dark, without the benefit of lights or a friendly reception team in place to meet them on the ground.

In early Delta operations, the teams were limited to advanced reconnaissance and were immediately withdrawn by helicopter if discovered. But as their numbers and proficiency increased, Delta teams were allowed to continue their operations after contact with the enemy, as long as they broke contact or annihilated the force they engaged. These teams acted independently, often attacking small targets that they could handle without outside reinforcement or support.

Straight Shooting

When John Wayne was in Vietnam doing research for *The Green Berets*, he was presented with a Jarai bracelet by a Montagnard tribe. He wore that bracelet in every film he made until his death in 1979.

The Apache Force and the Eagle Scouts also had their beginnings at this time. The Apache Force was conceived as a combined force of Special Forces men and indigenous troops who performed advanced reconnaissance and then helped orient American or South Vietnamese entering the region. This orientation included terrain walks, map analysis, briefings on local Viet Cong tactics, and an extensive review of enemy activity in the area to date. Members of the Apache Force usually accompanied American or ARVN units into the field for the first several days of combat in a new area.

The Eagle Scouts, like the Apache Force, were capable of deep reconnaissance, orientation, and combat missions and could be moved by helicopter as well.

Project Omega and Project Sigma

Encouraged by the success of Delta, Project Omega and Project Sigma were organized to perform the same type of mission, but on a much larger scale. Sigma consisted of 900 Civilian Irregular Defense Group troops and 125 U.S. Army Special Forces personnel; Omega had 600 CIDGs and 20 Special Forces troops. Both Omega and Sigma included a reconnaissance element, a reaction force, and an advisory command.

The reconnaissance units included Roadrunner teams—four indigenous troops who conducted long-distance deep-reconnaissance missions along the trails used by the Viet Cong to infiltrate the South. Because they spoke the language and were disguised as Viet Cong or PAVN, these troops were able to gather intelligence about enemy deployment, create maps, and call in air strikes against enemy installations and troop concentrations. Some Roadrunner teams not only wore the uniforms of the regional People's Army of Vietnam, but they also were armed with appropriate Soviet-made weapons as well. They even carried forged paperwork that "proved" they were communist troops.

Straight Shooting

The troops of Project Sigma also trained for a special mission. They were trained to carry out raids on communist prisoner-of-war camps. Although the troops of Project Sigma participated in several raids, none were successful in recovering American or allied prisoners.

Backing up the reconnaissance teams was Mike Force, the Mobile Strike Force Command, consisting of 150 airborne-qualified CIDG personnel led by 20 to 25 Special Forces officers and men. Mike Force companies were deployed to exploit contacts with the enemy, to aid in the extraction of compromised recon teams, and to perform reconnaissance-in-force missions.

Vietnam-era Huey helicopter.

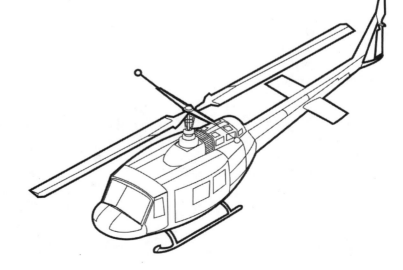

Incident in the Tonkin Gulf

On the afternoon of August 2, 1964, the U.S. Navy destroyer *Maddox*, which was on a reconnaissance cruise off the coast of North Vietnam, was unsuccessfully attacked by three communist torpedo boats. Two nights later, a second attack against the *Maddox* may or may not have been launched.

President Lyndon Johnson, believing that such an attack took place, ordered retaliatory air strikes against North Vietnamese targets on the afternoon of August 5. More important, Johnson demanded—and quickly obtained—the Tonkin Gulf Resolution from Congress, authorizing him to do whatever was necessary to stop communist aggression in Vietnam. President Johnson used this resolution to dramatically escalate the war in Vietnam. The first stage of this escalation involved the deployment of the first expeditionary units of the United States Marine Corps.

After the Tonkin Gulf Resolution was passed, the size of the war, as well as the Special Forces activity in Vietnam, increased exponentially. While members of the Special Forces still trained ARVN units and indigenous forces, that mission became but one of many. Soon the entire 5th Special Forces Group was moved to Vietnam, with permanent headquarters in Nha Trang. By February 1965, the Special Forces war in Vietnam belonged to the 5th until it returned to Fort Bragg in 1971. Within two years of the Gulf of Tonkin Resolution, the first Project Delta, Apache Force, and Eagle Scout missions were mounted, followed by Projects Sigma and Omega.

> **CAUTION**
>
> **FUBARs**
>
> Although the U.S. Congress passed the Tonkin Gulf Resolution nearly unanimously, suspicions that President Johnson misled legislators about the attack on the *U.S.S. Maddox* rocked Washington and ultimately damaged Johnson's credibility with Congress, the press, and the American people. The resolution was repealed in 1970.

During this period of intense buildup, the Special Forces established 254 joint U.S./ARVN camps, most defended by a dozen or so Special Forces A-Team members in command of hundreds of native troops. These camps quickly became heavily defended strong points, often located in the heart of hostile territory. The camps were built to defend Vietnamese civilians living in the region. Many of these camps were deliberately established near the borders of Laos, Cambodia, and North Vietnam, where the Viet Cong filtered into the South to terrorize the populace and strike at the ARVN and U.S. military units struggling to maintain a foothold in the territory.

Some of the fiercest, most violent firefights of the Vietnam War took place in and around these camps. At places such as Song Zoai and Plei Mei—and especially at Nam Dong—the communists threw everything they had at the Green Berets, only to be thrown back into the jungle.

The Least You Need to Know

♦ The long-simmering crisis in Vietnam was the first test of the U.S. Army Special Forces.

♦ The Green Berets established effective programs to train the indigenous peoples of Vietnam to battle communism.

♦ Many successful military operations were planned and executed by the Green Berets in Vietnam.

♦ The Tonkin Gulf Incident of August 1964 increased the size and ferocity of the war.

8

Endgame in Vietnam

In This Chapter

- ◆ At the battle of Nam Dong
- ◆ Winning the hearts and minds of the Vietnamese
- ◆ Rogues and snake eaters in Vietnam
- ◆ A loss of honor: the Rheault Incident
- ◆ The final fate of the indigs

After some early success, the services of the Army Special Forces were much in demand. As the war in Vietnam grew in size and scope, the Green Berets struggled to keep up. In time, their resources were spread so thin that the rigorous standards required of Special Forces candidates were relaxed. Some who became Green Berets failed to live up to the high standards of their predecessors, and by the end of the Vietnam War, the once-noble reputation of the Green Berets had been severely damaged.

Despite the scandals that rocked the Special Forces' high command, the Green Berets managed to mount a final, heroic mission deep into enemy territory before they departed Vietnam forever.

In this chapter, I'll examine the three defining events of the Army Special Forces' involvement in the Vietnam war—the Battle of Nam Dong, the Rheault Incident, and the Son Tay Raid.

The Battle of Nam Dong

After the Gulf of Tonkin Resolution, the war in Vietnam intensified. The Army Special Forces became more active, adding new responsibilities to their original mission.

Meanwhile, the Green Berets continued to train, advise, and command indigenous troops waging their own war against the North Vietnamese. Many of these battles were fought in the vicinity of the Special Forces camps established in South Vietnam. These camps were fortified strong points meant to protect the local population and prevent the enemy from claiming new territory. One such battle, fought at a joint camp called Nam Dong, provided the U.S. Army Special Forces with its first decorated hero of the Vietnam War.

Nam Dong was situated just 24 kilometers from Laos—a dangerous location. The 12 Americans, 1 Australian, and 300 Vietnamese soldiers based at the camp were there to provide security and improve living conditions for about 5,000 Vietnamese civilians in the region. Nam Dong was built in a remote corner of the country, perilously close to both the Laotian border and the border of North Vietnam. Thirty-year-old Capt. Roger Hugh Charles Donlon of Saugerties, New York, commanded the U.S. Special Forces detachment in the camp.

At 0226 (2:26 A.M.) on the morning of July 6, 1964, Nam Dong was subjected to an intense predawn mortar barrage, followed by a fierce and sustained ground assault by 800 to 1,000 Viet Cong guerrillas. The attack didn't totally surprise Captain Donlon. There had been increased enemy activity around the camp for a week or more, and the locals seemed nervous and frightened. But the surest indication that Viet Cong guerrillas were in the region came on the morning of July 5, when one of Donlon's *tripwire patrols* found the corpses of two village chiefs who had been friendly to the Americans.

Special Ops Jargon

Tripwire patrols involved searching out Viet Cong units that infiltrated South Vietnam from Laos and Cambodia.

At 2:26 A.M., Captain Donlon had just finished his rounds and stepped through the door of the mess hall when the entire building shook and then collapsed around him. The shock of the explosion from a half-dozen mortar rounds threw Donlon through the door. Outside it was pandemonium—the command post was ablaze, and the rattle of small arms and machine-gun fire could be heard from every side of the camp's perimeter.

The 300 South Vietnamese soldiers and 40 Nungs were already returning fire as the guerrillas charged the perimeter, so Captain Donlon and his team sergeant, "Pop" Alamo, battled the fire and tried to salvage the weapons and ammunition.

Suddenly, a mortar detonated near Donlon, throwing him into the air and blowing off one of his boots. He crawled to a mortar pit, spied the enemy from the cover of his trench, and moved forward with ammunition and supplies to another mortar pit. A second round exploded, blowing Donlon off his feet and destroying the equipment he carried, except for his AR-15 rifle. Ignoring a serious shrapnel wound to his left arm and abdomen, Donlon crawled to an advance position and saw the enemy charging through the main gate, less than 20 yards in front of him.

For the next five hours, Captain Donlon moved from position to position, delivering much-needed ammo to the beleaguered defenders. Despite severe wounds, Donlon directed fire and encouraged his indigenous troops to fight on. When Sergeant Alamo was wounded, Donlon tried to pull him from the front, only to be hit yet again by a mortar shell that wounded him and killed the sergeant. Donlon fought on, even as shrapnel pierced his leg, his face, his abdomen, and both his arms.

The battle left 55 of the South Vietnamese and Nung defenders dead, with 65 more wounded. Sgt. Pop Alamo and Sgt. John Houston of the Special Forces both died, leaving behind pregnant wives back home. Though outnumbered three to one, Captain Donlon's indigenous troops did not let him down, and Donlon's A-Team would become one of the most highly decorated units in U.S. Army history. Captain Donlon was awarded the first Congressional Medal of Honor of the Vietnam War—the first awarded since the Korean War of the 1950s. Each member of Captain Donlon's Green Berets team was decorated. The Distinguished Service Cross was presented posthumously to Sgt. "Pop" Alamo and Sgt. John Houston, and four other A-Team members were awarded the Silver Star.

Straight Shooting

During the 14-year war in Vietnam, Special Forces troops earned 17 Medals of Honor, 60 Distinguished Service Crosses, 814 Silver Stars, 13,234 Bronze Stars, 235 Legions of Merit, 46 Distinguished Flying Crosses, and too many Purple Hearts (medals awarded for combat wounds) to count!

On December 5, 1965, all nine surviving members of Team A-726 joined Captain Donlon in the East Ballroom of the White House, where President Lyndon Johnson draped the Medal of Honor around the team leader's neck. Donlon's photograph later appeared on the cover of *The Saturday Evening Post.* It was Captain Donlon's remarkable performance under fire that set the standard for all Special Forces troops for the remainder of the Vietnam war.

The Other War

Civic action was an important component of the Army Special Forces pacification program in Vietnam. From the start, the Green Berets promoted social and economic development in the areas of their control. They provided medical care, conducted English language classes, and distributed food and supplies in impoverished areas. This process was commonly known as "winning the hearts and minds" of the Vietnamese people.

Civic action projects included the construction of schools, medical centers, wells, roads, bridges, and irrigation and sanitation canals. Agricultural experts, under the protection of military patrols, helped modernize Vietnamese farming techniques. All the while, the Special Forces troops gathered intelligence and mounted patrols in the contested areas, forwarding the military goals along with the social agenda.

As the war progressed, the U.S. Marine Corps developed its own pacification and civil action program. One program, called County Fair, was quite successful. It involved gathering up Vietnamese villagers and staging a party for them—complete with food, pro-government propaganda shows disguised as entertainment, inoculations against disease, and complete medical checkups. Identity cards were issued to the villagers, and these cards were rechecked intermittently, in an attempt to root out North Vietnamese infiltrators.

Special Ops Jargon

The pacification effort in Vietnam was known as **"the other war"** because two wars were being fought in parallel—one a struggle to defeat the enemy and the other to build a new nation out of the ashes of war.

Whether the Marine Corps' program was modeled after the actions of the Special Forces is not known, but County Fair was so successful that the regular Army created civic action programs of its own, including the successful Hamlet Programs in the Ia Trang Valley.

Whatever the origins of these other pacification and civil action programs were, there is little doubt that the U.S. Army Special Forces started the ball rolling when it began to minister to the needs of the indigenous people, even as they trained them to fight the communists.

Rogues and Snake Eaters

Retired Col. David Hackworth, recalling his experience with the Special Forces, remarked in an interview on Fox News in November 2001 that many members of the Green Berets who fought in Vietnam seemed to "have been dragged out of the brig, handed a rifle and a hat, and told they were now in the Special Forces" (Fox News Channel *Fox and Friends*, 11/23/01).

Although this assessment may seem unduly harsh, there is certainly an element of truth in Colonel Hackworth's comment. During the Vietnam War, the Army Special Forces expanded rapidly—too rapidly to maintain the high recruitment standards formerly in place. Although the pool of talented, qualified soldiers was limited, the need for special operations forces increased as the war in Vietnam expanded. By necessity, recruiting standards became lax, but the result was that the Army Special Forces in particular lost much of what made them special in the first place.

Much of what was wrong with the Army Special Forces in Vietnam had to do with the nature of the war itself, along with the type of warfare Special Forces soldiers engaged in.

Operating independently, deep in enemy territory—and out of touch with their commanding officers—Special Forces troops made life-and-death decisions to accomplish their goals. Sometimes those decisions were questioned, especially as U.S. public opinion turned against the war.

Army Special Forces soldiers who dealt with the government in Saigon were sometimes tainted by the contact. There was corruption at every level of the government in Saigon, and officers of the Special Forces had to deal with that corruption every day. To get things done, the Americans bent—or even broke—the rules from time to time. Sometimes this was done for the greater good, and sometimes it was done for more nefarious ends. The Green Berets were also suspect because of their perceived close contact with the "black" and "rogue operations" of the CIA.

Finally, some members of the Special Forces actually fostered a macho, tough-guy image that may have served them well in Vietnam but that ultimately damaged the reputation of *all* members of the U.S. Army Special Forces. The Green Berets, probably because of their formidable reputation back home, were held in contempt by the men of the "regular" Army, and when interaction occurred, fights were common.

 FUBARs

Besides the political corruption in Saigon, there was corruption inside the Civilian Irregular Defense Groups. Resources were often diverted and misused, and appropriations were stolen or misspent.

In Vietnam, the term "snake eater" became a pejorative used to describe the "hell-for-leather," macho antics of the Green Berets, in an effort to diminish the mission and the abilities of the Special Forces members. Ultimately, Special Forces soldiers began to reject the name "Green Berets" because of the negative connotations associated with the Vietnam era. Today, Special Forces soldiers prefer to be called just that—Special Forces. In their own eyes, they are "the quiet professionals" who reject the notion that they are just regular troops with macho attitudes who wear really cool hats.

The Rheault Incident

Col. Robert B. Rheault assumed command of the 5th Special Forces in May 1969. He served as the commander of all Special Forces units in Vietnam for less than two months, after which he was relieved of his command, was placed in the brig, and faced a general court martial on charges of murder.

Sometime in early 1969, a man named Thai Khac Chuyen, who worked for the Americans as an agent in Project Gamma, was identified by the CIA as a North Vietnamese Army intelligence operative. His photograph was found on a roll of film captured in Cambodia.

In the picture, Chuyen was in the company of other NVA intelligence picture. It was soon confirmed that Chuyen was working as a double agent and had compromised some elements of Operation Gamma. Because Project Gamma was a cross-border, intelligence-gathering operation targeted at Cambodia, its operatives were privy to much classified information, and the implications of Khac Chuyen's treason were truly staggering.

With Colonel Rheault's knowledge and approval, Thai Khac Chuyen was detained and interrogated. Then the suggestion came down from a CIA liaison that Chuyen should be "eliminated." Colonel Rheault was given a cover story to supply him with plausible deniability. Chuyen was assassinated on June 20, 1969, and his corpse was dumped into Nha Trang Harbor. Things started to unravel when an intelligence sergeant involved in the incident had second thoughts and confessed his own involvement in the assassination.

Creighton Abrams Springs His Trap

Gen. Creighton Abrams, commander of all U.S. forces in Vietnam and no friend of the Special Forces, summoned Colonel Rheault to Saigon headquarters. When questioned about the incident, Rheault repeated his cover story, not realizing that it had already been blown. Rheault insisted that there was no truth to the rumor that Chuyen had been murdered. Unfortunately, Abrams already knew the truth, so Colonel Rheault was exposed as a liar and relieved of his command. As a result of this decision, Abrams was universally despised by members of the Special Forces. There was purportedly a plot by the First Special Forces Group in Okinawa to break Colonel Rheault out of the stockade where he was temporarily held, and some Green Berets even planned to sabotage Abrams's vacation villa in Bangkok.

General Abrams was looking for an excuse to kick the Green Berets out of Vietnam, and Colonel Rheault handed it to him. Rheault and the Gamma participants were jailed in Long Binh, and the 5th Special Forces Group was summarily booted out of Vietnam. Although charges were dropped when members of the CIA refused to testify about the incident (probably to save their own butts), the damage to Colonel Rheault's career and the U.S. Special Forces was already over.

By March 1971, the 5th Special Forces Group was gone from Vietnam and returned to its former headquarters at Fort Bragg. The Civilian Irregular Defense Group program was turned over to the ARVN, where it eventually withered and died.

No Future for the Green Berets in Vietnam

Colonel Rheault was offered another command, but he elected to retire from the military, maintaining all the while that what he had done was right and proper under the circumstances. Given the savage and unpredictable nature of the war in Vietnam, the colonel was probably correct. Meanwhile, General Abrams began to realize just how much he had relied on the Special Forces for intelligence gathering in Cambodia, Laos, and North Vietnam. He was compelled to secretly bring back some Green Berets, to resume their former duties.

Although Special Forces troops remained in Thailand, where they launched secret raids into North Vietnam, they never again attained a high level of military activity in South Vietnam, and their indigenous training programs came to a halt. By the end of 1972, the role of the Green Berets in Vietnam had officially ended.

Operation Kingpin: The Raid at Son Tay

Before the Special Forces departed Vietnam for good, they conducted one final mission— a mission that sent a message to the communist government in Hanoi and boosted the morale of American prisoners of war who subsequently learned about the operation.

In May 1970, air reconnaissance photos revealed the existence of two active prison camps, both just 20 miles west of the North Vietnamese capital of Hanoi. The camp at Son Tay was the largest. It was surrounded by rice paddies and by elements of the 12th North Vietnamese Army Regiment, totaling 12,000 troops, an artillery school, an air defense installation, and Phuc Yen Airfield, where communist MIG fighters were based. Photos taken by a high-altitude SR-71 Blackbird further revealed a large *K* drawn into the dirt. The letter *K* was a prearranged code for "come and get us," indicating that American POWs were actually being detained in the camp.

The prison camp itself was situated among tall trees to obstruct aerial view. The prisoners were housed in four buildings in the main compound. Three observation towers guarded the camp's approaches, and the area was surrounded by a 7-foot wall. The central compound was kept small to prevent U.S. helicopters from landing and rescuing the POWs.

Brig. Gen. Donald D. Blackburn, who had trained Filipino guerrillas to fight the Japanese in World War II, suggested that an all-volunteer Special Forces unit move in and rescue the

Americans. To accomplish the mission, Blackburn chose Col. Arthur D. "Bull" Simons to lead the raid. Simons began to train 100 Special Forces volunteers at Fort Bragg for the operation, scheduled to launch in November, after the monsoon rains. Colonel Simons selected Capt. Richard "Dick" Meadows to lead the ground assault team, which was to land inside the prison compound. Speed was the key to success—any delay would give the enemy time to scramble fighters from nearby Hanoi or move elements of the 12th North Vietnamese Army Regiment into position to stop the raiders.

A full-scale mock-up of the prison camp was constructed at Eglin Air Force Base, Florida, where Special Forces troops trained secretly and at night. By day the training area was dismantled to elude detection by Soviet satellites. On November 18, the force moved to Thailand and took up residence at a CIA compound at Takhli. Out of the original 100 volunteers, 56 were selected to carry out the mission—and only Colonel Simons and three others knew what that mission was.

The Raid Begins

On the night of November 21, 1970, the Son Tay raid was launched. Using in-flight refueling, six helicopters flew across Laos into North Vietnam, to approach the camp under cover of darkness—even as various diversionary air attacks were occurring all around Hanoi and across North Vietnam.

A single HH-3H helicopter, code-named Banana I, carried the first assault group. The team's job was to crash-land in the center of the prison, among the tall trees. As the helicopter came down, the pilot realized that the trees were taller and thicker than anyone had thought from the recon photos. The helicopter's rotors ripped into them "like a big lawn mower" as the chopper crashed to the ground.

The assault team poured out of the crashed chopper, led by Special Forces Capt. Richard Meadows. They gunned down the Vietnamese guards and then a group of PAVN regulars who attempted to flee through the east wall. Then 14 men entered the prison compound to rescue the prisoners.

A short distance away, Colonel Simons's chopper had landed at the wrong site. Instead of landing near the prison camp, the team had come down near a barracks filled with North Vietnamese regulars! Colonel Simons and his men poured out of the choppers and killed a hundred PAVNs who had been awakened by the sound of the chopper landing outside. When Simons dived into a trench for cover, a North Vietnamese regular jumped in next to him. The Colonel pumped six rounds from his .357 Magnum into the enemy trooper, killing him instantly.

Meanwhile, Meadows radioed the bad news. There were "negative items" in the camp—no American prisoners. It turned out that the heavy monsoon rains had flooded part of the camp and fouled the wells. Without fresh water, the camp was abandoned by all but a skeleton force, and the POWs had been transferred to Dong Hoi, a camp closer to Hanoi, way back in the middle of July.

As the Special Forces men moved back to their choppers, they left hundreds of dead and wounded PAVNs behind. The Americans suffered only one casualty—a crew chief had broken his ankle in the hard helicopter landing among the trees. Although the raid was an intelligence failure (*someone* should have figured out that the POW camp had been empty for over four months!), it was a tactical success. The Americans had landed, fought hard, and rained death down on the enemy while taking no casualties of their own.

Straight Shooting

American prisoners in Vietnam languished under inhuman conditions. Most were housed in Hoa Lo, the notorious "Hanoi Hilton," where there was little food or opportunity for exercise. Most POWs were held in total isolation—their only human contacts came during the frequent interrogation sessions and beatings by their captors.

Positive Results of the Son Tay Raid

At Dong Hoi, 15 miles away from Son Tay, the American POWs who had been moved in July were awakened by the sound of surface-to-air missiles being launched and quickly realized that their old prison camp was being raided. Morale among the prisoners improved significantly when they knew that something was being done to free them.

More important, the boldness of the Son Tay raid sent a clear message to Hanoi that the American military was outraged by the treatment of its prisoners of war and would go to any lengths to bring them back home. The communists realized that if emaciated and brutalized American POWs were paraded in front of the television cameras, world opinion might turn against them. Within days of the raid, all of the Americans held in remote, outlying camps were gathered together in Hanoi. Suddenly POWs who had spent years in isolation found themselves sharing a cell at Hoa Lo with fellow Americans. The interrogations and beatings subsided, and the prisoners began to get more nutritious food. Short of complete liberation, the failed Son Tay ended up being the best thing that happened to the POWs during their long captivity.

Shop Talk

By 1970 there were 450 known prisoners of the North Vietnamese and nearly a thousand American servicemen listed as missing in action. Some POWs had been imprisoned for over 2,000 days—longer than any servicemen had ever spent in captivity in any war in America's history.

In 1979, Colonel Simons came out of retirement to help H. Ross Perot free two employees from the Iranian revolutionaries holding them hostage. Colonel Simons pulled off that rescue and then moved the hostages 450 miles to the Turkish border and freedom. He died of heart complications three months later. Today, the Arthur "Bull" Simons Memorial—a bronze statue of the man in full Vietnam-era battle gear—stands at Fort Bragg, North Carolina, a testament to one of the great heroes of the U.S. Army Special Forces.

This Is the End

The Son Tay raid ended the Army's Special Forces' direct action in Vietnam. On March 1, 1971, just four months after the failed prison camp raid, the 5th Special Forces Group moved its headquarters out of "The Trang" and back to Fort Bragg, North Carolina. Some USSF forces remained in-country as instructors, training indigenous troops in unconventional warfare. Teams from the 1st Special Forces Group, for instance, continued to train ARVN and Cambodian soldiers until February 22, 1973, when the 1st Special Forces Group finally pulled up its tents and ceased operations in southeast Asia.

Within two years, the U.S. government ended *all* direct military involvement in southeast Asia as President Richard M. Nixon's *Vietnamization* program moved into high gear. Inevitably, the government in Saigon collapsed under the weight of its own corruption and mismanagement, along with the flood of Soviet weapons and supplies that flowed into North Vietnam after the Americans departed. In April 1975, after a bold spring offensive, the communist government of North Vietnamese achieved its military goals in South Vietnam, captured Saigon, and "united" the country.

Special Ops Jargon

Vietnamization was the American term for the process of progressively turning responsibility for the conduct of the Vietnam War back over to the South Vietnamese. Though the move was well intentioned, without direct military intervention, financial assistance, or material aid from former American allies, the defeat of the Saigon government was inevitable.

The Vietnam conflict was really four parallel campaigns: the massive ground war in the South; the air war against targets all over Vietnam, but specifically in the North; the many covert actions all over Vietnam and spilling into Laos and Cambodia; and the propaganda war fought to win the hearts and minds of the Vietnamese people. Although they successfully carried out hundreds of covert missions behind enemy lines, the U.S. Army Special Forces really excelled in the war for the hearts and minds of the people. The Green Berets were perhaps the only element in the U.S. military that practiced the art of persuasion. The paramilitary training they provided, along with the medical, educational, and humanitarian activity, resulted in the denial of the Viet Cong and PAVN of certain regions of the Vietnamese countryside that would otherwise have fallen.

The Final Fate of the Indigs

Because of their training, the Montagnards and other indigenous peoples continued to resist the communist government in Hanoi for many years, right into the mid-1980s and beyond—without help or support from outside countries, including (shamefully) the United States. The Montagnards, in particular, paid a terrible price for their alliance with the Americans. The casualty rate among Montagnard strikers was catastrophic, and the communists murdered thousands of villagers, most of them noncombatants, during and directly after the war. The best estimates are that one third of the one million Montagnards who saw combat during the Vietnam conflict were casualties of the war, and 85 percent of their traditional lands and villages were forcibly evacuated or abandoned. This forced resettlement campaign imposed on them by the communist government in Hanoi effectively destroyed the fabric of Montagnard culture.

After the war, the U.S. government turned away from the Montagnards and never looked back. Today, former Green Berets such as George E. Dooley work tirelessly to resettle persecuted Montagnards in the United States, despite much resistance by subsequent U.S. Administrations, especially during the Clinton years.

Unfortunately, even as the Green Berets were winning the psychological war in Vietnam, the U.S. military was losing the propaganda war at home. By the end of the 1960s, radical antiwar protestors were repeating the propaganda of the enemy, and the national media was repeating it, too—on the front page of the local newspaper and on the nightly news. It turned out that the home front was where America was most vulnerable. Hearing the negative news coming out of Vietnam and the cries of outrage coming from college campuses, Americans became increasingly disenchanted. When Americans figured out that their own government had been misleading them about the war for many years, they were overwhelmed with disgust. The Vietnam War, and the way it was waged caused deep rifts in American society that still exist today.

Inevitably, when the longest war in the nation's history finally ended in defeat for America's ally, someone had to pay the price. Of course, the pundits and politicians who were in charge of things weren't about to blame themselves. Instead, they looked around for a scapegoat and found one pretty quickly. Ultimately, America's armed services paid the price of failure. For the U.S. military in general and the Special Forces in particular, tough times lay ahead. The lean years were about to begin.

The Least You Need to Know

- One of the most highly decorated units in the Vietnam War was the Green Berets who defended Nam Dong.

- Lowering of acceptance and training standards led to an erosion in the effectiveness and reputation of the Green Berets serving in Vietnam.
- The Rheault incident further damaged the honor and reputation of the U.S. Army Special Forces.
- After South Vietnam fell to the communists, the indigenous people trained by the Green Berets suffered horrible repression.

Chapter 9

The Lean Years

In This Chapter

- ◆ The Army Special Forces battle for survival
- ◆ Civic action at home: the SPARTAN program
- ◆ Crisis erupts in Iran
- ◆ Operation Just Cause: A second chance
- ◆ Special Forces action in the Gulf War

After the U.S. defeat in Vietnam at the hands of what Henry Kissinger once described as a "fourth-rate power," there was a very loud and very public backlash against the U.S. military. The Army, Navy, Air Force, and Marine Corps became America's scapegoats for the nation's humiliation in southeast Asia and were punished accordingly. Funding was cut, the military was downsized, and many valuable, experienced officers were forced to take early retirement—their services were no longer required by their country. There was a general de-emphasis on special operations during the post-Vietnam era. As the Army high command concentrated once more on conventional warfare, it turned away from the jungles of Asia toward the growing Soviet threat in Europe.

And, like the rest of the military establishment, the Special Forces suffered for their "sins" in Vietnam. Although the other Special Forces groups—the Navy SEALs, the Air Force Special Operations, and the Army Rangers—played a role in the disastrous outcome of the Vietnam War, the Green Berets were the largest and most visible group and thus an easy target.

In this chapter, I'll examine the lengths to which the Army Special Forces went to survive the post–Vietnam War backlash against the military, and how the Green Berets reinvented themselves in the decades following the war.

A New Battle for Survival

One consequence of the Vietnam War and the diminished recruiting standards instituted by the Army Special Forces during that conflict was that the Green Berets had acquired the image of a bunch of undisciplined armed thugs running uncontrolled, murderous rogue operations all over southeast Asia. This stereotype, however unjustified it may have been, translated into the dissolution of over one half of the U.S. Army's Special Forces Groups as America's involvement in Vietnam was winding down. The 3rd Special Forces Group was the first casualty, shutting down in December 1969. The 6th was demobilized in 1971, and the 8th was shut down in June 1972. The 1st Special Forces Group managed to hang on until 1974 before it was demobilized. Even worse, the Special Forces reserve was completely eliminated, along with hundreds of trained and experienced reservists. Although the 1st and the 3rd *were* eventually reactivated, during this period there were calls by pundits and politicians to eliminate the Special Forces groups entirely.

FUBARs

Former U.S. diplomat, historian, and foreign policy critic George F. Kennan called the Vietnam War "the most disastrous of all of America's undertakings over the whole 200 years of its history."

The change in attitude toward America's elite forces was even apparent in the popular culture. Once the hero of popular fiction, comic books, and motion pictures such as *The Green Berets*, by the late 1970s members of the Army Special Forces were more likely to be portrayed as villainous, rogue operatives who were part of some shadowy government conspiracy—or worse. In the 1978 film *The Deer Hunter*, a gaunt Green Beret sergeant becomes the symbol of death and destruction in the lengthy wedding sequence that opens the movie. Sylvester Stallone's *Rambo* pictures didn't help the reputation of the Special Forces, either.

Forever Loathed?

The hostility toward the U.S. Army Special Forces that began in the Vietnam era still persists today. One of the most outrageous media assaults on their integrity and honor came from CNN and *Time* magazine in the late 1990s, when these two national news organizations published unsubstantiated accounts that accused Special Forces personnel of using chemical weapons to kill defecting American soldiers in Cambodia in the early 1970s. Known as "the Operation Tailwind Scandal," the story was later proven to be a fabrication. However, the fact that the story appeared at all may serve as proof of the depth of animosity toward (and ignorance about) America's Special Forces community.

Learning to Adapt and Overcome

It was only due to the diligent, determined efforts of a few visionaries within the military establishment that the Special Forces survived the bleak period after the Vietnam War. Things were grim for the U.S. military with the slashing of budgets during the administrations of Gerald Ford and James Earl Carter. Those Special Forces units that managed to survive did so despite funding deficits, diminished capabilities, and rock-bottom morale.

A few former Army Special Forces soldiers were able to adapt to changing times and moved on to other pursuits, some within the military. During the 1970s, as the quality of America's armed forces deteriorated, a number of former Special Forces NCOs who possessed years of valuable knowledge and experience accepted assignments with regular Army units, where they raised training and fitness standards even as they restored order and discipline in the chaotic ranks of the U.S. Army. Unfortunately, the number of such postings was finite, and many experienced Special Forces officers were forced into early retirement. Others, like Maj. Dick Meadows, a decorated hero of the Son Tay raid, did a stint as an Army instructor, retired in 1977, and then was hired to help create the antiterrorism unit called Delta Force in the late 1970s.

> **Shop Talk**
>
> Retirement didn't mean the end of defense work for former Army Special Forces Maj. Dick Meadows. After working as a consultant during the creation of Delta Force, Meadows was recruited by the CIA and sent on an undercover assignment in Tehran during the Iranian Hostage Crisis.

Civic Action at Home: The SPARTAN Program

In an effort to prevent the further erosion of the Special Forces and the emasculation of their once-formidable capabilities, the Special Forces command established a unique social program designed to demonstrate the multiplicity of talents these units possessed. The Special Proficiency at Rugged Training and Nation-Building (SPARTAN) program was meant to show that America's Special Forces were not outmoded and that they had the ability to achieve positive results in peacetime as well as during war.

SPARTAN mimicked the work of the Depression-era Civilian Conservation Corps (CCC). Special Forces troops, many with years of combat experience in southeast Asia, moved into depressed areas of the United States in an effort to raise the standard of living among impoverished people. Under the aegis of the SPARTAN program, the 5th and 7th Special Forces Groups worked with Native American tribes in Florida, Arizona, and Montana. They built roads and bridges, established medical facilities, and provided free medical care and treatment to impoverished citizens of Hoke and Anson Counties in North Carolina.

SPARTAN was a noble effort and one that fit the socially conscious times in which it was conceived. But it was also a waste of experienced combat troops who would have been better suited for other duties. SPARTAN was hardly what the Special Forces were designed for. Although there were a few ongoing SF operations in Lebanon, Africa, and Central America in the 1970s, morale and recruitment continued to decline through the dark years of Jimmy Carter's presidency.

Crisis Erupts in Iran

By the 1970s, Iran was on its way to establishing the only Western–style-leaning government in the Middle East besides Israel's. That progress ended in 1978 when fundamentalist Islamic militants and revolutionaries led by the Ayatollah Khomeni toppled the government and established a theocracy. The Shah of Iran, a friend and ally of the United States, fled the country, which quickly descended into chaos.

On November 4, 1979, a mob of Iranian "students" stormed the U.S. embassy in Tehran and took the staff and the Marine Corps security contingent hostage. In all, 52 Americans had been seized by the Iranian Revolutionary Guard. After months of negotiation and a stalemate that all but paralyzed the floundering administration of Jimmy Carter, the newly certified 1st Special Forces Operational Detachment—Delta was ordered to mount a rescue.

Though not a part of any Army's Special Forces Group, the failure of Delta Force to rescue the hostages, and the tragic outcome of the raid, pointed out America's tactical weakness among *all* of its once-proud Special Forces units. Modeled after Operation Thunderbolt, the Israeli raid on Entebbe, America mounted Operation Eagle Claw, a bold and ambitious attempt to rescue the Embassy hostages—far too bold and ambitious for the U.S. military to accomplish after the benign neglect of the post-Vietnam era. While the Israelis lavished resources and provided extensive training to their special forces units, America had consigned its Special Forces units to the scrap heap of history!

Shop Talk
In 1976, the Israeli special forces raided Entebbe Airport in Uganda, where 103 hostages off a hijacked airliner were being detained. The hijackers, scores of Ugandan guards, and the Israeli commander of the commando team were killed. All but one of the hostages were rescued.

Although Delta Force was a trained counterterrorist organization, it was forced to yield to the demands of "joint operability"—in other words, involving untrained personnel from the Navy, Marine Corps, and Air Force—all of whom lacked the skills necessary to accomplish a complex secret operation such as Operation Eagle Claw.

When Eagle Claw was finally launched, bad weather and mechanical failure dogged the raiding party. The entire operation was finally aborted when several participating aircraft dropped out and other aircraft crashed into one another at a remote refueling airstrip dubbed Desert One. Although eight American servicemen paid the ultimate price in that failed operation, some good came out of it, too. After the disaster, the military made an all-out effort to improve the lot of America's Special Forces.

The monumental failure of Operation Eagle Claw and the rise of new insurgencies in Africa, Central America, the Middle East, and Asia highlighted the need for better Special Forces capabilities in the U.S. military. To meet these challenges, the Army injected a new spirit into the Special Forces. The qualifications became tougher, in an effort to recruit the highest-caliber soldiers. In June 1983, the Army authorized a new, exclusive uniform tab for the Special Forces to wear on the left shoulder. On October 1, 1984, the Army established a separate career field for Special Forces; on April 9, 1987, the Army Chief of Staff established a separate branch of the Army for Special Forces officers.

Under President Ronald Reagan, the growth of U.S. Special Forces capabilities rivaled that of the Kennedy years. During the 1980s, Special Forces teams were deployed to dozens of hot spots around the globe. They proved to be particularly successful in El Salvador and Honduras, where Special Forces activity prevented the Sandinistas from spreading their communist revolution across the borders to these neighboring countries. Special Forces missions varied from training allied armies to defend themselves against insurgents, to providing humanitarian aid to Third-World countries on almost every continent.

> **CAUTION**
>
> **FUBARs**
>
> Maj. Dick Meadows, working undercover in Tehran to support Eagle Claw, was not informed that the operation had been aborted. He read about it in the local newspapers. Left hanging by the CIA, Meadows was forced to extract himself out of Iran with no outside help.

Operation Just Cause: A Second Chance

Throughout the 1980s, under Ronald Reagan's firm hand, the U.S. military rebuilt, even as the Special Forces reorganized. The 1st and 3rd Special Forces Groups were reactivated, and funding improved for special operations across the board. In 1987, the U.S. Congress ratified the Nunn-Cohen Amendment, which created SOCOM (discussed in Chapter 10, "The Coming of the U.S. Special Operations Command"). From that point onward, the Special Operations Command controlled all of the special operations forces of the Army, Navy, and Air Force, streamlining the command structure while effectively creating a new branch of the U.S. armed services—one comprised exclusively of special operations forces. The first test of the new, improved Special Forces came in December 1989 in the Central American nation of Panama.

Much misery could have been avoided if the United States had maintained its strategic control over the Panama Canal. Unfortunately, President Jimmy Carter signed an agreement handing over the U.S.–built canal to the Panamanian government by 1999. Any political instability in the Central American region could jeopardize the Navy's ability to move its fleet during a crisis.

Panamanian dictator Manuel Noriega was a longtime friend of the United States. As a military officer, he had taken classes at the U.S. Army School of the Americas in the Canal Zone and, in 1970, became commander of G-2, the Panamanian Guard's intelligence branch. He maintained close ties with U.S. Army intelligence, the CIA, and the Drug Enforcement Agency (DEA). After the death of his mentor, dictator Omar Torrijos in 1981, Noriega became commander of the Panamanian Defense Forces (PDF) and the most powerful man in Panama. After that, he provided a safe haven for the deposed Shah of Iran and helped the United States deal with the Sandinistas by providing assistance to the Contras attempting to overthrow the Nicaraguan communists.

But in 1989, Noriega lost his bid to become leader of Panama in a free and open election. Instead of stepping down, he seized complete control of the government. The DEA, meanwhile, accused Noriega of drug trafficking. Tension between Panama and the United States increased until on December 15, the National Assembly of Panama declared that a state of war existed with the United States. In the days that followed, U.S. military personnel and dependents stationed in Panama were harassed; then a U.S. Marine Corps lieutenant was murdered by Panamanian government thugs.

Noriega continually used terror tactics to maintain control after he voided the election results and grabbed power. A coup mounted against him failed in October 1989, sparking bloody reprisals. After the coup, Noriega relied on paramilitary units called Dignity Battalions to frighten and brutalize his political rivals. The situation in Panama was spinning out of control when President George H. W. Bush decided that the United States could no longer countenance the belligerent strongman.

Special Forces in Panama

On December 20, 1989, President Bush ordered the mobilization of Operation Just Cause, up to that time the largest deployment of the U.S. military since the end of the Vietnam War and the largest *single contingency operation* since World War II.

Special Forces units actually spearheaded the invasion of Panama. Before the first waves of America's conventional military units landed, advanced special forces teams raided command-and-control facilities, traded shots with the Panamanian Defense Force units in brutal and costly firefights, seized communications facilities, captured scores of prisoners, and eventually helped to track down Noriega himself when the former dictator became a fugitive. Primary objectives in Panama were achieved quickly, and order was restored in mere days. The American troops began to withdraw by December 27. Manuel Noriega is currently serving a 40-year sentence in a Florida prison for drug trafficking.

Although there were hundreds of American casualties and at least a thousand Panamanians killed, the United States deposed a vicious and unpredictable dictator, kept the Panama Canal safe for passage by U.S. shipping, and restored representative government to the nation of Panama. The specter of America's defeat in Vietnam had nearly been expunged.

Special Ops Jargon

A **single contingency operation** is organized and concerted military activity undertaken to achieve a single goal. In Operation Just Cause, that goal was the capture of Panama's Maximum Leader, Manuel Noriega.

Special Forces in the Persian Gulf War

By 1990, Iraq was reeling under its economic woes. After a decade of war against Iran, its military was one of the most formidable in the region, but its government was nearly broke, despite the nation's vast oil reserves. To solve this problem, Iraqi dictator Saddam Hussein sent his troops across the border of neighboring Kuwait in July 1990 to annex its oil fields and subjugate the Kuwaiti people.

On November 29, 1990, the United States obtained United Nations Security Council authorization for the nations allied with Kuwait "to use all necessary means" if Iraq refused to withdraw by January 15, 1991. Meanwhile the United States deployed close to a half million military personnel and their warplanes, tanks, ships, helicopters, and artillery to Saudi Arabia. General H. Norman Schwarzkopf, a Vietnam veteran and the commander of Operation Just Cause, was appointed to lead the campaign to liberate Kuwait.

Now, as overall commander of Operation Desert Shield/Storm, Gen. H. Norman Schwarzkopf did not want the U.S. Special Forces cluttering up *his* war. Recalling the antics of the undisciplined rogues and snake eaters in Vietnam, as well as their dismal performance at the invasion of Grenada, where Navy SEALs drowned after a nighttime insertion, Schwarzkopf stubbornly refused to give any Special Forces units a role in America's largest military adventure since World War II.

Shop Talk

The Persian Gulf War had two distinct phases. The multinational buildup of forces in the region was called Operation Desert Shield. The bombing of Iraq and the land war to liberate Kuwait that followed was called Operation Desert Storm.

Gen. Carl W. Stiner, the commander-in-chief of the U.S. Special Operations Command (USSOCOM) at that time, had other ideas. Stiner flew to Schwarzkopf's headquarters in Riyadh, Saudi Arabia, to present his plan for how best to use the resources of the Special Forces in the war against Iraq. A strong proponent of conventional forces, General Schwarzkopf expressed concerns that the presence of special operations troops might disrupt his carefully conceived plan. When General Stiner further suggested that he might move SOCOM command from McDill Air Force Base in Florida to Riyadh, Schwarzkopf's ego was threatened and he strongly rejected Stiner's plan. USSOCOM's commander was suddenly an unwelcome guest in Saudi Arabia.

Scud Busters in Iraq

As hostilities commenced, General Schwarzkopf rejected nearly every request that Special Forces units made to join the fight. Of the nearly 60 direct action suggestions made by the 5th Special Forces Group, all but a few were flatly rejected. The general finally changed his mind when Saddam Hussein began to fire Scud missiles at Israel. Hussein's launching of these *Scuds* was meant to unravel the delicate political alliance forged by the United States to prosecute the war, more than it was to damage Israeli cities or kill its citizens—although death and destruction *did* result from these crude missile attacks.

After several Scud attacks on the suburbs of Tel Aviv, the Israeli government threatened to attack Iraq on its own unless something was done to stop the missiles. The United States knew that such a move by Israel would unravel the delicate political coalition that President Bush had created to fight the war. In exchange for assurance that Israel would stay out of the conflict—at least for the time being—George Bush promised the Israelis that America would mount "the darndest search-and-destroy effort that's ever been undertaken" to uncover and eliminate all Iraqi missile sites. That proved to be a nearly impossible task, however, because the Scuds were being fired from truck-mounted mobile launchers in western Iraq—launchers that could be broken down and moved less than 10 minutes after the missile left the launch rail.

Special Ops Jargon

Gulf War **Scuds** were variants of the basic Soviet-made, short range ballistic missile. Iraqi Scuds had added fuel tanks and smaller warheads. They were primitive, with no internal guidance system. Crews aimed by estimating the distance to the target and then adjusting the direction and elevation of the launcher.

Scuds were launched from the 29,000-square-mile wilderness of western Iraq. "That's the size of Massachusetts, Vermont, and New Hampshire all put together," Schwarzkopf explained to a journalist in the region, insisting that "there's not much point putting people (special operations units) on the ground to try and find 9, maybe 10 trucks." Eventually pressure from Washington compelled the general to change his opinion.

Faced with mounting political pressure and the knowledge that the British had already unleashed their own unconventional warfare units to track down the Scuds, Schwarzkopf relented and allowed America's elite to finally enter the war. By the time the ground war was launched in January 1991, the U.S. Special Forces had penetrated deep into enemy-held territory. Green Berets from the 3rd and 5th Special Forces Groups conducted deep-reconnaissance missions to make sure the terrain in Iraq was suitable for the passage of Schwarzkopf's tanks. Side by side with their counterparts in the British Special Air Service, units of the U.S. Special Forces also hunted Scuds, performed search-and-rescue missions, captured and interrogated prisoners, and gathered critical intelligence.

Straight Shooting

Although General Schwarzkopf eventually permitted the Special Forces to participate in Desert Storm, he still didn't trust them. Special Operations Forces were forced to operate under highly restrictive rules and over-sights that no other branch of the military had to endure.

Into the Twenty-First Century

By the close of the Persian Gulf War, even a skeptic like General Schwarzkopf was forced to acknowledge the valuable service provided by America's Special Forces. Now, with two successful conflicts behind them, America's fighting elite had a much brighter future. Decades of uncertainty had finally ended. After the formation of SOCOM, and after their successes in Panama and the Persian Gulf, America's Special Forces were now a permanent component of the U.S. military, ready to serve their country whenever and wherever the need arose.

The Least You Need to Know

◆ After America lost the war in Vietnam, the Special Forces struggled to remain an important component of the U.S. Army.

◆ Battling bureaucratic indifference and public hostility, the U.S. Special Forces managed to endure.

◆ The once-formidable reputation of America's special operations forces suffered another blow after the failure of Operation Eagle Claw in 1980.

◆ Despite draconian funding cuts, personnel shortages, lowered morale, and the hostility of the Army's high command, the Special Forces performed well in Panama and Iraq.

Part 3

The U.S. Army Special Forces

Now that you have caught a glimpse of the long history of America's Special Forces, it's time to turn your attention to the command structure, disposition, and operations of the U.S. Special Forces as they exist today.

After four decades of uncertain existence, the creation of the U.S. Special Operations Command (USSOC) in 1987 ensured that elite unconventional warfare units would always be an important component of America's military structure.

To understand America's special operations forces at the dawn of the twenty-first century, it is necessary to start at the top, with the joint unified command called SOCOM—the command headquarters for the entire spectrum of America's Special Forces. After that, I'll focus on the Army Special Forces today, which still remain the largest and most visible component of America's unconventional warfare capability.

Rangers of
Note in History

Served in European
Theater in WWII

Tries to keep
bear from stealing
picnic baskets

10

The Coming of the U.S. Special Operations Command

In This Chapter

- ◆ The defining moment of Carter's presidency
- ◆ The Nunn-Cohen agreement
- ◆ The basic structure of the U.S. Special Operations Command

After the failed rescue attempt of the American hostages held in Iran, Congress moved to drastically restructure the face of America's elite Special Operations Forces. Gathering all groups under one umbrella command—and essentially creating a fifth branch of the armed services—the Special Forces of the United States were reborn.

In this chapter, you'll see how America's unconventional warfare groups were united under a single command following the disastrous attempt to rescue the U.S. Embassy personnel held hostage in Iran, and how that revamping of America's Special Operations Forces changed the way those groups are funded, trained, and deployed.

The Iranian Hostage Crisis

It was April 1980. After six months of vacillation, President Jimmy Carter finally decided that it was time to rescue the 53 American hostages who had been held prisoner in Iran since militant students, egged on by the revolutionary government of Ayatollah Khomeini, stormed the Embassy in Tehran and seized them. It was the defining incident of Carter's presidency. Since that terrible moment, the Carter administration had been paralyzed. The hostages had taken center stage, at the expense of all other concerns.

Like John F. Kennedy before him, Carter turned to America's Special Forces groups in an effort to free the Americans. Unfortunately, those were the very groups that Carter—and Gerald Ford before him—had worked so hard to decimate. By 1979, the Special Forces were at less than 60 percent of their strength at the close of the Vietnam War. In fact, the entire military had been hit with postwar cuts that had stretched their resources thinner and thinner. As it turned out, the military had neither the capability nor the personnel to execute the complex, joint-services rescue operation called Operation Eagle Claw.

> **CAUTION**
>
> **FUBARs**
>
> When Carter took office in 1977, he instituted his "Georgia approach" to government management. In the case of the intelligence agencies—especially the CIA—that meant layoffs of hundreds of experienced personnel. So it was that the CIA lacked the manpower and resources to monitor the deteriorating situation in Iran.

Over two nights, April 24–25, 1980, special operations aircraft penetrated Iranian airspace. The planes were C-130s, some configured to carry fuel bladders and others used as transports to bring in the Delta Force assault teams and then fly out the teams and the American hostages after the rescue was complete. On that second night, U.S. Navy RH-53D Sea Stallion helicopters, launching from the *U.S.S. Nimitz*, were to rendezvous with the airplanes at a secret location in the Iranian desert called Desert I. They were ordered to fly at no higher than 200 feet to elude Iranian radar, but that altitude flew them directly into a fierce *haboob* (dust storm). Sand choked engines, and two helicopters malfunctioned. Two other choppers lost sight of the task force in the dust cloud and were out of the mission.

Suddenly the entire operation was over an hour behind schedule. Even worse, there were only six helicopters still functioning—the bare minimum necessary to successfully accomplish the mission. The operation was dealt a final blow when another Sea Stallion helicopter malfunctioned. Now there weren't enough available helicopters to carry out the rescue.

As Desert I was being evacuated, the Sea Stallions kicked up a lot of dust. In the blinding clouds, one helicopter's rotor struck the cockpit of a parked C-130, and both aircraft burst into flames. Eight men died and more were wounded. Orders were given to blow up the remaining helicopters that couldn't get off the ground, but word never reached the demolition teams. Iranian troops later captured sensitive plans that revealed the location and identities of several Delta members working in the country to help the operation, and they were nearly captured.

All told, five Air Force personnel and three Marines lost their lives at Desert I. The mission was an intelligence and planning disaster. Those who calculated the time involved in the helicopter flight were off by hours. There was not enough advance reconnaissance on the ground in Iran, and even the Air Weather Services had failed to forecast the ferocity of the dust storms.

> ### Shop Talk
>
> Effective joint military operations have three main benefits: They are *economical* because resources are not duplicated among the services; they are *efficient* because good ideas, intelligence-gathering capabilities, and weapons-development systems are shared by all; and they are *effective* because "jointness" results in a more prepared, more flexible, and more powerful military.

But any chance of success was jeopardized by the "joint" nature of the operation. Air Force, Navy, and Marine Corps pilots all were involved, but it was later discovered that many of these aviators lacked the special training necessary to conduct night landings or maneuver their aircraft on the ground in the darkness.

The Marine Corps pilots of Operation Eagle Claw were especially vulnerable to accident. They lacked the skills and training necessary to conduct night operations. Navy mechanics were also at fault. They failed to place dust filters on the helicopters in anticipation of desert operations. Had the mission been staffed by better-trained, more experienced Special Forces personnel, the disaster at Desert One just might have been avoided.

The Nunn-Cohen Amendment

Out of the ashes of this debacle came the first restructuring of the United States military since the 1947 National Security Act. The first action was the Goldwater-Nichols Act, passed in 1986. It established a joint military, restructuring the various commands under a group of unified commanders-in-chief (CINCs) who are responsible for a particular mission or geographical region.

Unfortunately, the Goldwater-Nichols Act did not mandate a similar restructuring of the Special Forces—it only suggested it. The reorganization of America's Special Forces did not become a reality until 1987, when an amendment to Goldwater-Nichols was introduced by Sam Nunn (D–Georgia) and William Cohen (R–Maine) and eventually was enacted by Congress.

Shop Talk

The Marine Corps was excluded from Nunn-Cohen because the Corps had long encouraged the development of Special Forces, including its Force Reconnaissance Teams and other units, all of which are now part of the Marine Expeditionary Unit Special Operations Capable Forces deployed all over the globe.

The terms of the Nunn-Cohen Amendment created the U.S. Special Operations Command (USSOCOM), which now controls all the special forces units of the three services—Army, Navy, and the Air Force. The Marines, already mission-capable, were excluded. In essence, the Nunn-Cohen Amendment established a de facto *fifth* branch of the United States armed services—one able to stand shoulder to shoulder with the other unified commands and worthy of the same funding considerations. However, unlike the Army, Navy, Air Force, and Marine Corps, USSOCOM is an all-special operations capable branch that provides far more "bang for the buck" than conventional forces. With the creation of USSOCOM, all of America's elite forces became members of an all-elite, four-star command.

The Structure of the U.S. Special Operations Command

USSOCOM is based at MacDill Air Force Base, a few miles from Tampa, Florida. The Commander-in-Chief of the U.S. Special Operations Command (CINCSOC) is usually a general of the U.S. Army, reflecting the size, scope, and continuing importance of the Army's Special Forces groups compared to all the others. USSOCOM receives its own funding from the annual Department of Defense budget, so the Special Forces no longer have to squeeze their parent services for necessary resources and funding.

Unlike the other commands, USSOCOM does not have a service or geographical affiliation. While EUCOM covers Europe, PACOM covers the Pacific, and CENTCOM covers the Middle East, South Asia and Northern Africa—the so-called Muslim world—USSOCOM's responsibilities encompass the entire world and include the full compliment of missions, from small unit action, to counterterrorism, to full-scale global conflict. This is rather ironic because USSOCOM is the smallest unified command. While CENTCOM can draw on a half million personnel, USSOCOM has about 35,000 active-duty personnel performing a variety of duties at MacDill and elsewhere. There is also an additional pool of 12,000 National Guard and reserve special operations forces personnel available, if needed. Because of its global reach, USSOCOM is divided into five component commands with different geographic areas of responsibility. The following list presents the geographical breakdown of USSOCOM.

The geographical breakdown of USSOCOM

◆ **Special Operations Command, South (SOCSOUTH)** is part of the U.S. Southern Command (SOUTHCOM) and is responsible for actions in Latin America and the Caribbean.

◆ **Special Operations Command, Atlantic (SOCACOM)** is part of the U.S. Atlantic Command (USACOM) and is responsible for actions in the United States and the North Atlantic Basin.

◆ **Special Operations Command, Europe (SOCEUR)** is part of the U.S. European Command (EUCOM) and is responsible for actions in Europe, West Africa, Israel, and southern Africa.

◆ **Special Operations Command, Central (SOCCENT)** is part of the U.S. Central Command (CENTCOM) and is responsible for actions in central and southwest Asia, eastern Africa, and the volatile Middle East—minus Israel.

◆ **Special Operations Command, Pacific (SOCPAC)** is part of the U.S. Pacific Command (PACOM) and is responsible for actions in the Pacific Basin and eastern Asia.

CINCSOC owes no affiliation to any parent branch of the armed services, and it commands a collection of Special Forces units from the Army, Navy, and Air Force. However, each Armed Service's special operations units are grouped into separate component commands within USSOCOM. These components *do* retain close ties to their parent service.

The Component Commands under CINSOC

◆ **The U.S. Army Special Operations Command (USASOC)** is based at Fort Bragg, North Carolina. USASOC is the largest single component command, composed of the Army Special Forces Command, the 75th Ranger Regiment, the 160th Special Operations Aviation Regiment, the John F. Kennedy Special Warfare Center and School, the U.S. Army Civic Affairs and Psychological Operations Command, and the U.S. Army Special Operations Support Command.

◆ **The Naval Special Warfare Command (NAVSPECWARCOM)** is based in Coronado, California, near San Diego, with detachments stationed around the world. NAVESPECWARCOM controls the Sea, Air, Land Teams—the legendary Navy SEALs—and their support groups, which include special boat squadrons, submarines, and other seagoing delivery vehicles. NAVSPECWARCOM units operate like the U.S. Navy and perform special operations missions in the oceans, seas, river basins, and along the coast all around the world.

◆ **The Air Force Special Operations Command (AFSOC)** based at Elgin Air Force Base, Florida. This component is composed of helicopter and transport aircraft units. Its primary mission is to prepare landing zones and airfields in advance of the special operations units entering the area of operation. AFSOC also transports special operations units from other commands to their areas of operation and then provides resupply and support operations in the field for those units. AFSOC possesses a formidable armada of specialized attack-and-insertion and intelligence-gathering aircraft, as well as a ground force made up of special tactics squadrons.

◆ **The Joint Special Operations Command (JSOC)** is based at Fort Bragg, North Carolina. Antiterrorism is the primary function of this multiservice, interdepartmental command. Based at Fort Bragg, North Carolina, JSOC has a small command staff responsible for counterterrorism training and operations of the U.S. Army's Delta Force, the Navy SEAL Team Six, and elements of the Federal Bureau of Investigation's Hostage Rescue Team. JSOC remains one of USSOCOM's most shadowy and secretive components.

Of course, there are overlapping regions of control and responsibility, but this breakdown will serve as a general blueprint of the world of the USSOCOM.

Straight Shooting

The USASOC numbers were around 23,000 men—half of the 46,000 men serving in America's elite Special Forces units.

So it is that a SEAL assigned to NAVSPECWARCOM but under the overall command of USSOCOM may be ordered by CINCSOC to work with PACOM but be detached for counterterrorism training with JSOC before moving—via AFSOC—to his new assignment with SOCCENT, under the operational command of CENTCOM.

Are you with me? Great!

In the next chapter, I'll focus on the various Special Forces components within the U.S. Army Special Operations Command (USASOC) as they exist today.

The Least You Need to Know

◆ Out of the ashes of Desert I came the Nunn-Cohen Amendment, which reorganized America's Special Operations Forces.

◆ The Nunn-Cohen Amendment established the U.S. Special Operations Command, which unifies all branches of the special warfare units under one commander.

◆ Under the U.S. Special Operations Command, America's elite Special Operations Forces unite to form a de facto fifth branch of America's armed services.

Chapter 11

Introducing the U.S. Army Special Operations Command

In This Chapter

- ◆ The six components of USASOC
- ◆ The Special Forces Command
- ◆ The 160th Special Operations Aviation Regiment
- ◆ The Special Operations Support Command
- ◆ The John F. Kennedy School of Special Warfare
- ◆ The Civic Affairs/Psychological Operations Command

With approximately 23,000 personnel, the U.S. Army Special Operations Command (USASOC) is the largest component of USASOCUSSOCOM. Their command headquarters is housed in a large, ultra-modern building inside the Fort Bragg compound, right next to the XVIII Airborne Corps and the 82nd Airborne Division's headquarters. Today the USASOC trains, equips, deploys, and sustains Army Special Operations Forces worldwide—which makes them one of the most active commands in the United States military. From October 1997 to May 1998, 21,326 Army Special Forces personnel were deployed to 102 countries, where they conducted over 3,000 missions, including peacekeeping, humanitarian assistance, de-mining and mine-awareness, and foreign internal defense operations.

In this chapter, I'll outline the structure of the Army's Special Operations Command, their responsibilities, and their mission profiles. We will also take a peek at the elite 160th Special Operations Aviation Regiment, and the 75th Ranger Regiment—two vital elements of the USSOC today.

The "Six Pack"

The U.S. Army Special Operations Command (USASOC) is divided into six components—sometimes called the "six pack"—that together encompass the full spectrum of modern special warfare operations. They are listed here, from smallest to largest:

♦ The Civil Affairs and Psychological Operations Command

♦ The Special Operations Support Command

♦ The U.S. Army John F. Kennedy Special Warfare School and Center

♦ The 160th Special Operations Aviation Regiment

♦ The 75th Ranger Regiment

♦ The Special Forces Command

The Special Forces Command

The Special Forces Command (SFC) is the brains of the Army special operations community; the 75th Ranger Regiment (see Chapter 13, "The 75th Ranger Regiment") is its muscle. The SFC is the home of the Green Berets today, although Special Forces soldiers do not cherish that name as they once did because of its somewhat negative connotations stemming from the Vietnam era. With approximately 10,000 active-duty personnel and a larger reserve, the SFC is the largest unit of both SOCOM and USASOC. Within its ranks are both active-duty and National Guard Special Forces groups. There is also an active-duty and reserve Chemical Reconnaissance Detachment (CRDs), specially trained to deal with all chemical and some biological actions and emergencies.

Shop Talk

The SFC has the highest operational tempo (OpTempo) of any unit in SOCCOM. As a rule, special operations forces spend up to six months of every year " in the field." Compared to Navy personnel, who spend 6 out of every 18 months at sea, the unconventional warfare units work longer and harder than anyone else.

Presently, the SFC breaks down into 10 separate Special Forces Groups (SFGs), responsible for various geographic regions or particular types of operations.

SFC Special Forces Groups

- **The 1st Special Forces Group** is based at Fort Lewis, Washington, with forward-deployed units in Okinawa. This SFG provides special operations services to PACOM and SOCPAC.

- **The 2nd Special Forces Group** is based at Fort Bragg, North Carolina, and provides SOF services to EUCOM and SOCEUR operations in western and southern Africa, with detachments supporting operations for CENTCOM and SOCCENT when needed.

- **The 5th Special Forces Group** is based at Fort Campbell, Kentucky, today, but was once headquartered in Nha Trang, South Vietnam. The 5th SFG has seen the most combat, due to its involvement in the Vietnam War. Today the 5th SFG supports CENTCOM and SOCCENT in east Africa, the Middle East, and central and southwest Asia, its old stomping grounds.

- **The 7th Special Forces Group** is based at Fort Bragg, North Carolina, with a forward detachment in Puerto Rico. It provides SOF services for SOUTHCOM and SOCSOUTH in Latin America and the Caribbean Basin.

- **The 10th Special Forces Group** is based at Fort Carson, Colorado, with a forward detachment sitting in Germany. The 10th is America's original Special Forces group, the first such unit formed back in 1952. True to its eastern European roots, the 10th still provides services for Europe for EUCOM and SOCEUR.

- **The 19th Special Forces Group** is based at Draper, Utah, and is composed of units from the western United States. The 19th SFG is one of two National Guard Reserve Special Forces Group, and it supports operations for PACOM, SOCPAC, CENTCOM, and SOCCENT.

- **The 20th Special Forces Group** is based in the steel town of Birmingham, Alabama. It is the other reserve SFG, composed of units from the eastern United States. It provides services for SOUTHCOM and SOCSOUTH in the Caribbean.

- **The 56th and 801st Chemical Reconnaissance Detachments** are based at Fort Campbell, Kentucky, and Fort Bragg, North Carolina respectively.

- **The 445th Chemical Reconnaissance Detachment** is based at Fort Meade, Maryland, and is one of two reserve units composed of personnel from the eastern United States, where it provides CRD services.

- **The 900th Chemical Reconnaissance Detachment** is based at Fort Carson, Colorado, and is the second reserve CRD unit, staffed by and serving the people in the western United States.

These special warfare groups couldn't accomplish their mission without getting to the battlefield. Providing transportation for special operations is the responsibility of the 160th Special Operations Aviation Regiment—the famed Night Stalkers.

The 160th Special Operations Aviation Regiment

One of the most technologically advanced unit of the special operations forces today, the 160th Special Operations Aviation Regiment (SOAR)—known as the "Night Stalkers"—provides the aviation support required to insert Special Forces teams into their theater of operation, night or day, and in any kind of weather. Of course, with a nickname like the Night Stalkers, it is obvious that the 160th specializes in night operations, in which its array of advanced sensors, night-vision goggles, navigational equipment, weapons, and crew skills means that the Special Forces will have the technological edge in black of night.

To accomplish their mission, the Night Stalkers fly various types of specially modified helicopters, with three types of assault helicopters as their mainstay:

◆ **The MH-47D/E Chinook** is a specially modified version of the long-range, heavy-lift, twin-rotor Boeing MH-47 Chinook helicopter used by the regular Army. But the 47D/E is equipped with specially designed equipment, including terrain-following radar (TFR) for low-level infiltration, forward-looking infrared scanners (FLIR), electronic countermeasures (ECMs)to elude antiaircraft radar and missiles, and an in-flight refueling probe. The 47D/E is capable of carrying up to 20 Special Forces personnel into action and is equipped for "fast rope" operations.

◆ **The MH-60L "Enhanced" Black Hawk** is flown by the 160th to insert troops of the Army Special Forces or the 75th Rangers. It sports twin 7.62mm miniguns, AN/AAQ-16 FLIR imager, AN/ALQ-144 omnidirectional infrared jammer, two pintle mounts for machine guns, and an M-130 flare/chaff dispenser tied to the missile detector. The **MH-60K Pave Hawk,** flown by Air Force special ops, is also available for tasking. This aircraft is based on the UH-60 Black Hawk used by conventional Army forces. The Pave Hawk has the same mission package as the SpecOps MH-47D/E Chinook (TFR, FLIR, ECM, refueling probe, and so on), but it carries a smaller payload a shorter distance. The Pave Hawk can also be configured to fire Hellfire antitank missiles, and possesses jammers, flare/chaff dispensers, and machine guns to defend itself. Like the Chinook, the Black Hawk and Pave Hawk are both equipped for "fast rope" evacuations.

◆ **The AH/MH-6 "Little Bird"** is the hottest addition to the 160th aircraft fleet. The precise details and operational capabilities of this light attack, assault, and surveillance helicopter based on the H-6/MD-500 series helicopters built by Boeing are still classified. That said, the Little Bird is reportedly equipped with FLIR systems and armed with air-to-ground rockets and perhaps a 7.62mm, six-barrel minigun. This variant is also useful for infiltration into urban areas because of its small size, and chopper is equipped with "fast rope" capabilities.

FUBARs

If the nighttime-insertion capabilities of SOAR existed in 1980, the disastrous collision at the secret base at Desert 1 in Iran would have been avoided.

The MH-60 K/L Pave Hawk helicopter.

In the past, the United States military has had only limited success at night fighting. The special skills employed by the Night Stalkers is a huge leap forward in the evolution of the Army's night-combat capabilities.

The Origin of the Night Stalkers

After the failed hostage rescue attempt in Iran, the U.S. Army sought to radically improve its special operations aviation capabilities. Volunteers familiar with the UH-60 Black Hawk were selected from the 101st Aviation Brigade out of Fort Campbell, Kentucky. Over the next two years, this group developed tactics, techniques, guidelines, and procedures for conducting special operations. Intensive training began in June 1980 for long-range, low-level flying at night with primitive, full-faced AN/PVS-5 night-vision goggles. As the men's skills improved, the mission profiles became more complex and challenging. On April 1, 1982, this all-volunteer group was designated the 160th Aviation Battalion—informally known as Task Force 160.

In October 1983, Task Force 160 received its baptism of fire during Operation Urgent Fury, the invasion of Grenada. Within 36 hours of first notification, the 160th off-loaded at the forward staging area in Barbados in preparation for the launching of its first combat operation. Some elements of Task Force 160 assaulted the Richmond Hill Prison and others were dispatched to secure Sir Paul Scoon, the Governor General of Grenada, at his residence. Despite heavy fire and the loss of one aircraft, the twin missions were accomplished.

Straight Shooting

During Operation Prime Chance, from 1987 to 1989, Task Force 160 protected ships passing through the Persian Gulf. The 160th Special Operations Aviation Group (Airborne) operated their helicopters just 30 feet above sea level at night, using night-vision goggles and forward-looking infrared (FLIR) devices.

Operation Just Cause, the invasion of Panama, followed in December, 1989. Over 440 personnel from the 160th were deployed from their winter quarters at Fort Campbell to the sweltering heat of Panama without blinking. They participated in a preinvasion air assault and insertion of combat controllers at Torrijos-Tocumen Airport. Four AH-6 attack helicopters from the 160th assaulted the Panamanian Defense Headquarters, where one of them was shot down. The pilots survived the crash, evaded capture, and were eventually recovered by friendly forces.

With two successful missions under their belt and the formation of the Special Operations Command, the Nightstalkers were headed for bigger things. On May 16, 1990, the 160th Special Operations Aviation Regiment was born. The first deployment of this new regiment was mere months away.

Night Stalkers in Desert Storm

When the Iraqi Army invaded Kuwait on August 2, 1990, the 160th was put on alert. The unit was deployed to the Persian Gulf on September 3 and was based at King Khalid International Airport. During Operation Desert Storm, the 160th provided fire support for the preinvasion ground assault into Kuwait and Iraq. It also provided refueling aircraft for the AH-64 Apaches from the 101st Airborne Division and conducted combat search-and-rescue (CSAR) operations in support of downed Allied pilots. At one point, helicopters from the 160th successfully recovered a downed F-16 pilot who was more than 60 miles inside of Iraq—the only successful rescue of the war with night-vision goggles.

> **Shop Talk**
>
> One of the Night Stalkers' hairiest missions during Desert Storm involved the extraction of a Special Forces A-Team that had been compromised. The mission was conducted by a single helicopter in broad daylight, in the middle of a fierce firefight.

"Black Hawk Down!"—Disaster in Somalia

In the summer of 1993, elements of the 160th were deployed to Somalia as part of Task Force Ranger. America's involvement in Somalia began with the Marine Corps peacekeeping mission in support of the United Nations forces in the region, but the mission was transformed by the Rangers into a bit of nation-building. During Task Force Ranger, a series of miscalculations by the Clinton administration in Washington, and a bifurcated military chain of command in Somalia, resulted in disaster for the men on the ground and in the air over Mogadishu.

Factional fighting in the streets of Mogadishu was limiting the effectiveness of the U.N. personnel in Somalia. One of the most egregious perpetrators was a local warlord (that is, gangster) named Mohammed Farah Aideed. On October 3, 1993, Rangers and Delta Force operators were dispatched by trucks and helicopters to raid an Aideed stronghold near the Bakara Market, and capture several of the warlord's trusted lieutenants. Things did not go according to plan.

During the action, two MH-60 Black Hawks were hit by rocket-propelled grenades while trying to insert two special operations forces. Both aircraft crashed into the crowded streets and narrow alleys of Mogadishu, in two separate locations. Desperate efforts were mounted to rescue the downed crews. At one point, an MH-6 landed in a narrow street between two closely packed buildings, near the wreckage of one MH-60. While the co-pilot rushed to rescue the survivors, the pilot held off mobs of armed Somalis who were attempting to capture or kill the trapped Americans with suppressive fire. Under intense fire, the MH-6 departed with one survivor.

FUBARs

As the Rangers moved out of their base toward Aideed-controlled territory around the Bakara market, Italian soldiers from the United Nations peacekeeping force may have warned the warlord that the Americans were coming by flashing the headlights on their military vehicles. Gen. Bill Garrison must also shoulder some of the blame for the mission's failure, because he launched the operation in broad daylight, in the late afternoon—a time when Aideed's heavily armed militiamen were in a highly agitated state, induced by a cocaine-like local narcotic called *khot*.

As rescue attempts were mounted, more Americans came under intense fire and were trapped in the town. In the most intense ground-war firefight since the Vietnam War, the men of the 160th distinguished themselves. Eighteen American servicemen were killed, along with hundreds of Somalis. One American soldier was held prisoner for 11 days before he was released, and some of the American dead were dragged naked through the streets, paraded in front of the international news cameras. Recently, it was learned that international Muslim terrorist Osama Bin Laden was involved in arming and training the Somalis for this operation. The U.S. Army still has unfinished business in Somalia.

The Night Stalker crest.

The Night Stalker Creed

Because their missions are so unique, the Night Stalkers have a culture and tradition all their own, as evidenced in the stirring text of "The Night Stalker Creed."

Service in the 160th is a calling only a few will answer, for the mission is constantly demanding and hard. And when the impossible has been accomplished, the only reward is another mission that no one else will try. As a member of the Night Stalkers, I am a tested volunteer seeking only to safeguard the honor and prestige of my country, by serving the elite Special Operations Soldiers of the United States. I pledge to maintain my body, mind, and equipment in a constant state of readiness, for I am a member of the fastest deployable Task Force in the world—ready to move at a moment's notice anytime, anywhere, arriving on target plus or minus 30 seconds.

I guard my unit's mission with secrecy, for my only true ally is the night and the element of surprise. My manner is that of the Special Operations Quiet Professional; secrecy is a way of life. In battle, I eagerly meet the enemy, for I volunteered to be up front where the fighting is hard. I fear no foe's ability, nor underestimate his will to fight.

The mission and my precious cargo are my concern. I will never surrender. I will never leave a fallen comrade to fall into the hands of the enemy, and under no circumstances will I ever embarrass my country.

Gallantly will I show the world and the elite forces I support that a Night Stalker is a specially selected and well-trained soldier.

I serve with the memory and pride of those who have gone before me, for they loved to fight, fought to win, and would rather die than quit.

Night Stalkers Don't Quit!

The Special Operations Support Command

Without effective logistics, no military operation can end in success. The Army's Special Operations Support Command (SOSCOM) provides spare parts, supplies, special weapons, ammunition, and many other necessary supply services for the Army's front-line Special Forces units.

SOSCOM is divided into two major components:

- **The 528th Special Operations Support Battalion** based at Fort Bragg provides the basic logistical supply and service functions for the United States Army Special Operations Command.

- **The 112th Signal Battalion,** also at Fort Bragg, is responsible for servicing a wide range of communications, data-processing, and networking requirements for USASOC.

The John F. Kennedy Special Warfare Center and School

The John F. Kennedy Special Warfare Center and School (JFKSWCS) is the Army's special operations university. The JFKSWCS conducts the complete spectrum of special operations training, including the development of leadership skills, language skills, and military doctrine. Located at Fort Bragg, the JFKSWCS is housed in two structures—Bryant Hall and Kennedy Hall—and operates "off-campus" training sites and facilities across the country.

Named to honor the "father of America's Special Forces," the JFKSWCS graduates approximately 10,000 students annually. Beyond military strategy and tactics, students study history, civil affairs, foreign languages and cultures, regional differences, psychological operations, medical techniques, satellite communications, engineering, mathematics, philosophy, and comparative religion.

First established to support the training and selection of Special Forces personnel, the JFKSWCS has evolved into a center of learning for the entire USASOC community. Today the JFK Special Warfare Center and School is the institutional keeper of all Army Special Forces knowledge and is responsible for a wide range of training, procurement, design, and development tasks for all of the Army's Special Forces community. The JFKSWCS maintains an extensive library, archives, and a small museum, and it issues *Special Warfare*, an authorized, official quarterly publication for military professionals inside the Special Forces community. The JFKSWCS also operates subsidiary and field schools around the country that teach special skills such as scuba diving and free-fall parachute jumping.

The JFKSWCS strives for excellence as it instills courage, ingenuity, and innovation to its students. Graduates move on to the other commands in the USASOC with a high degree of specialized knowledge and skills that cannot be acquired anywhere else in the United States military.

The Civil Affairs/Psychological Operations Command

Persuasion is the key tool of propaganda warfare, and the art of persuasion—through public relations, advertising, rhetoric, and white propaganda and the black kind—is what psychological operations (psyops) is all about. If you can persuade the enemy to surrender, you don't have to defeat him on the field of battle because you have already won the war for his heart and mind.

The U.S. Army's repository of knowledge and expertise in the field of propaganda is the Civil Affairs/Psychological Operations Command. With headquarters at Fort Bragg, this command is composed of two active-duty groups and seven reserve units.

At the core of the Army's CA/PSYOPs active-duty capability is the 4th Psychological Operations Group, based at Fort Bragg. The 4th is supplemented by the Second PSYOPs Group, a reserve unit based in Parma, Ohio; and the 7th PSYOPs Group, a reserve unit based in San Francisco.

The 96th Civil Affairs Battalion is also based at Fort Bragg and is the only active-duty Civil Affairs group in the U.S. Army. It is supported by two large reserve brigades—the 358th Civil Affairs Brigade from Norristown, Pennsylvania; and the 361st Civil Affairs Brigade from Pensacola, Florida—and three smaller reserve units, including the 351st Civil Affairs Command based in Mountain View, California; the 352nd CA Command in Riverside, Maryland; and the 353rd CA Command based in the Bronx, New York.

The Least You Need to Know

- ◆ The U.S. Army Special Operations Command is divided into six components.
- ◆ Together, the six components of USASOC encompass the full spectrum of modern special warfare operations.
- ◆ The Special Forces Command (SFC) is the home of the Green Berets and the brains behind USASOC.
- ◆ The John F. Kennedy Special Warfare Center and School is the Army's special operations university.

The U.S. Army Special Forces Training Regimen

In This Chapter

- ◆ Recruiting requirements of the Army Special Forces
- ◆ The Special Forces Assessment and Selection course
- ◆ The three phases and final exam requirements of the Q course
- ◆ Into the teams

Fewer than 5 percent of active-duty U.S. Army personnel meet the rigorous entry requirements of the Special Forces. Because the training is so extensive—and expensive—candidates are expected to meet and exceed a series of stringent physical and psychological challenges before they can even qualify for the training.

And once Special Forces training begins, more candidates will be forced out through a high rate of attrition. Those who fail will return to their old units. Those who succeed will one day earn the symbol of the Army Special Forces—the coveted Green Beret.

In this chapter, I'll examine the extensive and sometimes grueling selection and training process which ensures that the U.S. Special Forces will find the best possible candidates to serve with the Green Berets.

Requirements for a Special Forces Recruit

Recruiters within the Special Forces face the nearly impossible task of finding and training nearly a thousand men every year. Faced with this challenge, the Army has stubbornly refused to lower its high recruiting and training standards. Instead, they have aggressively stepped up recruitment, searching high and low for quality—and qualified—new recruits to replace those who have retired. And although the Special Forces want professional and capable soldiers to fill the ranks of "quiet professionals," the typical Special Forces recruit is not some overmuscled, super-athlete—*those* types are more commonly found in the Army Rangers or the Navy SEALs!

Generally, Army Special Forces soldiers lack some of the confrontational and aggressive qualities of the other special operations forces. Eschewing macho antics and overly destructive behavior, Army Special Forces personnel prefer to blend in to their environment while they observe the people and situations they come in contact with. Their language skills and cultural and regional training make them more sensitive to the nuances of the people with whom they deal. And like CIA agents, Army Special Forces soldiers often go "undercover," wearing the clothing and affecting the mannerisms of the local population.

Needless to say, these skills and talents are not usually present in the young, which is why the average Special Forces soldier is in his 30s or 40s, with years of military experience and worldly knowledge—and often a failed marriage—behind him.

What does it take to become part of America's fighting elite? More than most people are capable apparently, because less than 5 percent of active duty military personnel can even *qualify* for Special Forces training, and only about 3 out of 10 candidates will actually complete the grueling Special Forces training course to graduate. In fact, after the rigors of recruitment, selection, and qualification are over, a 3-percent graduation rate may actually be optimistic! And for potential candidates, things only get harder after they complete the Q course and receive their Green Berets. A Special Forces soldier can expect to spend up to six months a year away from his home and family, with a fair chance of getting killed, captured, or wounded on some far-off shore that no one has ever heard of back in the United States.

The following list shows the *minimum* requirements necessary for a soldier to qualify for Army Special Forces training.

Straight Shooting

A limited number of foreign military officers also participate in Special Forces training. They are selected by their own governments and are trained at U.S. taxpayer expense.

Minimum Requirements for a Special Forces Recruit

◆ **Men only:** The congressionally mandated Title 10 restrictions deny women the opportunity to serve in front-line combat units in the United States military. Because the Special Forces are nearly always serving on the front lines, the Special Forces community is for men only.

◆ **Racial and ethnic background:** There are no restrictions, but minority recruitment has become a higher priority in recent years. To "blend in," the Special Forces operative must look like a local. Since the fall of the Soviet Union and in light of growing overseas commitments where Arabic, Asian, African American, or Hispanic soldiers are required to mingle with the population, recruiting minority candidates has become increasingly important.

◆ **Physical fitness:** Although the Army wants its personnel to be in top physical shape, the Special Forces are not looking for raw strength in a candidate as much as they want endurance skills and mental toughness. Intelligence is a more important factor than physical strength for today's Special Forces soldier. Think triathletes, long-distance runners, and swimmers more than body builders, wrestlers, or football players. In fact, swimming is recommended because it builds upper-body strength—and all SF personnel are required to stay afloat and move easily through the water.

◆ **Rank and maturity:** Special Forces personnel are generally older and more mature than the U.S. military average. Entry into the Special Forces is restricted to officers who have attained the rank of captain or first lieutenants already selected to become captains, and enlisted personnel who have reached the rank of sergeant or "promotable" sergeant (someone who has been selected for promotion but has not yet been promoted); all must have good records and be considered "promotable." Most begin SF training in their late 20s or early 30s. Those specialists who apply and are accepted will achieve the rank of sergeant by the time they have finished the Q course.

◆ **Military experience:** Although candidates are recruited from nearly every branch of the Army, most Special Forces recruits have served with the infantry and completed airborne training and often Ranger training as well. But recruits also come from the signals, supply, and armor units of the Army. Aviators and military doctors are not accepted into the Army Special Forces because they are too valuable an asset to endanger in the high-risk world of "ground-pounding" special operations—their skills are better utilized in a special operations aviation regiment like the 160th.

◆ **Airborne training:** All Special Forces units include an airborne designation, which means that everyone who is considered for recruitment either will have graduated from the Army Airborne School at Fort Benning, Georgia, or is prepared to do so prior to special operations training. This can be a major hurdle because airborne training is one of the toughest regimens in the military. If you are afraid of heights or are unwilling to jump out of a perfectly good airplane with only a silk parachute on your back, then it's best to consider another field of endeavor!

♦ **Education:** If a Special Forces recruit doesn't have a college degree, he will soon earn one—the Special Forces like to have highly educated men in their ranks. Officers who already possess a college degree can expect their education to continue. Most Special Forces officers are expected to earn a post-graduate degree, and some earn more than one. Enlisted personnel are expected to achieve their own undergraduate or graduate degrees, and to attend night or continuing education courses.

♦ **Language skills:** By the time a Special Forces recruit graduates and joins his first unit, he will have learned at least one foreign language. Some of these languages are quite common (such as Spanish, French, or German), while others require a year or more of extensive study to master (think Chinese, Japanese, Arabic, or Tagalog). Recruits who apply for training already knowing at least one foreign language have a distinct edge over other potential candidates.

♦ **Interpersonal and communication skills:** Special Forces soldiers must feel comfortable dealing with other people, communities, cultures, and races—interpersonal skills are an important part of their job description. Although "people skills" might seem trivial, in the Special Forces they are essential. Special Forces personnel must also possess the communication skills required to share their knowledge—and their point of view—with others.

In addition to these attributes, a Special Forces recruit also benefits from having solid combat experience; real, measurable leadership abilities; adaptability; and vision.

The Special Forces Assessment and Selection Course

Today the successful training of a single Special Forces soldier takes about a year and costs over $100,000. Those who can't cut the mustard have to be weeded out early to avoid wasted effort, resources, and capital. Not surprisingly, the attrition rate during Special Forces training is high, and much of it is accomplished through the Special Forces Assessment and Selection (SFAS) course. Potential candidates—about 300 of them at a time—face the SFAS course, which is held four times a year.

Shop Talk

Col. Nick Rowe was a Green Beret serving in Vietnam when he was captured. He spent five years as a prisoner of war before he escaped and made his way back to the American lines. He was killed 25 years later by a bomb planted by Filipino insurgents.

The training is conducted at the Col. Nick Rowe Special Forces Training Facility at Camp MacKall, among the pine trees and rolling sand hills of North Carolina, west of Fort Bragg. It is here that the recruits endure the rigors of the Special Forces Assessment and Selection course, the biggest hurdle before they get to the actual Special Forces Qualification Course—the infamous "Q course"—a special event that will highlight one's talents and abilities and ensure one's career in the Special Forces—or put an end to it very quickly.

"Twenty-four days of pure hell" is how one anonymous Special Forces officer described the Special Forces Assessment and Selection course, a harsh, unforgiving test of spirit, body, and mind designed to weed out the less qualified and push those who make the grade forward, to the actual Q course and the next level of Special Forces training. Over the 24 days of the SFAS course, candidates will suffer the tortures of hell, including physical and mental challenges, limited nutrition, sleep deprivation, endurance tests, and competency exams. Under the harshest conditions imaginable, they will be expected to perform field-craft exercises, accomplish menial (and not-so-menial) tasks, and successfully complete assigned performance goals.

To fool returning candidates and those who possess "inside knowledge" (such as readers of this book), no two SFAS courses are ever the same. Events, goals, times, durations, and trials are constantly changed and rearranged. "It's like Christmas," said an anonymous Special Forces graduate of SFAS. "There's always a surprise." Candidates' sleep patterns are interrupted early and often during the assessment and selection phase, so sleep deprivation hits recruits fast—usually in the first week.

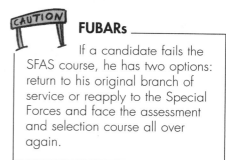

FUBARs

If a candidate fails the SFAS course, he has two options: return to his original branch of service or reapply to the Special Forces and face the assessment and selection course all over again.

The average SFAS course includes the following challenges:

- **Obstacle courses** that incorporate barriers, walls, crawls through buried sewer pipes, rope climbing, and jumps. Candidates with negative traits such as claustrophobia or fear of heights are quickly eliminated.

- **Marches** take place daily, and many are conducted with 50-pound packs. Candidates march day or night through all types of weather and are never informed how long or how far they will be expected to go in a given exercise.

- **Runs** occur daily, some with heavy packs. Medium-distance runs usually begin the candidate's day.

- **Orientation and field-craft exercises** begin in the second and third weeks of the SFAS course. Candidates are expected to orient themselves and maneuver to a geographical point within a given time frame using only a compass, a protractor, and a map. Like the marches, this exercise can take place day or night, in any type of weather.

- **Situation and reaction exercises** confront candidates who are already deprived of sleep and nutrition, and probably near the edge of physical collapse, with a difficult problem to overcome. These problems range from fording a river without getting wet to moving a crippled vehicle a mile or more on muscle power and simple engineering tricks alone.

◆ **Team cooperation exercises** test a candidate's ability to work with others. Like the situation and reaction exercises, the recruits are given a common goal and told to accomplish it. Those who become impatient with their mates or who fail to become a team player are weeded out.

By the second week of the SFAS course, nearly half of the original 300 candidates have been bounced. Most fail during the endless runs or long marches, or suffer from extreme sleep deprivation and can no longer continue. When a candidate reaches his limit, he lets the training instructor know by raising his hand. The candidate is quickly isolated from the rest before being discharged.

Sometimes candidates are injured. If the injury is slight (a cut, a pulled muscle, and so on), participation in the Q course continues. If it is more severe (broken limb, concussion, and so on), the candidate is dropped but usually is permitted to reapply for the Special Forces training after recovery.

At the end of the twenty-fourth day, those who endured all the rigors and hardships of the SFAS course are given an invitation to the Special Forces Qualification Course (Q course). The Q course does not begin right away. Often candidates are given up to a year to recover from the SFAS course and improve the skills in which they were most weak.

The Qualification Course

Once a candidate passes the SFAS course, he has proven himself to possess the talents and aptitudes necessary to one day become a Special Forces soldier—but he is not in the Special Forces yet! The candidate still has to survive the Q course, a tough training regimen that turns a qualified and experienced soldier into a basically trained Special Forces soldier who is ready for active duty with a Special Forces group.

The Q course is divided into three phases:

◆ **Phase I** centers on basic skills and training. It lasts for 39 days and is designed to provide a common level of field skills for all candidates, no matter what the background or previous service specialty may have been.

◆ **Phase II** divides the original group according to the candidates' military occupational specialty. This phase varies in length, depending on the complexity of the training.

◆ **Phase III** lasts 38 days and is designed to familiarizes the candidates with the basic tactics of unconventional warfare. This phase ends with a large-scale field exercise called Robin Sage.

> **Shop Talk**
>
> Today the Q course is similar to the training offered 50 years ago, when Col. Aaron Bank established the training regimen for America's first SF unit, the 10th Special Forces Group.

Phase I

Phase I is conducted at Camp MacKall and the Col. Nick Rowe Training Facility. This phase teaches the candidate how to plan, supply, conduct, and lead a squad-sized patrol through an assigned mission in a given period of time. Candidates are required to accurately navigate cross-country with a full combat load and according to the prearranged schedule—night or day, no matter what the weather is.

The first 21 days focus on land-navigation skills, field craft, and patrol basics. While it is a given that once they are on active duty most Special Forces soldiers will rely on a NAVSTAR global positioning system (GPS), such luxuries are forbidden when they are undergoing the Q course—in real combat, satellites may fail, batteries run down, and GPS devices may be destroyed by enemy action. During Q course, navigation must be done by the sun, the moon, and the stars with a compass, protractor, and map. This is followed by a four-day course on marksmanship, first aid, and the field-craft skills that many of us learned in the Boy Scouts. The third week is for learning patrol tactics and observational skills.

Special Ops Jargon

Special Forces candidates are encouraged to learn how to measure distances with **Ranger beads,** a simple field abacus that is hung around the neck, a belt, or a uniform.

The fourth week of Phase I is dedicated to learning the basics of field reconnaissance and setting up ambushes, followed by another week of field exercises meant to test the proficiency of each candidate. The skills learned in the previous weeks are tested in real field environments. During this phase of the training, the students are broken into six-man teams and dispatched to the countryside to perform mock reconnaissance, ambushes, and other simulated exercises.

By day 32, candidates are ready to begin platoon operations, followed by another field exercise to test their proficiency—this time with 12-man teams dispatched to the forest to run several different types of missions. On the thirty-ninth day, Phase I is completed, and those who didn't fail move on to Phase II.

Phase II

During Phase II, the candidates begin to focus on their unique specialty. This phase is often conducted at other facilities. For this phase, 18-series courses are available, varying in length from six months to a full year. Candidates can become officers (18A), weapons sergeant (18B), engineer sergeant (18C), medical sergeant (18D), communications sergeant (18E), and so on. While learning, candidates are urged to hone their teaching skills because they will be called upon to train foreign military personnel or insurgents in their particular specialty at some future date.

Failure is still an option. Because Phases II and III are complex and expensive, candidate screening is intense during Phase I of the Q course. Those who flunk out *may* be permitted to try again—but only once! A second failure means they are sent back to their old assignments.

The specialty fields available are ...

- **Officer training,** which is a six-month course designed to take officers from the conventional military units and turn them into Special Forces leaders. Candidates learn the elements of unconventional warfare—including guerrilla warfare and insurgency operations—as well as mission assessment, mission planning, and logistics.

- **Weapons training,** which is designed to teach advanced weapons skills for a wide range of special ordinance. These candidates—all sergeants or higher—are expected to master the operation and maintenance skills necessary to use every kind of weapon, from handguns to rocket launchers to Stinger missiles.

Shop Talk
During weapons training, Special Forces candidates not only learn how to use weapons from the U.S. military arsenal, but they also are expected to master those firearms used by other militaries around the world.

- **Medical training,** which is the longest of the training courses, lasts a full year. Run by the Special Operations Medical Training Battalion at Fort Bragg, the course teaches candidates quick response to trauma—gunshot wounds, shrapnel wounds, stabs, and so on. Near the end of this course, these future medical sergeants are sent to hospitals in Tampa, Florida, or the Bronx, New York—violent, inner-city urban areas where they get real, hands-on experience with trauma injuries.

- **Engineering,** which centers on basic construction and demolition skills. The course teaches candidates—again, all sergeants—how to build things and then blow them up.

- **Communications,** which is a six-month course on all types of communications, from Morse code to advanced computer networking to encryption techniques.

- **Operations/Intelligence,** which covers the intelligence gathering, logistical elements, tactics, and strategic planning that precede any special warfare operation.

Phase III

Though only 38 days long, Phase III of the Q course is the most intensive part of Special Forces training and ends with a "final exam" called Robin Sage. In the first few days of this phase, officers learn "intelligence preparation of the battlefield"—or how to understand the terrain, evaluating possible targets—while the sergeants learn about mission and operational planning. This is followed by a refresher course on air, parachute, and helicopter operations; and day 11 features an airborne insertion (parachute) exercise. This is done because, in two weeks the Robin Sage Field Exercises, commence. During Robin Sage, Special Forces candidates are expected to use all of the skills they learned—and more.

Leading up to Robin Sage are more lectures on unconventional warfare, cross-cultural communications training, and weapons instruction. On day 16, candidates begin their preparations for Robin Sage. This preparation includes days of simulations, rehearsals, and exercises—all done in isolation. Finally on day 23, the final exam begins.

Final Exam: The Robin Sage Field Exercise

The Robin Sage Field Exercise is held four times a year and is designed to simulate the missions of the Jedburgh Teams of World War II (discussed in Chapter 2, "The Special Forces of World War II"). Jedburgh Teams were parachuted into occupied France by the OSS prior to the D-Day invasion in 1944. Once on the ground, they linked up with resistance groups to aid them in their fight against the Nazis. This is a difficult and dangerous type of mission, and it is exactly what these Special Forces candidates have trained for. By the end of the Q course, these students of war are more than ready to test what they've learned in simulated combat.

Robin Sage is a large exercise and involves all the candidates, many of their instructors, hundreds of active-duty and reserve Special Forces soldiers, several airplanes, a dozen helicopters, and hundreds of square miles of North Carolina's Uwharrie Forest to execute. Among the sand hills and pine trees, the candidates are given a final opportunity to prove that they have what it takes to join America's fighting elite. The Robin Sage Exercises, or simulations like them, have been carried out by the Army Special Forces for over 40 years.

> **Shop Talk**
>
> Rural, retirement, and vacation communities around Camp MacKall donate their land for use by the Special Forces during Robin Sage, and it isn't all that unusual to find a Special Forces soldier in camos crouching among the trees near your front yard!

Robin Sage involves the infiltration of an imaginary nation called Pineland, where unorganized bands of resistance fighters are trying to overthrow an oppressive government. Local residents, called the Pineland Auxiliary, play the role of Pineland civilians, to keep the feel of the exercise real. Each exercise lasts 15 days and involves enormous expenditures by the Air Force and Army aviation units to support the simulated infiltration and resupply missions throughout the simulated campaign.

In preparation for Robin Sage, the instructors and staff assemble a number of 12-student units. There can be as few as 9 teams for this exercise or as many as 12, depending on the number of candidates who have remained in the training thus far. These 12-man units are called Operation Detachment Alpha Teams, popularly known as A-Teams. The ODA Team is the basic building block of the Army Special Forces. As in real combat missions, the ODAs in Robin Sage are carefully balanced teams composed of men trained in various specialties. And, like a real mission, the ODA is composed with a duplicate mix of personnel—two weapons specialists, two communications specialists, and so on—so that in the field the team can be evenly split to create two combat ODAs with the same mix of skills and capabilities as the original. These capabilities include a vast array of martial and marksmanship skills, along with expertise in civil action, communications, trauma medicine, and civil engineering.

FUBARs

Operational Detachment Alpha Teams used to be called A-Teams, but since the television show of the same name appeared in the 1980s, the term has fallen out of favor among Army Special Forces personnel.

Once the ODA teams have been selected, they are given their assignments. Each team is required to link up with a particular insurgency organization—called a G-Band—win its trust, join the guerrillas, build a rapport with the insurgency leaders, and attempt to organize them into more effective fighting units. During the course of these events, the ODA teams will join in a simulated attack on an enemy "target" somewhere inside of Pineland. All of this is accomplished under the watchful eyes of the instructors, who observe and evaluate each team—and each member of that team. One Observer/Controller

(O/C) is permanently attached to each ODA and can provide guidance and advice. Other O/Cs evaluate specific events, such as the first meeting with the insurgents (active or reserve Special Forces troops vividly acting the part of unorganized, sometimes blood-thirsty guerrillas who will make life for the candidates difficult indeed), an ambush, infiltration, reconnaissance patrol, or evacuation.

As on an actual mission, the candidates are divided into teams. Bravo units—in this case the instructors—remain behind at "headquarters," except for the observers, while Alpha teams (the candidates) are deployed into the field. The Robin Sage Exercise begins on a Saturday night with the insertion of the 10 to 12 student ODA teams into the North Carolina wilderness. Some will ride in on trucks or row in with a rubber boat. Others will

Special Ops Jargon

Operational Detachment Bravo (ODB) units are headquarters staff members who coordinate and control the action of several Operational Detachment Alpha (ODA) units in the field.

parachute into Occupied Pineland from C-130s supplied by the Air Force Special Operations Command. Still others will fast-rappel down ropes from UH-60 Black Hawk helicopters. To keep things from getting too boring and routine, instructors often switch infiltration methods at the last possible moment. Often the instructors provide additional hurdles for the ODA teams to overcome, all while evaluating the candidates' performance and adaptability as their schedules and missions begin to unravel.

As soon as they arrive at the landing zone or assembly point, the ODA teams count heads and get themselves oriented to the region—knowing full well that they are already being stalked by teams belonging to the opposing force (OpFor teams are composed of members of the 82nd Airborne Division or other XVIII Airborne Corps units). Before the sun comes up, the ODAs are expected to meet up with their assigned G-Band, and bury the bulk of their food, supplies, and ammunition where it is safe but can easily be retrieved. The safety of this supply cache may mean the difference between graduation or failure for the candidates—or life and death in an actual combat mission.

Once the ODAs have linked up with their guerrillas, they have to be introduced to their leader—dubbed the G Chief. Playing the role of a local warlord, an experienced Special Forces officer puts the candidates through the ringer for them to "win his support." This is an intense period for the ODAs, but it is up to them to win the G Chief's trust. This may take days of interaction, and during the negotiations the "guerrillas" will try to steal their food, ammunition, or weapons. Even the secret cache is not safe from looting. All through this awful ordeal, the ODAs must remain calm, must never threaten their relationship with the G-Bands, and must never be insensitive to their culture. During this phase of the exercise, the candidates learn firsthand that patience is a virtue!

In time, the officers of the ODA team are taken to a meeting with a powerful guerrilla chieftain, played by a member of the Pineland Auxiliary. At this meeting, the candidates are expected to explain official U.S. policy as it relates to Pineland, America's plans for the liberation of the region, how the ODAs can help, and so on. Finally, around the fourth day, the ODA teams are allowed to begin their real work—teaching the guerrillas new military skills and tactics while attempting to forge them into something like a legitimate military force.

Near the end of the first week, the ODAs, combined with the G-Bands, stage a raid or ambush on the OpFor unit. The ODAs plan and help execute the mission while guiding the insurgents through each step. After that, the ODAs teach helicopter/airborne landing zone procedures to the G-Bands so that they can be resupplied from the air. Then a combined ODA/G-Band force mounts a precision raid on an enemy infrastructure target such as a bridge, a dam, a mock railroad juncture, or a power plant. The Robin Sage exercise ends with the linkup of the "invading" force as Pineland is liberated, followed by the difficult task of convincing the guerrillas to give up their weapons and become good citizens.

Straight Shooting

ODAs try to convince the guerrillas to join the New Pineland Army, explaining that they will be paid, will have military records, and may receive pensions or positions in the new government—if the guerrillas are victorious. Of course, G-Bands resist any effort to make them behave like a civilized army.

When all those missions are accomplished, the ODAs are extracted and returned to their base, where they write and file their reports and await the judgment of their instructors and O/Cs. Those who have successfully completed the Q course return to Camp MacKall for a dinner and awards ceremony, where they are inducted into the First Special Forces Regiment and presented with their Green Berets. They also receive a badge for the front of their berets, which represents the Forces Group to which they have been assigned.

More School, Then into the Field

After completing Q Course, graduates still continue their education—usually at language school, where they learn the words and culture of their geographic areas of operation. For a posting at EUCOM, future ODA team members may learn Russian, Czech, Hungarian, German, Portuguese, Polish, Arabic, or French. For PACOM, they may take courses in Chinese, Russian, Korean, Thai, Indonesian, and, of course, Tagalog. At SOUTHCOM, Spanish and Portuguese are preferred, and for CENTCOM—the hottest posting of all at the time of writing—graduates learn Arabic, Persian, Farsi, Pushtu, or Urdu.

After language school, Special Forces soldiers must attend the Survival, Evasion, Resistance, and Escape School (SERE) back at Fort Bragg. This course teaches high-risk personnel how to elude capture, survive imprisonment, and endure torture. Needless to say, the curriculum at SERE is highly classified.

> **Shop Talk**
>
> A typical Special Forces soldier can expect to spend between three to six months overseas—and to spend the rest of his time honing his skills and learning new ones.

There is hardly time to breathe before the fresh Special Forces personnel are sent to advanced parachute training at Military Free-Fall Course, conducted at Yuma, Arizona. It is at this joint training center that members of all the Special Forces learn the fine art of "free fall" parachute jumping (see Chapter 13, "The 75th Ranger Regiment"). From there it's on to an ODA team, where they carry out the missions for which they were trained with honor, courage, and consistency.

The Special Forces Creed

The Special Forces Creed has inspired Army Special Forces candidates and graduates for half a century:

> I am an American Special Forces soldier. A professional! I will do all that my nation requires of me.

I am a volunteer, knowing well the hazards of my profession. I serve with the memory of those who have gone before me: Rogers's Rangers, Francis Marion, Mosby's Rangers, the First Special Service Forces and Ranger Battalions of World War II, and the Airborne Ranger Companies of Korea. I pledge to uphold the honor and integrity of all I am—in all I do.

I am a professional soldier. I will teach and fight wherever my nation requires. I will strive always, to excel in every area and artifice of war. I know that I will be called upon to perform tasks in isolation, far from familiar faces and voices, with the help and guidance of my God.

I will keep my mind and body clean, alert, and strong, for this is my debt to those who depend upon me. I will not fail those with whom I serve. I will not bring shame upon myself or the forces. I will maintain myself, my arms, and my equipment in an immaculate state, as befits a Special Forces soldiers.

I will never surrender, though I be the last. If I am taken, I pray that I may have the strength to spit upon my enemy. My goal is to succeed in any mission—and live to succeed again.

I am a member of my nation's chosen soldiery. God grant that I may not be found wanting, that I will not fail this sacred trust.

De Oppresso Liber

The Least You Need to Know

◆ Fewer than 5 percent of active duty Army personnel even *qualify* for U.S. Army Special Forces training.

◆ Fewer than 3 in 100 will actually complete the Army Special Forces training course and graduate.

◆ Special Forces members are more than mere warriors—they must learn a military specialty, learn at least one foreign language, and earn one or more college degrees.

◆ Even after a candidate earns his coveted Green Beret, his training continues.

Chapter 13

The 75th Ranger Regiment

In This Chapter

- ◆ The Rangers in Korea and Vietnam
- ◆ The structure of the 75th Ranger Regiment
- ◆ The Ranger Training Brigade
- ◆ The Ranger Creed

The elite U.S. Army Rangers possess a culture of their own, which is not surprising, given their long and distinguished tradition of service, their distinctive haircuts, and their "hoo-ah" battle cry. Though only a quasi-elite force, the Rangers must first endure a rigorous all-weather, airborne-capable training regimen that few complete.

The average U.S. Army Ranger ultimately ranks far above the typical Army grunt in the military hierarchy but just under the Green Berets. For many troopers, success in the Rangers is but the first stepping stone for advanced service in the Army Special Forces or even the ultra-elite antiterrorist Delta teams.

In this chapter, I'll explore the unique traditions and glorious history of the Rangers, and examine one of the most elite Army regiments of them all—the 75th Ranger Regiment.

"Rangers Lead the Way"

Based at Fort Benning, Georgia, the 75th Ranger Regiment is the second largest component of USASOC—after the Army Special Forces (the Green Berets)—with approximately 13,000 active-duty personnel. Descendent of the legendary Ranger battalions of World War II (see Chapter 2, "The Special Forces of World War II"), the 75th Ranger Regiment is composed of three specially trained, airborne-qualified battalions. The Rangers are trained and equipped to parachute out of an airplane, engage the enemy, and capture or annihilate juicy targets such as command-and-control facilities, airfields, communications arrays, and seaports. As they are fond of stating, "Rangers lead the way!"

Today the 75th Ranger Regiment ranks among America's elite military forces, but that wasn't always the case. After serving the United States during World War II, the Rangers were disbanded when the war ended. But it wasn't long before the Army realized that it had made a big mistake and set out to rectify it. Before a decade had passed, the Rangers were on the front lines of a brand new war.

Korea

After the communist North Koreans invaded the South on June 25, 1950, the United States entered the conflict on a limited basis. While the front lines were fluid, the first Ranger units since World War II were activated and trained at Fort Benning, Georgia, before being committed to combat. Impressed by their success at infiltrating enemy territory, U.S. Army Chief of Staff Gen. J. Lawton Collins ordered that one company of Rangers be attached to each Army division fighting in Korea, where they would infiltrate enemy lines to attack command posts, artillery, tank parks, and communication centers. These Rangers were well trained and could move themselves and their equipment 50 miles cross-country in 12 to 18 hours, depending on terrain. They received cold-weather training at Camp Carson, Colorado. Eventually six Ranger companies were dispatched to Korea, where they participated in every major battle from their arrival in late 1950 to their deactivation in the fall of 1951.

Straight Shooting

One of the six Ranger companies sent to Korea was the 2nd Ranger Company, the only all–African American Ranger unit in U.S. Army history.

Vietnam

In 1969, during the Vietnam War, the Long Range Reconnaissance Patrols (LRRPs) in Vietnam were designated as Rangers. Many in the Army felt that the Rangers should have a place in the Vietnam-era Army, and because LRRPs were doing Ranger-style operations, it followed that they should take the name of "Rangers" and receive the training. On February 1, 1969, two new Ranger companies—A at Fort Benning, and B at Fort Carson—were formed as part of the 75th Infantry Regiment.

In Vietnam, a typical LRRP mission lasted from five to seven days. The duration was never longer than a week because of the limits of human endurance—the six-man teams hardly slept in the field, and everything they required had to be carried on their backs. Usually the LRRP team was assigned a 4-square-kilometer zone in which to operate. On the final days of the mission, an ambush site was chosen. Once the trap was sprung and the enemy was engaged, LRRPs would move to their prearranged landing zone (LZ) and be extracted by helicopter.

By 1973, as the Vietnam War was winding down, Gen. Creighton Abrams ordered the formation of the first Ranger battalions since World War II, requiring that these new Rangers be airborne-capable. So it was that on January 31, 1974, the 1st Battalion (Ranger) of the 75th Infantry was established. Following on its heels, the 2nd Battalion (Rangers) was activated at Fort Lewis, Washington. The 3rd Battalion (Ranger) would not be activated until October 3, 1984.

Rangers were supposed to participate in the ill-fated attempt to rescue the American hostages in Teheran, but the mission was aborted before they could enter the action. Rangers went on to serve as the lead elements in the invasions of Grenada (Operation Urgent Fury) and Panama (Operation Just Cause). Although their participation in Operation Desert Storm is still classified, the Rangers were highly visible when, in December 1991, Company C of the 1st Battalion of the 75th Infantry Regiment parachuted into Kuwait in broad daylight, where television news cameras recorded the action—a reminder to Iraqi dictator Saddam Hussein that the Rangers could respond quickly to crisis and were prepared to halt any further threats to the security of the region.

The 75th Ranger Regiment Today

Today the 75th Ranger Regiment is America's premier strike force, capable of moving across any terrain and enduring any hardship required to complete their mission. In just 18 hours, the 75th Rangers can move to any region of the world to perform light infantry tasks and conduct and support special operations missions. Despite the terrain and climate, these Rangers can infiltrate and assault their target by land, sea, and air.

The typical Ranger mission requires initiative, depth, agility, and synchronization above and beyond those skills found in conventional light infantry units. Surprise is the key to the success of a Ranger mission, and many of their operations are carried out at night and during poor weather conditions, when the enemy is less vigilant and can easily be thrown off balance. Using stealth and concealment, Rangers have enhanced "survivability" on the battlefield.

FUBARs

Like all highly trained and skilled special forces groups, the Rangers should never be deployed for missions that can be accomplished by conventional forces. To do so is to squander an invaluable tactical and strategic resource.

Special Ops Jargon

Poop and snoop missions are long-range, long-duration Ranger reconnaissance missions deep into enemy-held territory. Such operations can last days or even weeks.

Rangers are trained to take full advantage of the terrain and choose the time and place to engage the enemy in combat. They employ different methods of insertion and attack to prevent the enemy from perceiving a pattern to their operations—which means that, above everything else, Rangers are unpredictable. Coupled with mobility, speed, and their superior firepower, this unpredictability often means that the Rangers can complete their mission before the enemy has the time and can martial enough resources to react.

The 75th Ranger Regiment consists of three battalions and a headquarters command. The 1st Battalion is located at Hunter Army Air Field, Georgia; the 2nd at Fort Lewis, Washington; and the 3rd at Fort Benning, Georgia. The regimental commander also has a special staff that includes a communications officer, a fire support officer, a surgeon, and a staff judge advocate to take care of legal matters. A weather officer from the U.S. Air Force and a tactical air control officer—usually from Air Force Special Operations—are also permanently assigned to the Ranger command headquarters. The backbone of this force are the Rangers themselves, who are well-trained to perform deep reconnaissance *"poop and snoop"* missions in any environment.

These three battalions rotate as the Ranger Ready Force—one month on, two months off. For the four months out of the year when a battalion takes its turn as a Ranger Ready Force, the designated battalion must be ready to deploy anywhere in the world within the designated 18 hour window. That means that supplies and ammunition must be secured on pallets, ready to be loaded onto transport planes and, if necessary, delivered or parachuted into the theater of operations from the air. The RRF battalion must be ready to recall all of its personnel from leave and assemble them in a matter of hours, in preparation for deployment into the combat zone. The following list presents a force breakdown of a Ranger regiment:

Regiment = 3 battalions

Battalion = 3 rifle companies, 1 headquarters company

Rifle company = 3 rifle platoons, 1 weapons platoon

Rifle platoon = 3 rifle squads, 1 machine gun squad

The Ranger tab.

The Structure of a Ranger Regiment

A Ranger regiment consists of three battalions. Each of these three battalions further breaks down into three combat companies and a headquarters company. A Ranger rifle company is comprised of 3 rifle platoons of 45 men each, with a weapons platoon of between 20 and 25 men. Each rifle platoon is made up of three rifle squads of three teams each and a machine gun squad. Squad leaders are staff sergeants, and team leaders are sergeants.

Sometimes specialists—with the equivalent rank to corporals—are allowed to be team leaders. The high number of NCOs among the Ranger teams ensures a good amount of individual initiative—a basic requirement for successful Ranger operations. Like the Marine Corps, the units of the Army Special Forces stress individual initiative, with the NCOs—corporals, sergeants, staff sergeants, and master sergeants—often leading an operation.

One potentially deadly hazard of Ranger operations is the lack of casualty evacuation capabilities in dire combat conditions. In an intense firefight—like the Battle of Mogadishu—an air evacuation of the wounded could threaten the mission goal by alerting the enemy to the Rangers' presence or location, or threaten the safety of the rescue personnel, who may face intense enemy resistance as they attempt to approach the evacuation point. To plug this gap, Rangers provide an extensive amount of medical care in the field. All team, squad, and platoon leaders learn basic first aid, including the use of hypodermic needles. Each squad also has a medic who has received extensive medical treatment training, but when his use as a healer is not required, the medic in a Ranger unit carries a rifle like everyone else. As you can see, serving in the 75th is much more stressful than doing time in a conventional Army unit—which is why the members of the 75th Ranger Regiment sometimes refer to themselves as *quadruple volunteers*.

Special Ops Jargon

The 75th Rangers are dubbed **quadruple volunteers** because they volunteer four times during military service: first for the Army, then for airborne school, again to join the Rangers, and finally for the honor of attending Ranger School, where, upon graduation, they receive their tabs. If the candidate is assigned to an actual Ranger unit like the 75th, they must complete additional training to receive a "scroll." According to the 75th Rangers, the Ranger tab is a school, but the scroll is a way of life.

The Ranger Training Brigade

Ranger training school is very difficult, and only one in four recruits makes it through the daunting regimen to earn the right to wear a curved yellow-on-black left-shoulder tab with the word *Ranger* emblazoned on it. Rangers who complete their training in the winter months get to sew on their tabs with white thread, an added honor that they well deserve! The goal of this torturous training is to screen out unfit candidates and to produce a tough, competent, independent-minded small-unit leader who can take up the reins of command in a combat situation and teach others the rudiments of Ranger tactics and strategies.

Straight Shooting

Ranger training is tough. Approximately 75 percent of the men admitted to Ranger training flunk out. Many Rangers who serve in the 75th are recruited from airborne units.

To re-create a realistic battle environment during Ranger training, the stress of combat is simulated by hunger, sleep deprivation, constant challenges, intense pressure, and a harsh physical environment featuring extreme weather conditions. At the end of the Ranger training course, the student is usually in the worst physical shape of his life. During training, the average weight loss by a candidate is about 30 pounds—which sounds pretty good but is a hell of a way to lose weight!

Teamwork is essential to pass Ranger training. All tasks are performed with two-man teams, and during the training, all candidates are considered equals—regardless of rank. This buddy system is important. It teaches Ranger candidates the importance of cooperation. No Ranger moves forward during a training course unless his buddy is with him.

All male officers and noncommissioned officers from American and allied services are eligible to apply for Ranger training. Applicants must be in excellent health and top physical condition. Airborne qualifications are desirable but are not required to join most Ranger units—students may train for parachute operations at a later date. Airborne proficiency *is* required, however, if a candidate wants to join the 75th Ranger Regiment, an elite regiment within this elite force.

Shop Talk

Approximately 60 percent of those who begin Ranger training come from the U.S. Army, 20 percent come from the other U.S. armed services, and 20 percent come from foreign countries. Candidates report to Ranger training without rank or service insignias because all students are regarded as equals.

To join the 75th Ranger Regiment, three and a half weeks of additional training is required. Most officers and enlisted men who join this elite regiment are recruited from airborne units. Candidates must complete the Ranger Indoctrination Program (RIP), a 26-day training program designed to eliminate the unqualified and unmotivated. RIP includes navigation tests, speed marches, intensive physical training beyond what they have already experienced, as well as courses on Ranger tradition and history. After completing RIP, the new Rangers go into the 75th for additional, hands-on training. All training is performance oriented, and done under stressful and sometimes hazardous conditions. Many of the candidates who complete RIP and join the 75th Ranger Regiment, see their time served in this unit as one stepping stone toward joining more elite groups like Delta Force or the Army Special Forces.

The Fun Begins

After orientation and the reams of paperwork have ended, candidates begin the Ranger Assessment Phase (RAP) of their training. This takes place at Fort Benning's *Camp Darby*—the "prisoner-of-war camp" located deep in the wooded hills of Georgia. There are no permanent structures here—students live and eat under the open sky, in all weather. There are five sites for field training exercises; the largest of them is called Cinder Block Village, which is comprised of two buildings and a wooden tower, all surrounded by a chain-link fence. The Darby Queen Obstacle Course is another semipermanent training structure, while the rest of the sites simulate mission objectives such as bunkers, missile installations, communications facilities, strongpoints, and enemy outposts.

Candidates begin by taking the Army Physical Fitness Test. They must be able to perform over 50 push-ups, over 60 sit-ups, and at least 6 chin-ups, as well as complete a 2-mile run—all in less than 15 minutes. Then come the three exercises that comprise the Water Survival Test. The 15-minute swim must be completed wearing fatigues, boots, and web equipment (canteen, ammunition pouches, and so on). During the submersion test, a candidate must submerge and remain underwater while discarding his rifle and equipment, and then swim to the poolside. Finally, a blindfolded candidate must walk off the end of a diving board, remove the blindfold, and swim to poolside without the loss of his equipment or rifle. He must be comfortable in the water at all times and show no fear.

After the fitness and water survival tests, the candidates are assigned buddies. A Ranger and his buddy work together throughout the course, although most candidates are compelled to change partners at least once during training because of the high rate of attrition. Following the Ranger Assessment Phase comes Ranger Stakes, which enables instructors to spot and remedy a candidate's weaknesses in weapons or communications proficiency.

Special Ops Jargon

Camp Darby is named for William O. Darby, the legendary commander of Darby's Rangers and the founder of the modern U.S. Army Rangers regiments. It was Darby who created the "Me and My Pal" training system during World War II.

Ranger Stakes

Ranger Stakes consists of 11 tasks meant to demonstrate how well candidates handle communications and light infantry weapons:

◆ **Tasks 1 through 3** test a student's ability with a machine gun. He must take the weapon apart and put it back together in a reasonable time, load the weapon, and then prepare it for firing.

◆ **Task 4** requires students to set a Claymore mine, run a wire to it, and then detonate the explosive—there's no bang, however, because all is done in simulation.

◆ **Tasks 5 and 6** involve communications. Students must send a radio message and then encode and decode a message using the KTC 600 operations code.

◆ **Tasks 7 through 9** involve proficiency with the basic weapon of the U.S. Army. Candidates must maintain and correct the malfunctions of an M16 rifle and then fire it. A Ranger's rifle must be in top condition at all times, and candidates seldom rest before they have cleaned and checked their rifles.

◆ **Tasks 10 and 11** involve the use of hand grenades and the M203 grenade launcher.

Straight Shooting

Ranger candidates who fail Ranger Assessment Phase are not permitted to continue the training. Those who display the proper "can-do" attitude might be permitted to try beating the assessment course again. Most are washed out of the program for good.

The third day of Ranger Stakes begins with the daily predawn run, and candidates must move at a pace of 1 mile per 8 minutes. This is followed by the confidence course, which is designed to build a candidate's agility and endurance. Troops climb a high log fence without ropes and then enter the worm pit, a shallow, muddy pond covered by barbed-wire—Ranger candidates must crawl on their backs and bellies under the knee-high wire, and things can get pretty messy. Finally, they climb rope netting and then slide down a single rope on the opposite side. This is followed by a map-and-compass navigation course similar to the one used by the Special Forces. For the Rangers there are both daylight and nighttime navigation tests.

Time for a Swim

The Ranger Assessment Phase ends with the Water Confidence Test. Candidates climb a crude ladder, walk across a log 30 feet above the ground, and then drop from a rope into Victory Pond—30 feet below! There is no time to rest before they climb a 60-foot tower and slide down a 200-foot inclined rope, right back into the water. These test is conducted no matter what the weather is—unless Victory Pond is frozen solid.

The next phase of Ranger training begins with an air assault from helicopters into a clearing near the camp's permanent structures. Candidates receive instructions on the fundamentals of combat patrols, deep reconnaissance, and advanced land navigation, while the physical training continues daily. Training intensifies as the days get longer—soon courses begin before 0500 hours (5 A.M.) and end as late as 0200 hours (2 A.M.). On three to four hours of sleep, candidates begin to feel the effects of sleep deprivation much more quickly. The long training day is meant to simulate real combat conditions.

Next the candidates run the Darby Queen Obstacle Course, 20 difficult and challenging obstacles scattered up and down a steep, wooded hillside. After that, their survival training begins. Students learn how to catch, cook, and eat rabbits—and because they have not been allowed to eat prior to their exercises, the men are plenty hungry and quite eager to skin and burn a cute little bunny!

Finally come combat exercises, which last four days and nights and feature a platoon of the 4th Ranger Training Battalion using Eastern Bloc weapons to simulate an enemy force. The enemy teams set up camp, post sentries, and remain vigilant while the candidates sneak up on them in day and night reconnaissance mission simulations. If a student is "killed" or captured, that failure is noted on the post-training evaluation.

Harsh-Weather Training

The Ranger combat exercise is followed by various types of climatic training, which are conducted at other facilities across the United States.

♦ **The 7th Ranger Training Battalion** at Fort Bliss, Texas, teaches desert survival tactics. Water procurement and preservation are stressed, followed by reconnaissance techniques in the flat terrain of the desert. Candidates learn how to penetrate barbed wire, clear a trench line, and assault a fortified bunker. During field exercises, candidates experience a simulated airborne assault, and meals are reduced to one a day to enhance real combat conditions.

♦ **The 5th Ranger Training Battalion** at Dahlonega, Georgia, specializes in mountain training. Candidates learn lower and upper mountaineering techniques. They learn about the various knots needed to secure ropes and climbing equipment, as well as techniques in belaying, rappelling, and so on. Candidates are expected to climb a cliff face in day or night, in any type of weather, with or without their rucksacks. Airborne operations are also conducted with some of the smallest drop zones of any military training facility. The instructors carry special tools for extracting men and parachutes from tall trees! Students plan and conduct ambushes and various types of reconnaissance missions—again, these exercises are conducted both in daylight and at night.

◆ **The 6th Ranger Training Battalion** at Eglin Air Force Base, Florida, is the Ranger candidates' next stop. Here they learn the basics of jungle warfare. By now their original numbers have been cut in half, and the heat and high humidity add to the rigors of training. (It's even worse in the winter. Florida swamps can get mighty cold.) Candidates learn how to spot and avoid reptiles, how to treat snakebites, how to carry out small-boat operations (with squad-sized Zodiac boats), how to ford streams, and how to survive 9 to 10 days in the Florida swamp. (They learn this by doing it!) Rations are cut, and sleep is permitted only four hours a day. This phase of Ranger training is considered by many to be the most grueling. It ends with a mock assault of Santa Rose Island by Zodiac boat. They attack by night, and as the candidates arrive at the island, they face a barrage of flares and fireworks—simulating an artillery attack—as they struggle onto the shore.

Graduation

Less than 30 percent of those who begin the Ranger training course actually complete it. Continued sleep deprivation, the chronic shortage of food, and the tough living conditions all take their toll on the candidates' mental and physical stamina. Those who graduate into the ranks of the Rangers know they have completed the most physically and mentally grueling training regiment in the United States Army.

Even after they receive their tabs, Rangers continue their training. Like their compatriots in the Army Special Forces, the Rangers have a very high OpTempo, as well as the most intense training schedule in the Army. Forty-eight weeks out of every year are spent in the field or downrange, learning new skills and honing the old. Rangers constantly train under tough, stressful, grueling, and dangerous conditions, including harsh-weather and live-fire exercises. Ranger units are often pitted against one another, using *MILES* simulators to raise their level of competitiveness.

Special Ops Jargon

MILES is short for Multiple Integrated Laser Engagement System, a training simulator in which optically safe laser transmitters mounted on rifles are used against laser detectors worn by individual soldiers or mounted on vehicles. This military version of the game "Laser Tag" is an effective training tool.

In addition to all the training, each Ranger battalion conducts readiness exercises two or three times a year. During these labor-intensive drills, they must assemble their personnel and equipment quickly and efficiently, for immediate movement. And just as in actual combat, they are then loaded into C-130s for a parachute drop into the target area and perhaps even follow-up combat simulations on the ground. After these exercises, the units are graded for speed and efficiency. It's hard work but worth the sweat because the reward of all this rigorous training is the finest special operations light infantry regiment in the entire world—the U.S. Army Rangers.

The Ranger Creed

The Rangers are fully aware of the traditions they must live up to, as eloquently outlined in the Ranger Creed:

> **R**ecognizing that I volunteered as a Ranger, fully knowing the hazards of my chosen profession, I will always endeavor to uphold the prestige, honor, and high "esprit de corps" of my Ranger Regiment.

> **A**cknowledging the fact that a Ranger is a more elite soldier who arrives at the cutting edge of battle by land, sea, or air, I accept the fact that as a Ranger my country expects me to move further, faster, and fight harder than any other soldier.

> **N**ever shall I fail my comrades. I will always keep myself mentally alert, physically strong, and morally straight, and I will shoulder more than my share of the task, whatever it may be. One hundred percent and then some.

> **G**allantly will I show the world that I'm a specially selected and well-trained soldier. My courtesy to superior officers, neatness of dress, and care of equipment shall set the example for others to follow.

> **E**nergetically will I meet the enemies of my country. I shall defeat them on the field of battle, for I am better trained and will fight with all my might. *Surrender* is not a Ranger word. I will never leave a fallen comrade to fall into the hands of the enemy, and under no circumstances will I ever embarrass my country.

> **R**eadily will I display the intestinal fortitude required to fight onto the Ranger objective and complete the mission, though I be the lone survivor.

> Rangers Lead the Way!

The Least You Need to Know

- With a long tradition of service, the U.S. Army Rangers have evolved into an elite special warfare unit.
- Qualifications for the Army Ranger are high, and candidates undergo one of the toughest training regimens of any military servicemen in the world.
- Ranger training involves activities in all types of climates and environments.
- Active-duty Rangers continue to train after graduation and spend 48 weeks a year in the field.

Part 4

The U.S. Navy SEALs

Today, the U.S. Navy SEALs are America's premier Special Forces nautical unit. In this part I will explore the origins of this tough, aggressive unit, which sprang from the Underwater Demolitions Teams of World War II. You will also learn about the creation of the SEALs during the Kennedy administration, study their operational history from Vietnam to Desert Storm, and learn about the demanding phases of Basic Underwater Demolition/SEAL (BUD/S) training—one of the most rigorous and challenging military training programs in the world.

Chapter 14

Introducing the Navy SEALs

In This Chapter

- The origins of the Navy SEALs
- The SEALs in action
- A closer look at the "Brown Water Navy"

Like the Army Special Forces, the U.S. Navy's Sea, Air, Land Teams were born during the Kennedy administration, though their roots stretch back to World War II. In this chapter we will meet the SEALs, examine their rigorous training, and explore their operational history.

The Origin of the Navy SEALs

The Navy SEALs were established during the Kennedy administration. At that time, nearly every branch of the United States military had formed its own special warfare unit in response to the president's belief that future wars would be small, contained conflicts in the Third World, fought by specially trained, unconventional warfare groups. The SEALs' origin, however, dates back to the Underwater Demolition Teams (UDTs) of Word War II.

In November 1942, the U.S. Marine Corps assaulted the Japanese-occupied island of Tarawa—"Bloody Tarawa," as it is known today. The American forces attacked without enough advanced reconnaissance of the ocean, reefs, or terrain, or credible intelligence about enemy defenses. Without even a fair knowledge of the shore, the beach reefs, and the tides around the island, the Marines launched their assault. The results were devastating for the landing force (see Chapter 2, "The Special Forces of World War II"). Although the Marines prevailed, losses were horrendous. Valuable lessons were learned, but at a terrible price. Never again would the Marines assault a beach before the Navy finished a thorough advance reconnaissance of the island and its defenses, followed by the destruction of the many obstructions built by the enemy.

To accomplish these difficult and dangerous assignments, the Naval Combat Demolition Unit (NCDU) was formed at Fort Pierce, Florida, in May 1942. Expert swimmers trained in demolitions and advanced reconnaissance tactics, these NCDU teams first saw action, ironically, in the European theater during the Normandy Invasion. In the Pacific theater, U.S. Navy UDTs were created to perform the same basic mission as the NCDUs, with equal success. By the end of the war, when the UDTs were eliminated, the Navy possessed 34 UDTs, with over 3,500 officers, enlisted men, and support personnel.

The UDTs were revived briefly during the Korean War, mostly in support of the September 1950 amphibious invasion of Inchon. After the invasion, as the communist North Koreans were in retreat, UDTs blew up bridges, railroad junctions, tunnels, and similar strategic targets far from the water. As their mission expanded, these UDTs performed guerilla operations behind enemy lines, parachute insertions, and other special missions quite different from those that they were originally created for. Such unusual missions are now part of the basic mission profiles of today's Navy SEALs.

The SEALs and the Navy Special Warfare Command

The SEALs are but one of *three* components of the Navy Special Warfare Command (NAVSPECWARCOM). The other two components are the Special Boat Squadrons (SBSs) and the SEAL Delivery Vehicle Teams (SDVs).

> **Shop Talk**
>
> The SEAL Delivery Vehicle Teams are a high-tech bunch. They are equipped with free-flooding mini-submarines that can carry six SEAL team members and can be launched from a submerged submarine. This vessel is capable of secretly transporting its passengers into an enemy harbor for sabotage missions.

The SEALs, the SBSs, and the SDVs have been fighting side by side for over 30 years, and each branch demands the same high training and performance standards of their personnel.

All U.S. special operations forces perform the same basic types of missions, although these missions are adapted to fit the particular talents and capabilities of the force carrying them out. Simply put, that means that the Army fights on land, the Navy on the water, and the Air Force in the air. However, with the introduction of universal special forces airborne capability, close-air support, and helicopter insertions, such distinctions are becoming less relevant.

The SEALs specialize in unconventional warfare operations in a maritime setting (which includes shores, lakes, rivers, and swamps). However, they also have airborne components and may operate 20 miles inland of any shoreline. If you think about it, that pretty much covers two thirds of the human population of the world because humans tend to cluster close to the water.

Although the SEALs use pretty much the same standardized weapons, parachutes, boats, dive gear, radios, explosives, and uniforms as the other special operations forces, their tactics are unique. Unlike the personnel in the other unconventional warfare branches—who focus on a particular combat *specialty*—members of a SEAL team are *generalists*. Each man in a SEAL team is capable of performing a variety of tasks, so SEAL teams can perform difficult and dangerous missions with a limited number of personnel.

Straight Shooting

Although the SEALs are one of the smallest communities in all of Navy Special Warfare Command—with only 1,500 to 2,000 active-duty personnel currently in service—they perform some of the most deadly and dangerous special ops missions imaginable.

Like Air Force Special Operations, the SEALs have consistently pushed the limits of technology. SEAL teams have been equipped with steadily improving innovations such as bubbleless, closed-circuit breathing equipment, underwater communications devices, and underwater weapons far beyond the spear guns and broomstick minisubs seen in a popular 1960s James Bond movie.

The Basic SEAL Mission Profiles

The mission of the Navy SEALs is to conduct unconventional warfare, counterinsurgency, and clandestine operations in maritime environments. There are five basic types of SEAL missions, and they are similar in profile to the missions performed by other SFGs:

♦ **Direct Action (DA):** "Direct Action" is really just a euphemism for *combat operations*. For the SEALs, direct action missions are usually of short duration and involve seizing, damaging, or destroying targets; rescuing hostages; or performing capture operations against facilities on the shore or afloat. This mission profile may include fierce but limited offensive combat operations against hostile forces operating near the shore or aboard ships.

♦ **Unconventional Warfare (UW):** Like the Green Berets, the Navy SEALs train, lead, and supply insurgent forces behind enemy lines. They have performed such missions in Vietnam, and they conduct them today in many friendly nations.

♦ **Special Reconnaissance (SR):** A SEAL's specialty is advance reconnaissance and covert surveillance operations, especially of hostile beachheads. SEAL teams perform beach surveys and establish advanced listening posts and observation posts. Like their forefathers in the UDSs, SEALs are trained to demolish shore obstacles and beach fortifications in advance of a planned amphibious landing.

◆ **Foreign Internal Defense (FID):** Training and advising the military, paramilitary, and law-enforcement personnel of a friendly nation are other responsibilities of the SEALs. They also provide civic action and economic development to such nations, but only in a noncombat environment.

◆ **Counterterrorism operations (CT):** SEALs conduct various types of operations against terrorist units and individuals. Some of these missions may be in direct response to a terrorist operation or may be geared toward prevention or deterrence.

To accomplish such a wide range of missions, the SEALs need to be agile, inventive, capable, and adaptable. SEALs are trained more rigorously than conventional military personnel, and like all special operations units, they are measured with a higher standard. The SEALs also require far more resources, man for man, to train, equip, and maintain than a conventional unit.

The SEALs in Action

On January 1, 1962, John F. Kennedy commissioned Teams One and Two of the newly christened Navy SEALs. Like the Green Berets, Teams One and Two were created to conduct special warfare and clandestine operations. Before long they conducted missions in support of U.S. Navy forces during the Cuban Missile Crisis and the Dominican Republic crisis.

Straight Shooting

The Rung Sat Special Zone (RSSZ) was a Viet Cong stronghold and one of the most difficult places in Vietnam to conduct military operations. SEALs deployed three- to seven-man hunter/killer teams that targeted VC boat traffic and land concentrations. SEALs sometimes waded through neck-deep mud to set up ambushes.

Impressive Results in Vietnam

In 1962, SEALs were also deployed to the widening conflict in Vietnam, where they operated out of Da Nang in an advisory role, primarily helping the Vietnamese navy. The SEALs trained Biet Hai naval commandos, who conducted unconventional warfare operations using armed and upgraded civilian junks, as well as the Lien Doi Nguoi Nhai (LDNN), the Vietnamese navy underwater demolitions teams.

But the real test of SEAL combat readiness did not come until 1965, when two platoons of SEAL Team One were deployed into the Rung Sat Special Zone—a region of dense mangrove swamp 7 miles south of Saigon, the capital of the Republic of Vietnam. There they established ambush sites and hunkered down to wait. After conducting a raid, as Viet Cong units returned by sampan to friendly territory in the Rung Sat Zone, SEALs ambushed them from shore. The VC were either killed or captured. Soon their operational routine was shattered and their grip over the local population was broken.

Before long, these SEAL teams went where no American or South Vietnamese had gone before—to the remote rivers, creeks, and channels where the Viet Cong had formerly operated in perfect safety. The SEALs established listening posts to collect information on VC movement, and they set up ambushes to stop North Vietnamese incursion into South Vietnamese-controlled area. These tactics were so successful that, by 1966, the Viet Cong could no longer operate safely in the Rung Sat Special Zone. Four additional platoons were soon sent to Vietnam—one to Nha Be, one to Binh Thuy, and another to My Tho, with a headquarters element established in the now-abandoned Subic Bay Navy base in the Philippines.

SEAL teams were coordinated and controlled by Detachment Alpha, which set up shop at Subic Bay. Detachment Bravo performed beach reconnaissance in the country; Detachment Charlie went aboard two submarines—the *U.S.S. Perch* and the *U.S.S. Tunney* (later the *U.S.S. Grayback* was also reconfigured to carry SEAL teams). Detachment Delta was deployed to Da Nang; Echo and Foxtrot went aboard the Amphibious Ready Group (ARG) standing watch along the Vietnamese coast.

However, it was Detachments Golf and Hotel that saw the most combat. They were responsible for river patrols, where the real action was found. SEALs conducted missions up to 20 miles inland, infiltrating hostile shores by swimming from submerged submarines or in small boats. Before the war in Vietnam ended, an entire squadron of UH-1 Iroquois helicopter gunships (a heavily armed version of the famed Huey) and OV-10 Broncos were allotted to the SEALs operating in the Mekong Delta.

SEALs were again deployed in 1966, first around Saigon and then in the heavily populated Mekong Delta. As with all SEAL teams in Vietnam, the platoons trained together, deployed together, and returned home together at the end of their six-month tours, which made for a unit cohesion far stronger than could be found among the conventional forces in Vietnam. These units performed independently and conducted their operations with little outside interference. Unlike the Green Berets, the SEALs avoided working with the South Vietnamese military as much as possible, preferring to gather

Straight Shooting

Vietnam-era SEALs had to complete the 25-week Basic Underwater Demolition/SEAL training (BUD/S) followed by 3 weeks of airborne training by the U.S. Army. Then they received training in small arms, hand-to-hand combat, land and water navigation, and other specialized skills. This grueling schedule mirrors the pace of SEAL training today.

their own intelligence and act without support from the Army, Air Force, or Army of the Republic of Vietnam (ARVN). But the SEAL missions often included members of the Vietnamese SEALs, who proved their worth and gained the Americans' trust.

SEAL teams played a key role in Operation Brightlight. From 1970 to 1972, they staged raids in enemy territory to free American POWs imprisoned in the Mekong Delta. Although many ARVN troops were rescued and caches of weapons were found and destroyed, not one American prisoner-of-war was ever located.

In the Mekong Delta, missions included up to 14 members but usually no more than 7. The SEALs mostly gathered intelligence in preparation for future military operations, remaining deep behind enemy lines for weeks at a time. They also mounted ambushes, conducted patrols, and occasionally participated in large joint military operations. In 1972, as America withdrew from the war, the last SEAL teams were withdrawn. They returned home with an enviable record of combat success. As with the Army Special Forces, the SEALs were quite effective within the limited confines of their mission profiles. Their covert operations set the tone for the conduct of U.S. Navy Special Warfare components of today.

> **Shop Talk**
>
> The SEALs in Vietnam produced impressive results with small numbers and low casualties. During the Vietnam War, 49 naval special warfare personnel were killed in action, and none was ever captured.

Failure in Grenada

After Vietnam, the SEALs were not immune to the general postwar decline experienced by the rest of the U.S. military, nor were they prepared for the missions to come. The failed hostage-rescue operation in Iran came as a wake-up call to the military establishment that things were not going in the right direction. That view was reinforced during Operation Urgent Fury, in which the U.S. special forces groups in general and the Navy SEALs in particular failed to perform up to the high standards expected of them.

When the Governor-General of Grenada, Sir Paul Scoon, was ousted by a Marxist revolution, the U.S. government feared that the tiny island nation would become another Cuba—an island fortress and a potential staging area for future Soviet military activity in the region. There was already mounting evidence that a Soviet buildup was imminent, so Operation Urgent Fury, the military invasion of Grenada, was hastily mounted in response to the crisis.

During Urgent Fury, one platoon of SEAL Team Six was assigned to perform reconnaissance on Point Salines, a narrow jut of land at the extreme southwest end of the island nation. There the Grenadans had built a new military airfield, and the SEALs were to determine the suitability of this base for future operations once it was in American hands. For this operation, 16 SEALs and their gear were to parachute into the ocean near the point, where PBLs (patrol boats, light) were waiting for them.

Things went wrong from the start. The SEALs were supposed to parachute into the ocean off Grenada's coast at dusk, but they arrived six hours late and jumped in near total darkness. In the blackness, linkup with the boats was nearly impossible. Despite the use of floatation devices, the SEALs were so overloaded that three members were dragged to the bottom by the weight of their packs and drowned. Others survived only by jettisoning their rucksacks and packs, which contained all their vital equipment. Instead of accomplishing their mission, the SEALs floated in the ocean all night, awaiting rescue by the U.S. Navy at dawn.

A second squad that parachuted during that same night lost one man to drowning but managed to locate and board its boat. The SEALs rowed ashore, made contact with an enemy patrol, and were forced to withdraw or risk compromising the entire invasion. They tried again the next night, only to have their boat malfunction. They waited, their vessel dead in the water, until the SEALs were picked up by a U.S. Navy destroyer at dawn.

One platoon from SEAL Team Four, meanwhile, had reached the shore and operated in direct support of the Marine Amphibious Unit preparing to assault the Pearls Airport, in the middle of the island. There they uncovered unsettling facts. The Grenadans were ready for the invasion and had heavily reinforced the airport with troops, light artillery, and armor. The SEALs also discovered that the beach the Marines intended to use was unsuitable for an amphibious assault—both bits of bad news, but at least the SEALs had determined these facts *before* the Marines attempted to hit the beach.

The SEALs from Team Six dispatched by helicopter to rescue Sir Paul Scoon couldn't locate the governor's house from the air, despite maps and photographs. After much confusion, they located the mansion and proceeded to the debarkation site—which proved to be unsuitable for a helicopter landing.

The SEALs, as well as Gov. Sir Paul Scoon and his family, ended up being pinned down in the governor's house by Cuban and Grenadan forces. Despite an attack by a AC-130 Specter gunship, the SEALs and the folks they "rescued" had to wait over 24 hours—completely surrounded by hostile forces—until a Marine Corps force arrived to relieve them.

Success in Panama

Fortunately, things went a little bit better for the SEALs who went into Panama for Operation Just Cause. If fact, things went smoother for all the special forces units involved in the Panama operation, mainly because USSOCOM had come a long way in the process of integrating the various branches of America's special operations force and because there had been an injection of badly needed funding and attention during Ronald Reagan's presidency.

The SEALs had two big missions during Operation Just Cause—both meant to prevent Panamanian strongman Manuel Noriega from fleeing the country. Task Unit Whiskey was ordered to seize the Panama Defense Force patrol boat *Presidente Porras*, while two platoons of SEALs were dispatched to capture Noriega's private jet, which was fueled and ready to spirit away the dictator from Punta Paitilla Airport. Things went like clockwork for the boat group, but the two platoons at the airport walked right into a genuine, 100-percent FUBAR.

<table>
<tr><td>

Shop Talk

Noriega may indeed have been planning to use the jet at Punta Paitilla Airport to flee Panama. The SEALs sent to destroy the aircraft ran into Panamanian Defense Force personnel, who were real pros. They caught the SEALs in the open and fired with deadly accuracy. Four Americans died in the firefight.

</td><td>

After multiple schedule and mission changes, and very little time to prepare or rehearse its action, Task Unit Whiskey launched from a staging area in Rodman Naval Station in Balboa Harbor, one of many U.S. Navy installations in the Panama Canal Zone. Using inflatable rafts, two SEAL platoons infiltrated the area around Pier 18, where Noriega's boat was moored. Supported by two PBRs (patrol boat, river), Unit Whiskey secured the area and disabled the boat.

At the airport it was a different story. When H-hour (the scheduled time for the attack) was pushed up 15 minutes, the SEALs at the airfield were forced to race a large detachment of Panamanian Defense Force soldiers

</td></tr>
</table>

to the hangar. The Americans lost, and a furious firefight ensued. Facing up to 50 Panamanians, the badly outnumbered SEALs still managed to destroy the aircraft. They also took many hits. Four SEALs were killed, eight were wounded, and after the engagement was over, it took over 90 minutes to medivac the wounded off the airfield.

Aggressive Reconnaissance During Desert Storm

The Persian Gulf has been a hot spot for the Navy SEALs for decades. During the war between Iran and Iraq that preceded Operation Desert Storm, SEAL teams were used to keep the shipping lanes open and safe for oil tankers moving fossil fuel out of the region.

Straight Shooting

U.S. Navy Commander Gary Stubblefield, a television network advisor during America's assault against the Taliban in Afghanistan following the World Center Attack on September 11, 2001, was the SEAL team leader in charge of the floating platform used for Operation Earnest Will and Prime Chance.

That sometimes meant protecting international shipping from mines, missiles, and even small attack boats. It was an impossible task without a permanent installation in the general area.

For Operation Earnest Will and Prime Chance, the SEALs established a kind of floating base packed with personnel from the Marine Corps, the Army, the Navy, and several Air Force forward controllers. The Army operated AH-6 "Little Bird" attack helicopters of the platform while the Marines defended the base itself. The Air Force directed air support that circled the floating "guardhouse" protecting the vital waterway.

While this base was in operation, the Iranians attempted to use several oil platforms to fire upon shipping, but the Marines quickly took them out. An operation by the SEALs against several Iranian-manned oil rigs was aborted when enthusiastic U.S. Navy gunfire meant to soften up the targets ended up obliterating them.

Shortly after Saddam Hussein invaded Kuwait, as American forces were building in the region, the SEALs performed aggressive advanced reconnaissance missions along the coast of occupied Kuwait. They were operating with elements of the SBS and used extremely fast, low-profile cigarette-shaped racing boats designated HSBs (high-speed boats). Not built for combat, HSBs were normally used by the Navy to train the crews of larger warships how to repel the enemy's small fast-attack boats. The SEALs converted these quick little boats for combat and used them very effectively.

The HSBs made dozens of night forays along the coast, testing Iraqi defenses and looking for a suitable landing place, in case an amphibious assault was required. SEALs swam ashore in chilly water and without Scuba or closed-circuit breathing gear to reconnoiter the beaches. When an amphibious assault was ruled out, the SEALs continued their work, to deceive the Iraqi leadership that a Marine landing force would eventually hit the Kuwaiti beaches.

The SEALs took the deception to such extremes that they actually mounted an elaborate mock invasion. On the night of February 23, 1991, SEALs used Special Boat Squadron HSBs to carry them and their Zodiac near the coast. In total darkness, the SEALs debarked with their rafts and rowed to within 500 yards of shore. Then they swam to the beach and strung a line of buoys identical to those used to mark amphibious landing zones. The SEALs also planted six satchel charges packed with 20 pounds of plastic explosives each. When they returned to the cigarette boats, the SEAL teams opened fire with machine guns and small arms, even as the satchel charges detonated along the waterline. The Iraqi defenders were so rattled that they began to fire back, certain that the D-Day landings had finally come!

> **Shop Talk**
>
> One night SEALs swam to the Kuwaiti shore, placed satchel charges along the beach, and then returned to their boats. At the appointed time, the SEALs opened fire. Adding to the cacophony were the satchel charges detonated by timers. The Iraqi shore defenses were stunned and disorganized by this aggressive diversionary action.

The "Brown Water Navy"

No discussion of the U.S. Navy special operations forces can be complete without mentioning the dedicated personnel of the SBS, also know as the "Brown Water Navy." The legendary SBS has worked closely with the SEALs for three decades and possesses a fleet of boats designed to take the battle close to the beach or up dangerous rivers—hence the designation Brown Water Navy.

Mission mobility for the personnel of Naval Special Warfare provides an interesting and diverse set of mission and vessel types for the men of the SBSs. The breakdown of these missions and vessels is as follows:

◆ **Coastal Patrol and Interdiction:** This type of mission requires the largest vessels in the SBS fleet. This is not a covert operation or clandestine insertion; coastal patrol boats must be large enough for a crew to operate for long periods of time in relative comfort yet possess the speed and firepower necessary to get the job done.

> **Shop Talk**
>
> The Special Boat Squadrons use a mix of surface vessels, including fast-attack boats, inflatable boats, and pump-jet propulsion craft capable of rapid movement in shallow water.

For operations of a short duration, flat-bottomed patrol boats are preferred. For longer missions, the 65-foot, 1960s-vintage Mk III Swift Patrol Boat—a fast, potent vessel with few amenities—is used. The vessel is seaworthy but can still be utilized for coastal and river patrols, and it can insert or extract a SEAL team. The Mark IV Sea Spectre, a newer, 68-foot patrol boat, is an improved version of the Mk III, with the same basic weapons and equipment, but it is more adaptable to various mission profiles.

◆ **Special Operations Support Missions:** This type of mission is conducted clandestinely and requires smaller, sleeker boats with low radar profiles, longer ranges, good fuel economy, and little in the way of amenities. Special operations support missions usually involve inserting teams into dangerous zones, and in today's joint service, that could just as easily be Green Beret ODA teams as SEALs.

For these types of missions, inflatable boats are often used. The Rigid Inflatable Boats (RIBs) are simple, cheap, and fast, and are used by the Army, Navy, and Coast Guard as well as the SBS. The Combat Rubber Raiding Craft (CRRC) is one of the most useful boats for this type of mission and is used by the Green Berets and the Rangers as well as the SBS. At only 15 feet long, the CRRC can move across the water at 20 knots, with a range of 65 miles on 80 gallons of fuel.

The most secretive vehicle in the SBS fleet is the submersible called the SDV Mk VIII, used for subsurface insertions. The SDV is like a little speedboat that operates underwater, with rechargeable batteries and an electronic propulsion motor. The SEALs ride inside, wearing their breathing gear for later insertion—although the SDV has its own air supply. They can be launched from a Dry Deck Shelter (DDS) attached to a submarine. A DDS is like a small hangar built on a submarine's deck, just large enough to hold the SDV and a chamber-connecting tunnel leading from the sub to the DDS for the swimmers to enter. The DDS is then flooded and the SDV is released.

◆ **Riverine Patrol and Interdiction:** This type of mission is a holdover from the Vietnam era. SEALs and SBS teams still conduct river warfare in the backwaters of the Amazon basin and elsewhere with a variety of river patrol craft. Today the SBSs operate with foreign military or law-enforcement personnel equipped and trained by special forces groups, often SEALs, working in the area of Foreign Internal Defense (FID).

Patrol boats, river (PBRs) have been used for this type of mission since Vietnam. They are designed for high-speed patrol and insertion operations in rivers and

Shop Talk
Riding an SDV submersible is a strange experience. The SEALs are packed tightly inside, the driver can't see ahead because of darkness or sediment in the water, and navigation depends primarily on instruments. The SDV provides more range and speed than swimming, but exposure to the cold and to ambient sea pressure puts tremendous physical strain on the divers.

bays. PBRs are heavily armed and armored, designed for combat at close quarters with special ceramic armor similar to the material used in tanks applied to the crew compartments. The 32-foot hull—with a beam of 12 feet—is made of reinforced fiberglass and is light enough to be transported on a C-5 Galaxy transport aircraft.

The Patrol Boat, Light (PBL) is a 25-foot military version of the Boston Whaler, an unsinkable little power boat with two engines and two heavy weapons—a .50-caliber machine gun and an Mk 19 grenade launcher. The PBL is light, fast, quiet, and air-portable.

The SBS also employs the Mini-Armored Troop Carrier (MATC), a small amphibious landing craft similar to the one that the Marine Corps has used to assault islands for decades, only much smaller. It has a flat, ramp bow that drops forward to disgorge 16 combat-ready SEALs onto the beach. The MATC has a water-jet propulsion system and a crew of three. The boat is fast and stealthy, with a low profile in the water to elude radar.

With loads of combat experience and the learning curve behind them, the SEALs and SBSs of today's Naval special forces are ready for rapid deployment and response, to defend American lives and interests in any maritime region in the world.

The Least You Need to Know

◆ The U.S. Navy's Sea, Air, Land Teams descended from the Underwater Demolition Teams of World War II and were created for special operations in a maritime setting.

◆ SEALs perform the duties of most special operations forces: direct action, special reconnaissance, foreign internal defense, counterterrorism, and unconventional warfare.

- After Vietnam, the SEALs participated in actions in Grenada, Panama, and Operation Desert Storm.
- SEALs serve with two other Navy special warfare units, the Special Boat Squadrons (SBSs) and the Swimmer Delivery Vessel Teams (SDVs).

The Navy SEALs Training Regimen

In This Chapter

- Requirements for Navy SEAL candidates
- The BUD/S training regimen
- Into the teams

Like the Army's Special Forces training, SEAL training is physically and mentally demanding—one of the toughest programs in the world. From the stiff qualifications through a grueling training regimen, the Navy screens potential candidates closely, weeding out those applicants who cannot make the cut. Only a chosen few will complete the training course to pin on the coveted gold eagle-and-trident symbol of the Navy SEALs.

What does it take to become a Navy SEAL? Only 26 of the hardest weeks of your life, weeks that will push you to the max both mentally and physically as you sweat, shiver, and suffer through a training regimen that resembles a diabolical new form of the classic Chinese water torture. Even those candidates who arrive at the training facility in Coronado, California, certain of what they'll face and ready to test themselves to the limit, are not prepared for the rigors, demands, and sheer intensity of the Basic Underwater

Demolition/SEAL (BUD/S) program—one of the most difficult, humbling, challenging, dangerous, enlightening, and brutal learning experiences in the world. In this chapter, I'll give you a taste of what it takes to make the cut and become a qualified SEAL.

Requirements for a Navy SEAL Candidate

As with most special forces training programs, only a select few candidates actually complete the program and graduate. Those who fail are often complemented for trying, and some are allowed to return for a second attempt. Like the Army's Q course, the first phase of the BUD/S program is an intense and uncompromising selection process that is calculatingly brutal and that deliberately ratchets up the stress and endurance levels so high that only the strongest survive.

The BUD/S course is nearly foolproof in its ability to weed out those candidates who don't quite make the grade.

SEALs are so tough that even their training program is risky. Injuries are common, some of them serious. During the most intense phase of the training, deaths occasionally occur.

FUBARs

Tragically, young men have died by drowning and from hypothermia while trying to become Navy SEALs. Although the U.S. Navy takes every precaution possible to ensure the safety of SEAL candidates, learning to become a SEAL is nearly as hazardous as *being* one. SEAL candidates spend an awful lot of time in the water. The Pacific Ocean can be very cold, even in the summer months. Yet SEAL training goes on all year round. SEAL trainees are expected to endure discomfort, and hypothermia is just one of the hardships they face. Even with a wetsuit—a luxury that is not always permitted—the cold of the ocean seeps into the flesh and bone of long-submerged candidates, sometimes lowering their body temperature to dangerous levels. Violent, uncontrolled shivering is a fact of life, and sometimes candidates come out of the cold water to dry in a colder wind. This is a form of torture intentionally inflicted by the instructors—again, it is not mere cruelty, but an endurance test meant to weed out the unfit.

Although the physical standards to qualify as a BUD/S candidate are quite high, it's mental toughness that will get him through the course successfully. And, yes, I said *him*. Like the other branches of America's elite special operations forces, the SEALs is a boys' club. Oddly, although many SEALs are superb athletes, small, skinny guys with the right mental attitude often make it through the course while stronger, more physically imposing candidates fail. A SEAL will explain that if you have the intestinal fortitude to endure the fatigue, the humiliation, the discomfort, and the fear experienced during the screening process, you can probably develop the physical strength required for active duty with the SEALs.

Volunteers for SEAL training come highly recommended. They must possess certain skills, have the enthusiastic endorsement of their commanders, and have plenty of time left in their enlistment. The latter is because it costs a lot of money to train a SEAL, and the Navy doesn't want to squander it on a candidate who will complete the BUD/S course only to quit the Navy for a more lucrative job in the private sector.

According to the written regulations, to qualify for SEAL training, a candidate can be no older than 28 years. However, this age requirement is actually one of the few things about SEAL training that is flexible. Several candidates in their early 30s have graduated, and two candidates successfully completed SEAL training at the ripe old age of 36. Many other qualifications are set in stone, however.

Potential SEAL candidates must have eyesight of at least 20/40 in one eye and 20/70 in the other—correctable to 20/20, of course—and no color blindness. Candidates must score high on the written tests and must pass a physical fitness exam that includes a swim test, during which candidates are expected to move through 500 yards of water—doing a breast or side stroke—in less than 12 minutes and 30 seconds, followed by a 10-minute rest. Then the candidate must do at least 42 push-ups in 2 minutes (followed by a 2-minute rest), 50 sit-ups in 2 minutes (with a 2-minute rest), 8 pull-ups with no time limit—but as fast as possible (followed by a 10-minute rest), and run a mile and a half in combat boots and battle dress uniform (BDUs) in 11 minutes and 30 seconds. All these physical tests must be completed in less than 60 minutes. Though there are short rest periods of up to 10 minutes between these physical trials, SEAL candidates will tell you that the rest periods seem to end far quicker than the actual physical tests.

During this test phase and BUD/S training, officers and enlisted personnel go through the same experiences together and both suffer equally. SEAL training is a team-building effort, and trust and respect must be developed up and down the chain of command. Usually between 35 to 40 officers and 225 to 250 enlisted personnel graduate BUD/S training each year to join the ranks of the SEALs or accept leadership positions with the SEAL Delivery Vehicle Teams (SDVs).

Shop Talk
SEALs are trained at the Naval Special Warfare Center in Coronado, California. This institution is the U.S. Navy's equivalent to the Army's John F. Kennedy Special Warfare School and Center at Fort Bragg, North Carolina. The Special Boat Service units there are affectionately known as the "Coronado Yacht Club."

BUD/S Training

Even after seven weeks of indoctrination programs, physical preconditioning, long hours spent in classes or running through the sucking sand of the beach, swims in the Pacific in hot and cold weather, push-ups, sit-ups, calisthenics, and assorted physical and mental tests, the candidate is still not ready to even *begin* BUD/S training!

SEALs Training: Phase One

The SEALs are trained at the Naval Special Warfare Center in Coronado, California, the Navy's equivalent to the Army's John F. Kennedy Special Warfare Center and School. The first phase of BUD/S training lasts nine weeks and involves the basic physical and mental conditioning of the candidate. There is running, swimming, and jaunts through a tough, complex O (for "obstacle") course that is designed to test physical strength, speed, agility, and mental toughness. During this phase, the minimum written and physical test requirements are raised each week, and all candidates are required to improve their written and physical test scores on a weekly basis—or face elimination.

Straight Shooting

Even quitting SEAL training can be humiliating. When a candidate has had enough, he stands on painted frog footprints and rings a brass ship's bell three times—and it's over. After he's gone, his helmet liner remains beside the bell, right next to the liners of those who have quit before him.

The O course looks like a big sandbox with lots of wooden poles assembled into a wide variety of simple structures. Trainees are assembled at the O course once or twice a week, for an hour or two at a pop. On command, each student runs the circuit of the course, starting with pole stumps set into the ground, their tops raised unevenly, about 2 or 3 feet above the deck. A candidate must run across the poles, jumping from one to the next without falling off.

From the last stump, a candidate leaps to the top of a low wooden wall, swings one foot over the top, and drops to the other side—only to start running again. Next up is a grid of barbed wire that the candidate crawls under. When he emerges, the candidate climbs a 50-foot tower on a loosely dangling rope net (which provides unstable footing), goes over the top, and then climbs down the other side.

"The Dirty Name" is next. Here candidates climb a pair of simple towers set in the ground 4 feet apart. The trainee goes up the first structure and jumps to the second, catching the crossbar across the chest. Many candidates break their first bone—a rib, usually—while attempting this hurdle. Although it's tough, this is not the end. There are other hurdles to conquer, including a 10-foot sand berm and a dip in the cold, cold ocean. After that, candidates are permitted by the instructors to dry off. This is accomplished by rolling in the sand.

Though torturous, the O course is not designed to inflict pain on the candidates. Instead, it is there to bolster their confidence. Those who master the O course feel that they have beaten the hardest physical and mental challenge they have ever faced. In time, those self-assured candidates will discover, to their shock and dismay, that things can get much, much harder. And at some point during Hell Week, they may even recall the wonderful days they spent on that beloved O course!

Hell Week Interlude

Hell Week begins with the sound of gunfire. Just before midnight on the fifth Sunday of their training, after five weeks of near constant activity that has exhausted the strongest of them, the candidates are awakened by the staccato pounding of an M-60 machine gun. As they leap from their bunks in shock and confusion, the night erupts around them, with the bright flashes of simulated artillery exploding all over the compound. The noise is disorienting, and the incessant shouts of the instructors are barely heard above the cacophony of simulated combat popping off outside.

What follows this rude awakening are five and a half days of almost constant activity. Sleep will become impossible, with the average candidate managing about 30 minutes of sleep in a 24-hour cycle. Candidates will *run* from one task or challenge to another, often after long bouts of physical training. They will eat on the run, but at least the food and water are plentiful. Their pace is so demanding that candidates will consume about 7,000 calories a day—and they will *still* lose weight. There will be boat drills, swims, obstacle courses, mud runs, rolls in the sand, and so on.

Straight Shooting

Sleep deprivation is dangerous. Without sleep, men risk mental and physical collapse. Officers, who make difficult command decisions on a daily basis, should take time to rest—even in a combat situation. T.E. Lawrence (Lawrence of Arabia) believed that an officer requires four hours of uninterrupted sleep to retain mental acuity.

Added to the training mix is an infamous event called Log PT, in which boat teams lift a 500- or 600-pound log, hold it over their heads for an extended period of time, toss it, or even do sit-ups with the log lying across their chests. The idea is to get the boat teams to work together as a team. After a few visits to Log PT, teams realize that if they work together, they can accomplish almost anything.

At dawn of the first day of Hell Week, training continues. The candidates do their usual load of work. But as the day wears on and night falls, the work continues unabated. The next morning, boat races begin. These races continue over the next seven days, in the bay and out in the ocean. The pace continues, and the candidates never see their bunks. Sleep deprivation begins to take its toll, and some begin to drop out. The purpose is to test mental toughness as well as physical stamina. As sleep deprivation sets in, candidates begin to hallucinate.

Shop Talk

During Hell Week, candidates are ordered to write a letter explaining why they want to become SEALs. After five days with no sleep and constant activity, the results are usually gibberish. The essays are returned to the graduates as a reminder of BUD/S training.

Soon other maladies begin to dog the candidates. Hypothermia and extreme overexertion are both a constant threat. An ambulance trails the candidates on long runs through sand and rolls in the mud of San Diego Bay, and a rescue team is nearby during the 3- and 5-mile swims around San Clemente Island. These precautions are necessary; despite them, deaths during this phase of training have occurred.

There is mental torture added to the physical trials. Slow runners are dubbed the "goon squad." Teams who fail to perform up to standards during Log PT are given the heaviest log—and the added stress of "special attention" from instructors and their peers. The injuries that candidates suffer, the intensity of activity, and the stress levels are all extreme for a reason: to mimic as closely as possible the physical and mental challenges of the battlefield. Once Hell Week is over, the candidates will notice that they have gained a measure of respect from the staff and instructors. The hard part is over.

After the candidates recover a bit, they begin to learn the basics of beach reconnaissance. Candidates wallow in the cold water as they survey the beach, measure the tides, and check the consistency of the sand or soil and other variables. Although this duty can be wet and miserable, it is the easiest part of BUD/S training they've experienced so far.

Straight Shooting

According to Commander Gary Stubblefield, BUD/S training is "the toughest military training in the world, and it's done that way on purpose …. Most of the people who make it through the program are not premier athletes—they are *normal* people who have the ability to stick with something."

SEAL Training: Phase Two

After hydrographic reconnaissance classes are completed, phase two of BUD/S training begins. In the following weeks, SEAL candidates will learn everything there is to know about diving operations. They will dive with scuba gear and closed-circuit breathing systems, become familiar with a wide range of operational gear, and study dive physiology until they are experts. Of course, along with that expertise comes the realization of just what can happen to a human body when it's subjected to the stresses and pressures of deep-sea diving.

Shop Talk

The military model of the Draeger BG-4 long-duration closed-circuit breathing apparatus is particularly suitable for long-term missions in a toxic environment. The unit is easy to clean and maintain, and it can quickly be prepared for reuse.

Today Navy SEALs no longer rely on the old-fashioned self-contained underwater breathing apparatus (SCUBA) their grandfathers went to war wearing. The new Draeger self-contained breathing apparatus (SCBA) rebreathing system has replaced the old-style mask and air tanks with a closed-circuit microelectronic unit that is lightweight and ergonomic and can provide up to four hours of constant underwater use for the wearer.

A closed-circuit SCBA operates on the principle of rebreathing the air sealed inside the breathing circuit of the SCBA. By rebreathing the scrubbed and filtered air, dive duration can be significantly extended. And because the system is closed, nothing is released—there are no telltale bubbles to give away a Navy SEALs' position. The exhaled air, containing carbon dioxide, flows through a soda lime scrubber that converts it into water. A further chemical process continually adds oxygen to the breathing air to replenish the oxygen that has been consumed by the wearer.

Along with the use of SCUBA and SCBA gear, candidates learn what they should do if some of their high-tech equipment fails. They learn about decompression and how to deal with the hazards of nitrogen narcosis. They discover the dangers of ambient sea pressure, lack of visibility, loss of regulators, and a hundred other real-life hazards of performing special warfare operations in an underwater environment. Candidates are taught how to navigate through the cold, dark, murky undersea environment in which SEAL operations usually take place. This part of BUD/S training is seven tough, physically and intellectually demanding weeks that will further cull the herd of potential SEALs.

It is now approximately four months into BUD/S training, and those who have stuck it out will be quite proficient in the basics of combat dive operations. In any country on Earth, they are qualified civilian divers capable of salvage operations the world over. Now that they can move about under water with ease, navigate through the most hostile waters, and use a wide range of high-tech underwater equipment, it is time for the candidates to learn how to be SEALs.

SEAL Training: Phase Three

Phase three of BUD/S training is the Demolitions/Recon/Land Warfare program. It is here that the candidates put their newly acquired confidence, strength, stamina, knowledge, and skills to the test in a series of exercises designed to simulate SEAL missions. During Demolitions/Recon/Land Warfare, candidates learn how to fight on land as well as master maritime combat. They learn navigation, map reading, explosives, small-unit tactics, rap-pelling and fast rappelling, and the strategy and tactics of reconnaissance patrolling. After four weeks of basic classroom instruction, the candidates deploy to San Clemente Island for five more weeks of intensive exercises.

On San Clemente, trainees are dispatched to eliminate a series of beach obstacles designed to block access to landing craft. They make hydrographic surveys of the area, mapping the location and type of obstacle they encounter. Then the candidates plan a mission to demolish the

> **Shop Talk**
>
> Beach obstacles have not changed much since World War II, when the Japanese placed concrete blocks and sank steel rails to rip out the bottom of Marine Corps landing craft. SEAL training on San Clemente Island involves learning how to clear such deadly obstacles.

obstacles with explosives. Trainees carefully calculate the quantity of explosives and the length of the fuse. They debark for their mission on rubber rafts and then dive to place the explosive charges. They link the explosives with detonation cords for a simultaneous blast, and then the divers are recovered. The explosions follow. The closer the candidates have gotten to their predicted blast time, the better—of course, the obstacles had better be gone, too.

These exercises more or less complete the six-month BUD/S training program. But bear in mind that six months is the *ideal* time it takes to graduate. Many candidates require a longer period of time to complete the training, due to the many injuries caused by the rigorous and brutal process of elimination. The Navy defends such tough standards, insisting that if the risk in training goes away, the mental stress and physical peril is also removed. Without those threats, many candidates would still wonder how they will respond under actual combat conditions, even if they complete the course. But after the high-intensity BUD/S training, they need wonder no more. More than a few SEALs have insisted that their combat missions were a piece of cake compared to the training it took for them to get there, which means that the instructors and staff of the BUD/S training program have done their jobs—and done them well!

Airborne-Qualified

Because the bulk of America's special operation forces are required to be airborne-qualified, SEALs candidates move on to Fort Benning, Georgia, for the three-week Basic Airborne Course. The first week involves general conditioning, with extra PTs to make the course less boring. Two weeks of learning basic military parachuting skills follow that. SEAL candidates learn the basic Parachute Landing Fall (PLF), how to pack and don their para-chutes, door positions, jumpmaster commands, exit techniques, emergency procedures, and so on. Some of the training is conducted in a 30-foot tower; some takes place in a mock-up of a C-130 interior.

Straight Shooting

Because the physical standards of the regular Army are lower than those required by the SEALs, Navy candidates find the first phase of the Basic Airborne Course to be easy. If they have a fear of heights, however, that phobia must be confronted to become airborne-qualified. Parachute jumps in daylight without combat equipment are called "Hollywood jumps" because they're simple, quick, and unreal, and they fill the sky with parachutes—which provides quite a show for the folks on the ground.

Week 3 is Jump Week, and five actual parachute insertions are required to pass. Three of them are daylight jumps without combat equipment. This is followed by a much tougher nighttime jump and a jump with loaded rucksack, rifle, and weapons container. The final jump comes on a Friday morning, and friends and relatives are permitted to watch the exercise from bleachers. They also can view the graduation ceremony, during which the instructors pin the silver wings of a qualified military parachutist on the shirts of their students.

Probation

After completing BUD/S training and the Basic Airborne Course, the candidates are still not fully qualified SEALs. Each candidate is assigned to a team, where he must complete a rigorous six-month probationary period. It is still possible to fail, and each candidate is closely monitored by instructors and his fellow team members. At the end of this probationary period, SEAL training is finally complete, and the graduates can pin on the gold emblem of Navy Special Warfare—the coveted "Budweiser." After a full year of conditioning, training, and probation, a Navy SEAL is finally born. Now fully qualified, the SEALs move into the teams—and into action.

 FUBARs

> Becoming a Navy SEAL does not put a candidate on a fast track to promotion—in fact, it's just the opposite. The SEALs share a "bad boy" reputation with the Green Berets. While not *entirely* warranted, the reputation certainly contains a grain of truth. So becoming a SEAL does not automatically lead to higher rank and probably *limits* a candidate's military career. Why does anyone do it? Mostly because Navy SEALs measure themselves against the highest standards of military performance.

Of course, the training continues. New techniques are always being introduced to the SEAL teams, and personnel can go on to many months of study at the Defense Language Institute (DLI) in Monterey, California, where they acquire the skill to speak Arabic, Estonian, Farsi, Mandarin, Korean, or one of the dozens of other languages required to operate successfully—and sometimes covertly—in a foreign country and culture. Even after a man is accepted into the ranks of the Navy SEALs, the training—like the action—never lets up.

The coveted "Budweiser."

The Least You Need Know

◆ SEAL training begins with a rigorous qualification process. The training is physically and mentally challenging, and the BUD/S course is one of the toughest military training regimens in the world.

◆ SEALs learn to use a vast array of underwater breathing apparatus and high-tech vehicles, as well as simple rubber boats.

◆ After a full year of training, SEALs enter the teams, where they will continue to hone their skills and train even as they perform difficult military operations.

Chapter 16

Into the Sea, Air, Land Teams

In This Chapter

- The active SEAL teams, Group One and Group Two
- Action in SEAL teams
- Breakdown of a typical SEAL mission

Once a SEAL completes his training, he will join a SEAL platoon from Group One or Group Two. Each SEAL platoon has 16 members—2 officers and 14 enlisted men, which can be broken down to two 8-man squads (or boat crews). This squad can further break down into two 4-man fire teams. The smallest SEAL unit is a 2-man team, known as swim buddies. A SEAL platoon receives support from the Special Boat Squadrons (SBSs) and the SEAL Delivery Vehicle Teams (SDVTs).

In the past, special units within the SEALs have performed top-secret missions—units such as Red Cell and SEAL Team Six. Some of the actions of those specialized SEAL units have been quite controversial. In this chapter, you will learn the breakdown of a typical SEAL platoon, experience what it is like to join a SEAL team on a combat mission, and uncover the operational history of Red Cell, and the highly secretive group called SEAL Team Six.

Group One and Group Two

Once a man becomes a Navy SEAL, he moves on to an active-duty SEAL team, where he will use all that he learned in BUD/S training to perform variations and combinations of the five basic SEAL mission responsibilities: direct action, unconventional warfare, special reconnaissance, foreign international defense, and counterterrorist operations. (For more details on these basic missions, see Chapter 14, "Introducing the Navy SEALs.")

A typical SEAL platoon consists of 16 SEALs, 2 officers, and 14 enlisted men—1 platoon, 2 boat crews, and 7 pairs of swim buddies. Usually the new SEAL will be posted into one of the three SEAL teams in either Group One or Group Two. (Occasionally, if his special skills or talents are needed elsewhere, he will join a SEAL team in forward deployment in a foreign country or aboard a U.S. Navy warship). Groups One and Two each include 3 SEAL active teams, 1 SBS, and 1 SDVT—all total, about 225 to 250 officers and men.

Group One operates out of Coronado, California, the location of the Naval Special Warfare Center, where the SEALs are trained. This group deploys its forces in the Pacific and Persian Gulf regions and is responsible for activities at the Special Warfare Center. The three SEAL teams assigned to Group One are Team One, Three, and Five.

Group Two operates from Little Creek, Virginia, and is responsible for operations in the Atlantic, Europe, and Latin America. Little Creek is also the home of the Special Warfare Development Group—a SEAL think tank where new tactics, weapons, communications systems, and dive equipment are tested. SEAL Teams Two, Four, and Eight are assigned to this headquarters.

SEAL Teams in a Nutshell

Ideally, a full SEAL team includes 10 platoons of SEALs, plus a small support staff from the regular Navy—radiomen, clerics, ordinance specialists, and regular Navy divers, in all about 20 non-SEAL personnel. There is a command element including the commanding officer, the executive officer, and the operations officer. They are all fully SEAL-qualified. Of course, situations in the military are seldom ideal. Training schedules, leave, and forward deployment cut the number of people actually available to participate in platoon action.

Each SEAL platoon (confusingly, this unit is also sometimes referred to as a "team") will have 16 SEALs assigned to it—2 officers and 14 enlisted men is the ideal. These are further grouped into squads of eight, each with an officer and seven enlisted men. The squads themselves are split into five teams of four men—the five teams each have two "swim pairs." The following list presents the breakdown of a SEAL team.

Breakdown of a SEAL Team

- ◆ Team = 10 platoons
- ◆ Platoon = 16 SEALs, 2 officers, 14 enlisted men
- ◆ Squad = 8 SEALs, 1 officer, 7 enlisted men
- ◆ Fire Team = 4 men, 2 swim pairs (buddies)

The eight-man squad has traditionally been the unit size of choice in the Navy SEALs, and they operate best with this small, tight, efficient unit.

SEALs are deployed all over the world, usually close to an explosive region or situation, to provide a combat-ready force for quick response. They are also deployed to train in environments not available in the continental United States. Among recent deployments— "dets," in SEAL jargon—Naval Special Warfare Unit Eight and Special Boat Squadron Twenty-six have been sent from their forward base in Panama to Latin America, to train antidrug troops in several countries. There are also large Naval Special Warfare detachments based in Alaska and Hawaii.

Because there are relatively few SEALs, the Navy has established five Naval Special Warfare detachments at forward positions, reasonably close to the many hot spots around the world. In an emergency, the local NSWUs are manned by extra SEAL staff from other bases and additional SBS teams; Swimmer Delivery Vehicles may even be flown in from the United States.

Two Special Warfare Units serve the European Command from bases in Spain and Scotland. The Pacific Command is served by Naval Special Warfare Unit One based in Guam. Naval Special Warfare Unit Eight serves the Southern Command out of Panama, while the detachments in Alaska and Hawaii are primarily training units.

> **Shop Talk**
>
> Naval Special Warfare Unit Eight, Special Boat Squadron Twenty-six, and SEAL Team Four make up the Mobile Training Teams (MTTs) sent to Bolivia, Argentina, Brazil, and Colombia, where drugs are manufactured. MTTs teach large numbers of local personnel effective drug-interdiction techniques.

Red Cell

One of the most controversial SEAL operations in recent years was dubbed Red Cell. Red Cell was a semicovert unit lead by former U.S. Navy Commander Richard Marcinko. Red Cell evolved out of the Naval Security Coordination Team. One of Naval Security's responsibilities is to assist U.S. Navy commands all over the world to improve their base, harbor, and ship security procedures to guard against terrorism, sabotage, and theft.

Red Cell's difficult and dangerous task was to behave like terrorists and attempt to break into secure U.S. military facilities, to highlight weaknesses in a local base or ship security procedures. Red Cell was bankrolled—to the tune of $4 million annually—through "black" (secret or disguised) funding and operated with a high degree of independence.

Straight Shooting

Naples in the 1980s was a dangerous place for U.S. military personnel, yet some U.S. Navy officers acted as if they were oblivious to that fact. To hammer home this point, Red Cell operatives would follow an officer who ignored security procedures and "ambush" him at a traffic light, usually by placing a sign on his vehicle that read, "You are one dead Navy asshole, sir."

In some cases, Red Cell exposed unforgivable lapses of security, usually capturing the moment on video for review by superior officers at the security hearing that almost always followed Red Cell activity. Of course, local Navy officers did not always welcome criticism from Red Cell operatives, and the program received a lot of bad buzz within the Navy. Today the SEALs operate several covert programs, including the shadowy, secretive Development Group that is responsible for SEAL Team Six. The activities of this Development Group, and other SEAL covert operations not named here, are all highly classified.

After his retirement, Commander Marcinko published his memoirs. Although *Rogue Warrior* became an international best-seller, some of Marcinko's bombshell revelations embarrassed the U.S. Navy in general and the SEALs in particular.

SEAL Team Six

The Naval Special Warfare Development Group is based at Dam Neck, Virginia, not far from Little Falls. Formerly known as SEAL Team Six, this unit is responsible for counterterrorist operations in the maritime environment. The origin of SEAL Team Six can be traced to the fallout from the 1980 failed hostage-rescue attempt in Iran called Operation Eagle Claw.

Little is known of the organization or deployment of this ultra-secretive unit. Created and formerly commanded by Commander Marcinko, who gave the unit its designation because it contained 6 units—90 men strong—that had previously received counterterrorism training—SEAL Team Six sprang from a two-platoon group known as Mobility Six. When that unit was demobilized, members joined SEAL Team Six for extended and enhanced counterterrorism action. Within six months of its formation, SEAL Team Six was declared operational and mission-ready.

Training for SEAL Team Six was conducted throughout the United States and overseas, at both military and civilian facilities. Experienced international teams—including Britain's SBSs and Germany's GSG-9—gave advice and instruction. The regimen was extensive and very much in the mode of the "train as you fight, and fight as you train" philosophy popular with most counterterrorism units. Subsequently, Team Six participated in a number of covert and overt operations during the 1980s. The unit soon gained a poor reputation for some of its antics, including womanizing.

SEAL Team Six was transformed into a component of the Naval Special Warfare Development Group in the late 1980s, after the founder of Team Six was convicted on various charges connected with unlawful acts perpetrated during operations—in essence, the Navy accused Commander Marcinko of going "rogue." Despite his legal troubles, Marcinko is still revered by members of the SEALs today and has become something of an unofficial spokesman for this elite Special Warfare unit.

According to the U.S. government, the Navy Special Warfare Development Group was established to oversee development of Naval Special Warfare tactics, equipment, and techniques, but this is only partially true. The unit is a component of the Joint Special Operations Command (JSOC) based at Pope Air Force Base in North Carolina, alongside other groups such as U.S. Army's Delta Force and the 160th Special Operations Aviation Regiment (SOAR). It is believed that the Development Group maintains its own helicopter support unit but trains with the 160th SOAR in support of ship assaults.

It is thought that the Development Group currently numbers approximately 200 personnel, broken down into 4 units that mirror regular SEAL structure. These units are Red, Blue, Gold, and a special boat unit, designated Gray. The types of missions that this unit conducts or has conducted in the past are, of course, highly classified.

> **Shop Talk**
>
> Under the leadership of Commander Marcinko, the unofficial motto of SEAL Team Six was "We get more ass than a toilet seat."

> **Shop Talk**
>
> Because of its compact size, the MH-6 "Little Bird" is particularly effective for use in ship assaults. The Little Bird is operated exclusively by the 160th SOAR, which may be why the Navy's Development Group operates alongside SOAR, a U.S. Army command.

A Typical SEAL Mission

The SEALs are ready to deploy to hot spots all over the world, to perform any of their basic mission profiles. But before they can go anywhere or do anything, somebody higher in the chain of command has to authorize, approve, and plan the deployment, campaign, or mission. The first step in any action is the issuance of a Warning Order, which could come from a superior officer, the U.S. Special Operations Command, or even the Commander-in-Chief.

Once a Warning Order is issued, the personnel involved are assembled and given a notion of what they will soon be asked to do and how they should prepare for that mission. The information is almost always incomplete but will include a brief description of the mission, the types of weapons and vehicles required, the establishment of a chain of command, and a schedule, including ample time for specific intelligence instruction and rehearsals. The idea behind the Warning Order is to give a unit a fixed amount of time to prepare—perhaps 12 hours or less. The platoon or squad leaders are expected to take a third of that time to create their own preliminary plan to carry out the operation and to allocate the other two thirds of the time to the subordinates to do prep work, study the intelligence, and carry out rehearsals.

SEAL deployments are almost always covert, so no one can notify family members of dispatch to some far-off location for an unspecified period of time. Eventually, when husbands and fathers don't come home from work, the families get the idea that something is up. They then tune in to the news with renewed interest, hoping to get an idea of where their loved ones have been sent. Eventually, someone from the Navy will officially notify them about the deployment, although details are never provided.

Each platoon has its own set of standard operating procedures, identity, reputation, subculture, strengths, and weaknesses—all based on the individual character, talents, and skills of the team members. This makes the planning and execution of a mission faster and more efficient than conventional military platoons because the duties, objectives, action on contact, and other individual responsibilities are an ingrained part of a company structure that does not need to be repeated or rehearsed.

Following a detailed orders brief, which can last minutes or hours, SEAL teams pore over intelligence material, communications intercepts, satellite imagery, or reports from agents in the field prior to the launch of an operation. Then they do a run-through of the operation— a kind of rehearsal that may entail a long briefing in the guts of a submarine on their way to the deployment area, or a complete acting out of the mission parameters in a full-size mock-up of the target area.

Infiltration

At this point, the SEAL platoon or platoons will begin infiltration into the area of action. This may mean a helicopter insertion, with SEALs fast-roping down a line to the ground, or it can mean jumping by parachute onto land or into the water, on or near the target. SEALs don't care for air insertions, but they will do them if they have to. Such insertions include high-altitude, high-opening (HAHO) and high-altitude, low-opening (HALO) insertions.

The HAHO technique allows a jumper to glide for many miles under a steerable canopy before he reaches the target. This is usually accomplished at night, when the SEAL is virtually free from the fear of detection. He is all but invisible to human eyes and will cause the same signature as a flight of birds on radar.

The HALO technique is much simpler. A jumper free falls for a long period of time before deploying his parachute very close to the ground. Both types of jump can begin so high that the jumpers require apparatus to breathe.

Straight Shooting

Parachute landings in water are dangerous—especially at night—and SEALs hate them. To enhance survivability, Navy SEALs prefer parachute canopies such as the MC-1, which can be steered and have some forward motion, so that they can have some control of the descent.

Most of the time, however, the Navy SEALs board a Zodiac boat or cram themselves, their equipment, and their weapons into a submersible minisub, which secretly moves through hostile waters to insert the teams near the target zone. They are, after all, *maritime* warriors.

Once everyone is in a Zodiac boat, they row or motor close to the shore but outside the surf zone. Then a pair of divers slips over the gunwales and into the water. These "scout swimmers" move to shore, to secure the landing area and signal the "all clear" once the beach is reconnoitered. When the Zodiac boat comes ashore, the SEALs debark and the boat is hidden or buried. The men assemble, count heads, and form a patrol as the SEALs move forward, toward the target.

On the Ground in Enemy Territory

Leading the patrol to its target is the point man, who is familiar with—or who has been briefed on—the lay of the land. A skilled land navigator, the point man's vigilance can mean the survival or annihilation of the entire team. He can avoid an ambush or walk right into one—survival depends on his skills, quick wits, and sharp eyes.

The preferred weapon of a point man in wooded terrain is not an M-16A2, a Car-15, or an Uzi—it's the military version of a standard 12-gauge shotgun packed with five rounds of "double-ought" buckshot, large, bullet-size pellets that spread out into a lethal cone of destruction, with a kill radius of about 100 meters. SEALs also utilize flechette rounds—shells packed with tiny steel darts in place of the buckshot. A third, heavier single-shot slug, accurate up to 5 or 6 feet, is useful for blasting open locked doors, disabling vehicles, or destroying electronic equipment.

The leader in a SEALs operation is one of the two commissioned officers in a platoon—a part of the team, yet, by necessity, aloof from it. His responsibilities are twofold: He must complete the mission and preserve his force. Sometimes these two duties are at odds. During a particularly hazardous action, he may well have to choose between the completion of the mission and the safety of his command. Officers in the Navy SEALS are trained at Annapolis or at the Officer Candidate School, but they still are required to earn the respect of the men under their command. Just because they salute you doesn't mean that you have earned their respect—SEAL commanders must display real competence and leadership skills, as well as perform as well or better than those under them, to earn the respect of fellow SEALs. During a march, the patrol leader takes a position near the front of the line, usually directly behind the point man—where he can appraise the situation and provide direction for the man on point and the squad behind him.

If trouble doesn't come on point, it will probably come from the rear of the patrol. That is why a sharp, vigilant SEAL is posted as "tail gunner," usually armed with a cut-down version of the standard U.S. military-issue M-60 machine gun. The tail gunner also carries a variety of other munitions and explosives to warn away the bad guys—tear-gas grenades, white-phosphorous grenades, a Claymore mine or two to rig as booby traps, and whatever else works best for the individual.

Mission Accomplished

Of the five basic types of SEAL combat operations, the most common involve reconnaissance (both deep and shallow), strike missions, raids, or ambushes.

Recon is a vital component of all combat operations. Despite the billions of dollars spent on high-tech intelligence-gathering systems mounted on satellites and high-altitude surveillance aircraft, there is still no satisfactory substitute for human intelligence (humint). Human intelligence involves real personnel entering the area at ground level, to scope out the scene and report what they see, hear, and sense. Deep reconnaissance (or strategic reconnaissance) penetrates to the heart of the target zone and often involves covert travel over land or insertions near the target. Shallow reconnaissance may be conducted on the fringes of the zone of operation and may be as simple as updating maps of the region in question. Both types of reconnaissance are important and remain the starting point of all successful special operations.

Strike missions are carefully planned and precision attacks mounted against a particular target. These missions are often carried out under difficult circumstances. Strike missions are usually undertaken when the United States government is concerned enough about "collateral damage" (hitting civilians or damaging or destroying nonmilitary targets) not to drop bombs from aircraft. A strike mission may involve direct action (engagement with the enemy), but covert action is preferred. If an engagement occurs, it is usually of limited duration and intensity. During a strike mission, SEALs neutralize security around the target, do what they have to do, and move out of the area quickly, before reinforcements arrive. Sometimes that involves demolition work, and the SEALs, like the other members of America's fighting elite, love to blow things up!

Raids are another matter. Though similar to the quick-in, quick-out action of a strike mission, raids are also designed to inflict pain on the enemy. Although the destruction of a specific target or the rescue of hostages may be the main goal of the action, during a raid the SEALs will not hesitate to engage the enemy and they will move with such precision that their foes might never know what hit them. Of course, during a hostage rescue, the shooting must be done with precision, or those who are the object of the rescue may become collateral damage themselves.

During the Vietnam War, the SEALs conducted thousands of ambushes. They are quite effective—if everything works as it is planned to work. The SEALs find a place where the enemy travels through on a predictable timetable. Then they establish a "kill zone," hunker down out of sight, and wait for the bad guys to show up. Discipline and timing are the keys to success. The SEALs must remain quiet, patiently waiting for the enemy to come to them. Claymore mines, grenades, and machine guns are all effectively employed during an ambush.

Exfiltration

When the SEAL mission is accomplished, the team reassembles and makes a quick trip to the extraction zone, where they will be lifted out of hostile territory by helicopter or picked up by boat or submarine. Under certain circumstances, SEALs may be extracted using the Stabilized Tactical Airborne Body Operations (STABO) harness. A helicopter hovers close to the ground and deploys a special harness. The SEALs all don harnesses similar to a parachute rigging and attach them to the line dropped by the helicopter. When everyone is belted onto the line, the helicopter lifts up and away—with the SEALs dangling from the rope below the aircraft.

Back at base, the SEAL teams get debriefed, file their after-action reports, return their weapons and equipment to the proper storage lockers, and stand down until the next Warning Order is issued. While waiting for a new mission, the SEALs learn new skills even as they hone the ones they already possess. They know that when the Warning Order comes, the cycle will begin again.

The Least You Need to Know

- SEAL platoons consist of 16 members, but the SEALs work best in tight 8-man squads.

- The Navy has organized the SEALs into two groups: Group One operates out of Coronado, California, and is responsible for deploying forces in the Pacific and Middle East.

- Group Two operates from Little Creek, Virginia, and is responsible for operations in the Atlantic, Europe, and Latin America.

- Red Cell and SEAL Team Six were top-secret units operating within the SEAL command structure.

Part 5

The U.S. Air Force Special Operations

The Army has the Rangers and the Green Berets, and the Navy has the SEALs. Rounding out those forces are the men of the U.S. Air Force Special Operations Command (AFSOC). The youngest member of the Special Forces community, the AFSOC has a surprisingly long and dramatic history, which began during World War II and continued through the Cold War, Korea, Vietnam, Desert Shield/Desert Storm, and beyond.

In this part I will provide an operational history of Air Force Special Operations, a peek at their high-tech arsenal, and an overview of the rigorous selection and training process used to create a modern "Air Commando."

Hey, who's the new guy?

Chapter 17

Introducing the U.S. Air Force Special Operations

In This Chapter

- ◆ The formation of the Air Force Special Ops
- ◆ The AFSOC basic mission profile
- ◆ The precursors of the AFSOC
- ◆ The decline and rebirth of the AFSOC after Vietnam
- ◆ A peek at the nine units of AFSOC
- ◆ Flying fixed-wing and rotary-wing aircraft of AFSOC

When you think of the U.S. Air Force, your mind probably fills with images of super-fast, high-tech jet fighters or sleek and stealthy black bombers racing across the silver-blue skies, unreachably high over the battlefield far, far below. But that is only because very few people know about one of America's most elite, most formidable, most technologically advanced special warfare groups— the U.S. Air Force Special Operations Command (AFSOC).

In this chapter, I examine the history of Air Force Special Operations from its humble beginning in World War II through Operation Desert Storm. I also explore the technological innovations which have changed the face of modern war.

The Birth of the Air Force Special Ops

On May 22, 1990, Gen. Larry D. Welch, U.S. Air Force chief of staff, redesignated the 23rd Air Force as Air Force Special Operations Command (AFSOC), responsible for the combat readiness of Air Force Special Operations Forces headquartered at Hurlburt Field, Florida. Forever afterward, this group would be the Air Force component of the U.S. Special Operations Command.

The new command consisted of three wings, the 1st, 39th, and 353rd Special Operations Wings, as well as the 1720th Special Tactics Group, the U.S. Air Force Special Operations School, and the Special Missions Operational Test and Evaluation Center. There are also Air Reserve components, including the 919th Special Operations Group (SOG) of the Air Force Reserve, based at Duke Field, Florida, and the 193rd SOG Air National Guard at Harrisburg Airport, Pennsylvania. With the issuing of the orders by General Welch, the Air Force Special Operations Command was born.

AFSOC's task is to support a range of activities from combat operations of limited duration and goals to long-term conflicts. It provides support to foreign governments and their military, while retaining a flexible mission profile that allows the Air Force Special Operations teams to respond to numerous threats and support a wide range of missions. AFSOC is committed to making continual improvements, providing Air Force Special Operations Forces for deployment worldwide and assignment to regional commands, and to conducting unconventional warfare, direct action special reconnaissance, personnel recovery, counterterrorism, foreign internal defense, psychological operations, and collateral special operations activities unique to the Air Force, such as Combat Search and Rescue (CSAR).

> **Shop Talk**
>
> Hurlburt Field, located on the western end of Eglin Air Force Base, Florida, is the home of the brand-new U.S. Air Force Special Operations Command headquarters. Hurlburt Field has been the traditional headquarters of the Air Force's unconventional warfare capabilities since 1961.

The AFSOC Basic Mission Profiles

AFSOC shares similar mission profiles with the other branches of America's special warfare elite.

◆ **Unconventional Warfare (UW):** During wartime, AFSOC may be tasked with directly supporting any resistance or guerilla force from the air or on the ground. This may be accomplished by infiltration operational units such as the Rangers, U.S. Army ODA teams, or SEAL teams into the combat area for the purposes of training, equipping, and advising or directing indigenous forces. AFSOC will also undertake a number of direct-offensive, low-visibility, covert operations on or above hostile territory.

◆ **Direct Action (DA):** This type of mission involves killing people and destroying things, usually during small-scale offensive actions of short duration. Such actions include seizure or destruction of target sites and the capture or elimination of enemy personnel. Such actions are usually carried out by the Special Tactic Squadron (STS) units. These units are highly trained and may employ raids, ambushes, or other small-unit tactics in the accomplishment of their mission goals. AFSOC may use mines, bombs, and other demolitions, or may conduct fire-support attacks from air, ground, or even sea assets. During such assaults, STS teams may lurk on the ground, to "paint the target"—using lasers pointed at the target to provide thermal guidance for precision-guided "smart bombs." One of the most common forms of direct action taken by AFSOC units is airfield seizure in hostile territory.

◆ **Counterterrorism (CT):** Offensive actions taken to prevent, deter, or respond to terrorism make up this mission. For the AFSOC, this includes intelligence gathering and threat analysis. In support of CT operations, fixed-wing and rotary aircraft are ideal for such missions. Pave Low helicopters are designed to deliver SOF troops through any terrain in any kind of weather, day or night. AC-130 Spectre gunships provide a formidable array of highly accurate and mobile firepower. And because AFSOC aircraft are air-refuelable, they can remain in the air over the operational area for long periods of time, to provide instant response when needed.

◆ **Foreign Internal Defense (FID):** This is the traditional mission of all branches of America's Special Operations Forces. AFSOC is equipped to provide expertise to other governments in support of their internal defense.

◆ **Psychological Operations (PSYOPS):** AFSOC is capable of conducting PSYOPS in conjunction with other special operations missions or support of SOF forces on the ground. Using specially configured aircraft, PSYOPS objectives can be achieved by providing intelligence, distributing leaflets, or doing media broadcasts.

◆ **Collateral Special Operations (CSO):** These include security activities, counter-drug operations, personnel recovery, and coalition support.

◆ **Combat Search and Rescue (CSAR):** A standard search-and-rescue operation, while intense, is nothing compared to a combat search-and-rescue mission. During civilian operations, the injured may be stabilized on the scene before being evacuated. But during CSAR operations, seconds matter. Casualties have to be located, stabilized, and evacuated in a hurry—and most likely under enemy fire. When seconds count, the STS teams spring into action. Almost all CSAR operations include "shooters"—Army Rangers, Army Special Forces, Navy SEALs, or Delta members on board the aircraft to provide security during the on-site rescue.

The Precursors of the AFSOC

The origins of the modern Air Force Special Operations Command can be traced to World War II. In August 1943, during a meeting between U.S. Army Gen. Henry H. "Hap" Arnold and British Adm. Lord Louis Mountbatten, assistance to British commando units operating in the China-Burma-India theater was discussed. General Arnold suggested the creation of a new, highly mobile fighting unit, complete with its own transportation and logistics. Lord Mountbatten agreed with the concept, and in time—and after many name changes—the 1st Air Commando Group (1 ACG) was formed in March 1944. Personnel in this operational unit were given the title "commandos" in honor of Lord Mountbatten, himself a former commander of the British commandos.

The 1st Air Commando Group

The actual task of forming this unit fell on two veteran fighter pilots, Lieut. Col. Philip G. Cochran and Lieut. Col. John Alison. Their task was to create a self-sufficient, highly motivated combat unit to support the activities of British Brig. Gen. Orde C. Wingate and his *Chindits* on long-range infiltration missions into Burma to battle the Japanese. Gen. "Hap" Arnold further ordered his pilots to get the job done, no matter what unorthodox means it took. "To hell with the paperwork," the general admonished them. "Go out and fight!" Alison and Cochran began recruiting immediately. To protect the covert nature of their operations, prospective candidates were given a minimum amount of information but were told that the missions would involve combat. As a nod to the unit's secrecy, the men adopted an unofficial patch—a black question mark on a white circle.

The unit began operations with a few C-47 Dakota transports and several CG-4A Waco gliders, but soon its inventory grew and expanded to include the quick-and-nimble P-51 Mustang and the invincible P-47 Thunderbolt fighters, along with B-25 Mitchell bombers, UC-64 Norsemen utility aircraft, and the L-1 Vigilant and L-5 Sentinel Liaison planes. The 1st Air Commando Group even used the YR-4 helicopter near the close of the war—the first-ever deployment of a helicopter into a combat environment. The Air Commandos also are credited with the first combat aircrew rescue by helicopter in military history, utilizing that same primitive YA-4 rotary aircraft. America's first Air Force special operations unit flew over hazardous mountains and vast jungles in Burma, China, and India to find and resupply the British ground forces in hostile territory. This was not always an easy task. The terrain was hostile to air insertion,

Special Ops Jargon

Chindits were a special warfare force raised in India by British Gen. Orde Wingate. Chindits specialized in making air assaults deep inside Japanese territory in Burma and then fighting their way back toward British lines, destroying everything in their path, while being resupplied by the 1st Air Commando Group.

and the British troops were highly mobile and never operated out of a permanent staging area. The 1st Air Commandos also evacuated Wingate's forces and provided limited air cover and striking capacity, if needed.

The 2nd and 3rd Air Commando Groups

The Air Commandos also performed a variety of conventional and unconventional combat and support missions behind Japanese lines, where they destroyed multiple ground targets and gathered vital intelligence. Because of the 1st Group's runaway success, two other Air Force special operations groups—the 2nd and 3rd ACGs—were eventually formed.

A tragic accident gave the 1st Air Commando Group its official motto. On February 15, 1944, during a hazardous, nighttime training mission, an accident involving a C-47 Dakota twin-engine transport plane and two Waco gliders claimed the lives of four of Wingate's commandos and three American airmen. The terrible incident could easily have shaken the British commandos' faith in the American Air Corps unit, but General Wingate's front-line commander sent a heartfelt letter to the Air Commandos telling them, "Please be assured that we will go with your boys, *any place, any time, anywhere.*"

Beyond the activities of the 1st, 2nd, and 3rd Air Commando Groups in the Pacific, Air Force units performed many missions in the European theater that mirror the unconventional and special warfare operations performed by AFSOC today. Combat Talon, for instance, had its forerunner in the highly modified, black-painted, four-engine B-24 "Liberator" bombers used by the 801st Bombardment Group, Army Air Corps. The crews of these aircraft, who were informally known as the "Carpetbaggers," were highly proficient in flying low-level, long-range, nighttime missions—often over hostile terrain and in poor weather. These gallant B-24 air crews gathered intelligence; delivered covert, three-man OSS Jedburgh Teams behind enemy lines; and dropped psychological warfare or informational leaflets on the civilian populations in hostile and occupied territory.

 Straight Shooting

During the Halyard mission, Air Corps special operations air crews dropped OSS agents into Yugoslavia, where they arranged for the return of downed Allied aircrews. Between June and August 1944, 400 American and 80 Allied personnel were recovered and evacuated by C-47 transports from covert airfields, with the help of Yugoslavian partisans.

The Air Resupply and Communications Service

After World War II, at the dawn of the nuclear age, the Army Air Corps evolved into the U.S. Air Force, to reflect the importance of long-range bombers in the delivery of atom and hydrogen bombs on faraway targets. Unfortunately, the Air Force high command could not visualize a future need for the Air Commando Groups, and all three of them were officially deactivated. They survived only in the imaginations of boys all over America, through the adventures of Milton Caniff's popular comic strip, "Terry and the Pirates."

Shop Talk

The B-29 Superfortress was used in World War II for long-range bombing missions over Japan. A B-29 christened the *Enola Gay* dropped the first atomic bomb on Hiroshima. During the Korean War, the Superfortress was used for long-range, covert parachute-insertion missions.

Special Ops Jargon

A secret team called Detachment 2 inserted **Rabbits** behind enemy lines with B-29s. These agents carried SCR-300 radios and provided crucial intelligence about North Korean and Chinese troop deployment. There was no way to extract these operatives—to get home, they had to cross enemy lines and reach friendly forces.

But during the Korean War, the Air Force again formed a unit to perform covert operations, this time for the newly organized Central Intelligence Agency (CIA). Under the direction of the Military Air Transport Service (MATS), the Air Resupply and Communications Service (ARCS) was created in February 1951. ARCS was primarily responsible for Air Force covert operations during the Korean conflict—or, in the jargon of the era, "special air missions."

The ARCS had a large inventory of aircraft in service, ranging from the huge B-29 Superfortress to the C-118 and C-119 cargo airplanes, to the tiny H-19 helicopter. The B-29 was especially useful as a long-range transportation platform for covert operation teams and intelligence agents. These vintage World War II bombers were reconfigured to allow the low-level insertion of a special operations team or human intelligence agent, dubbed *Rabbits*, by removing the bottom-rear gun turret and replacing it with a hatch. When the hatch was opened, it functioned as a windbreak, protecting the special forces teams who parachuted out of the airplane. The B-29 pilots would fly 500 feet above the ground, or even lower, to avoid enemy radar. To thwart visual detection, these hazardous missions were carried out in black-painted aircraft in the dark of night. The brave crews of these B-29s flew through the mountains of Korea at very low levels, without the benefit of modern forward-looking infrared systems (FLIRs) and terrain-following radar.

Detachment 2

Another secret Air Force unit operating during the Korean War was Detachment 2. This unit was the first to use the reliable C-47 Dakota transport plane as a bomber. The men of Detachment 2 rigged the interior of the fuselage with special racks and latch points under the plane, where two 75-gallon napalm canisters were mounted. Flying low and at night, the modified C-47s burned enemy supply convoys moving from North Korea into the South. These C-47s were also used for psychological assaults. A pair of C-47s with loudspeakers attached to the wings or chin blasted messages in Korean to the communist forces or dropped propaganda leaflets, followed by a strafing run by a pair of P-51 Mustangs—just to hammer the message home.

Despite the long record of success during World War II and Korea, the Air Force quickly moved to downsize its special operations teams as the conflict on the Korean Peninsula wound down. The Air Force was busy with its new mission—operating land-based bombers and intercontinental ballistic missiles of the Strategic Air Command (SAC). Yet the Air Force continued its role of supporting anticommunist uprisings by dropping weapons and supplies to the Tibetan guerillas battling the communist Chinese invasion of their homeland.

Using the brand-new Lockheed C-130 Hercules, Detachment 2 flew into Tibet from Thailand, across miles of uncharted mountain ranges at night through snow, fog, and generally inhospitable weather. Over the target area the unit dropped supplies, weapons, and ammunition to Tibetan guerillas and their U.S. advisors on the ground. Hundreds of these dangerous missions were carried out with no loss of personnel or aircraft. Little did the pilot of Detachment 2 know that another war against communism was brewing in the jungles of southeast Asia.

The 4400th Combat Crew Training Squadron

In the rush to create new U.S. special operations units during the Kennedy administration, Gen. Curtis E. LeMay, Air Force chief of staff, created the 4400th Combat Crew Training Squadron (CCTS) in 1961. Code-named "Jungle Jim," the 4400th CCTS was based at Eglin Air Force Base, Florida, at Auxiliary Field Number 9, now known as Hurlburt Field, the location of today's Air Force Special Operations Command headquarters. The unit started out with 350 officers and men and 32 aircraft—most of them vintage propeller-driven models left over from World War II. In November 1961, the 4400th CCTS was deployed to South Vietnam as part of Operation Farm Gate. It became the first U.S. Air Force unit to conduct actual combat operations in the Vietnam War. No longer did the Air Force fly missions for the CIA—the CIA created its own air resupply force, called Air America. Instead, the primary mission of the 4400th was to provide close air support for Army Special Forces units training anticommunist insurgents in the Central Highlands.

The Special Air Warfare Center

The war in southeast Asia—and the Air Force's mission there—quickly expanded. In response, General LeMay created the Special Air Warfare Center (SAWC) at Eglin in April 1962. The SAWC consisted of the 1st Air Commando Group, the 1st Air Combat Applications Group, and a combat support group. In 1963, the 1st Air Commando Group became a wing, as volunteers flocked in droves to the new unit. Operational strength jumped to over 3,000 personnel, with 6 squadrons. The Air Commandos added the A-1E Skyraider—the legendary *"Flying Dump Truck"*—to its arsenal. Soon the Skyraider became a common sight in the skies over Vietnam.

Special Ops Jargon

Although Air Force personnel referred to the A-1E Skyraider as **"Flying Dump Trucks,"** ground forces preferred to call them "Sandys" or "Spads." Whenever things got hot, ground troops knew that they could rely on the Sandys for air support, and downed pilots relied on them during search-and-rescue operations.

"Puff, the Magic Dragon"

It was during the Vietnam War that the evolution of the Air Force gunship began. The Air Commando Squadron based at Bien Hoa converted the first C-47 Dakota transport into the formidable AC-47 gunship, nicknamed "Puff, the Magic Dragon" because of its formidable fire-breathing capabilities—especially at night, when the gunship's weapons would literally light up the sky. Equipped with three GE SUU-11A/A Gatling miniguns capable of firing 6,000 rounds per minute, the plane had a crew of six, including a pilot, a co-pilot, a navigator, and three gunners to operate the many weapons. All of the Gatling guns poked out of the starboard side of the aircraft, so the pilot would bank the plane into a pylon turn and run a circle around the target on the ground, lacing every inch of an area the size of a football field with 7.62-mm rounds in just 3 seconds—a truly phenomenal rate of fire!

Straight Shooting

The call sign for the AC-47 "Puff, the Magic Dragon" gunship was "Spooky." That emblem is still used today by AC-130 Spectre gunship crews of today's Air Force Special Operations Command.

By 1965, the 4th Air Commando Squadron had 20 AC-47 gunships operating over Vietnam. They were especially useful in protecting remote Green Beret outposts from Viet Cong ground assaults. So was the AC-119G gunship, a converted C-119 "Flying Boxcar" that was delivered to the 71st Special Operations Squadron in 1969. The AC-119, called "Shadow," carried four 7.62-mm miniguns. During one memorable engagement, the AC-119Gs flew almost 150 sorties in support of remote Army Special Forces camps at Dak Pek and Dak Seang. The AC-119K variant was designated "Stinger."

Project Gunboat's Big Idea: The Spectre

As the AC-47s and AC-119s began to age, a new-generation gunship appeared in the sky. Using the C-130 Hercules transport aircraft as the basic platform, Project Gunboat designed an aircraft heavily laden with weapons and electronic devices and countermeasures. The result would come to be known as the AC-130A "Spectre" gunship. The first-generation Spectre carried four 7.62-mm miniguns, and later models were upgraded to wield four 20-mm M-61 Vulcan Chain Cannons. The Spectre also featured a FLIR system used to pick up heat signatures on the ground and a night observation device (NOD) and an image intensifier that magnified moon and star light to allow the NOD operator a clear view of the ground. A fire-control computer linked the gunsight, sensors, and guns into a coordinated weapons system, and lamps mounted on the fuselage were capable of giving off visible, infrared, or ultraviolet light to paint the battlefield.

With a crew of 13 or 14 men, the new Spectres were assigned to seek and destroy enemy supply convoys and trucks making their way down the Ho Chi Minh Trail. Among the Spectre crew were five navigators, one of whom served as an electronic warfare specialist to operate the Spectre's electronic defensive countermeasures, including flares. Another navigator was on the flight deck with the pilot, co-pilot, and flight engineer. The other three navigators made up the Sensor Team, which occupied "the booth," a small compartment inside the cargo compartment of the Hercules. Inside the booth, the navigators observed the world outside the aircraft through television screens and sensor monitors. With them in the booth were the fire control officer and three crew members who operated the many sensors, light amplifiers, and offensive weapons systems.

The AC-130 Spectre gunships were so successful at hitting Viet Cong supply convoys that they accounted for 44 percent of all the enemy vehicles destroyed in the 31 days of March 1969. In response, the Viet Cong increased air defenses along the Ho Chi Minh Trail by 400 percent, which didn't even slow gunship activity in the region. U.S. Air Force data confirms that the top three truck killers along the Ho Chi Minh Trail were the AC-130, the AC-119, and the F-4 Phantom fighter/bomber. During the 1969–1970 season, 20,000 North Vietnamese trucks were damaged or destroyed. As the war continued, more Air Force special operations personnel were deployed in-country, although they never accounted for more than 5 percent of the Air Force's total commitment to the region.

> **Shop Talk**
>
> Of the 12 Congressional Medals of Honor earned by Air Force personnel in the Vietnam War, 5 of them went to members of the U.S. Air Force Special Operations.

Air Rescue and Recovery Services

Air Force Special Operations Forces used helicopters in the Vietnam War. Especially useful were the rescue teams, who flew low over dangerous territory to rescue downed pilots. In January 1966, these Air Force rescue teams were formally organized under the Air Rescue and Recovery Services. Using a modified version of the Marine Corps' Sikorsky S-65 Sea Stallion, the ARRS became the premier combat rescue unit of the Vietnam War.

One of the most famous U.S. Air Force–supported special operations of the war was the 1970 Son Tay raid on Viet Cong prisoner-of-war camps (see Chapter 8, "Endgame in Vietnam"). Air Force Special Operations assets played a critical role in the attempted rescue of U.S. prisoners, and both Air Force and Army Special Operations Forces personnel carried out their assignments like precision machines, despite the fact that the mission was a tactical failure and no prisoners were liberated.

The Decline and Rebirth of Air Force Special Operations

As the conflict in southeast Asia began to wind down, the Air Force Special Operations Forces declined until, in June 1974, all of the Air Force special operations personnel were placed in a single unit—the 834th Tactical Composite Wing. By July 1975, the 834th was renamed the 1st Special Operations Wing, and by 1979 the 1st was the only U.S. Air Force Special Operations Force in existence.

The failed attempt to rescue the hostages held by Iranian "students" at the U.S. Embassy in Tehran in 1979 was a watershed event in the history of the American Special Operations Forces. After that very public failure, Jimmy Carter was summarily booted out of office and the government reassessed its special-operations capabilities and was found lacking. The hammer fell particularly hard on the Air Force because it was the aviation that bore the brunt of the responsibility for Operation Eagle Claw's disastrous failure. Because pilots were not trained for night operations, several helicopters became lost while heading for the staging area, delaying departure time, and jeopardizing the success of the mission. When the entire operation was cancelled and the forces were ordered home, a helicopter collided with a C-130 transport plane on the ground at the secret staging area in the Iranian desert, resulting in eight American fatalities. A review commission convened to examine the problem, and within a few years the entire special operations community was transformed.

On March 1, 1983, all U.S. Air Force Special Operations were consolidated into the 1st Special Operations Wing at Hurlburt Field. Active components consisted of the 8th Special Operations Squadron, operating MC-130 Combat Talons and HC-130 Hercules Tankers; the 16th Special Operations Squadron, operating AC-130 Spectre gunships; and the 20th Special Operations Squadron, using the MH-53 Pave Low and HH-53 Jolly Green Giant helicopters, along with Air Force Reserve and National Guard elements.

Operation Urgent Fury

The first test of this new organization came seven months later, during the October 1983 invasion of Grenada called Operation Urgent Fury. The 1st Special Operations Wing had two missions: MC-130 Combat Talons were tasked with delivering U.S. Army Rangers to Point Salines Airport, while Spectre gunships provided air-to-ground fire support. To capture the airfield, Air Force Combat Air Controllers made low-level parachute jumps from 500 feet, laden with nearly 100 pounds of critical equipment. Upon landing, they had to neutralize resistance, secure the area, establish a command-and-control radio net, and carry out air traffic operations for the follow-up forces at the airport and other places in Grenada. Meanwhile, Combat Control Teams (CCTs) performed as forward air control (FAC) for Air Force Spectre gunships, Navy fighters, and Army helicopter gunships.

FUBARs

During Operation Urgent Fury, Air Force special operations forces did not sustain a single casualty. The same cannot be said of the Navy SEALs, who lost four team members at sea during a "rubber duck" insertion.

Operation Just Cause

Next came Operation Just Cause, the invasion of Panama to oust dictator Manuel Noriega. During this campaign, Air Force special operations units were deployed heavily. Because of their surgical strike capabilities, Spectre gunships were used for close urban combat environments, avoiding friendly fire casualties or collateral damage. These Spectres were launched from the 16th Special Operations Squadron—christened the "Specters." (The 4th Special Operations Squadron are called the "Ghostriders" after the popular Marvel comic book character. Both units fly the AC-130 gunship.)

In May 1990, the U.S. Air Force Special Operations Command (AFSOC) was established. This was the final step in building a formidable new special operations force within the Air Force community. When Operation Desert Shield/Desert Storm began three months later, the Air Force was ready to respond.

Desert Storm/Desert Shield

It was the Pave Lows operated by the U.S. Air Force 20th Special Operations Squadron that fired the opening shots of the Persian Gulf War while executing a complex battle plan called Eager Anvil. The "Green Hornets" of the 20th—flying Pave Lows packed with FLIR, terrain-avoiding radar, geopositioning systems, and other sophisticated electronics—guided an assault force of Army AH-64 Apache attack helicopters to their target, the Iraqi radar installations that guarded the border.

The helicopters sped through the night, flying no higher than 50 feet above the ground (the nape of the Earth), on instruments alone. Relying on the Pave Low's computers and sensors, the pilots zigzagged through *wadis* (dry desert stream beds), around wandering nomad camps, and across the featureless terrain to hover over their target. Once over the Iraqi radar sites, the Apaches moved forward and took out the enemy radar with AGM-114 Hellfire laser-guided missiles. With these critical radar sites eliminated, a radar-free corridor was established and Coalition fighters and bombers began to stream through to hit targets deep inside enemy territory. This action by an Air Force special operations unit was the start of the air campaign—and the war.

Shop Talk

General Schwarzkopf's distrust of America's special operations forces did not extend to the Air Force. After being assured that special operations helicopters would destroy the Iraqi radar arrays in advance of the air war, General Schwarzkopf said to the colonel flying the mission, "Then you get to start the war."

In addition to this dramatic mission, the Air Force Special Operation Command's Combat Control Teams were responsible for all air traffic control in the Persian Gulf theater. Air Force units also performed direct-action missions, combat search and rescue, infiltration and extraction (the Air Force prefers the term *exfiltration*), air base ground defense, air interdiction, special reconnaissance, close air support, helicopter air refueling, and psychological warfare operations.

After the Gulf War, the Air Force Special Operations Command provided humanitarian assistance in northern Iraq to Kurdish refugees who fled to the mountains after the failed revolt against Saddam Hussein's Basra Party–controlled government in Baghdad. In July 1992, AFSOC units participated in NATO operations in Bosnia, and in December of that year they went to Africa for Operation Restore Hope in Somalia. More recently, Air Force special ops personnel have seen action in Afghanistan. Today the Air Force Special Operations Command stands ready to defend America's interests whenever and wherever they are threatened.

The AFSOC Units

The AFSOC has approximately 13,000 active, reserve, and National Guard personnel, with over 2,500 members permanently based overseas. The command operates more than a hundred fixed- and rotary-wing aircraft. Its mission is to provide mobility, surgical firepower, covert tanker support, and Special Tactics Teams to the U.S. Special Operation Command (USSOCOM). In times of crisis, units of AFSOC work in concert with U.S. Army and U.S. Navy special operations forces, including the Special Forces, Rangers, SEAL Teams, psychological operations (PSYOPS) personnel, Special Operations Aviation Regiments, and Civil Affairs units. Eight units compose the AFSOC today. Six are active-duty units, and two are reserve units.

The AFSOC Active-Duty Units

♦ **The 16th Special Operations Wing** is based at AFSOC headquarters, Hurlburt Field, Florida. The 16th is the oldest and most combat-experienced unit in all of AFSOC. This wing includes the 6th Special Operations Squadrons, responsible for the foreign internal defense unit; the 4th SOS, which operates the AC-130 U Spectre gunships; the 8th Special Operations Squadron, which flies the MC-130E Combat Talon; the 15th Special Operations Squadron, which flies the MC-130 H Combat Talon II; the 16th Special Operations Squadron, which flies the MC-130H Spectre gunship; the 20th Special Operations Squadron, which flies the MH-53J Pave Low III helicopter; and the 9th Special Operations Squadron, which is located at nearby Eglin and flies the HC-130N/P Combat Shadow.

♦ **The 352nd Special Operations Group** is located overseas, at the Royal Air Force base at Mildenhall, United Kingdom. The 352nd SOG is the designated U.S. Air Force component for Special Operations Command, Europe, and includes the 7th Special Operations Squadron, which flies the MC-130H Combat Talon II; the 21st Special Operations Squadron, which flies the MH-53J Pave Low; and the 67th Special Operations Squadron, which flies the HC-130N/P Combat Shadow. Included in this unit are the assault forces of the 321st Special Tactics Squadron.

♦ **The 353rd Special Operations Group** is based at Kadena Air Base, Japan. This unit is the Air Force component for Special Operations Command, Pacific. Included in the 353rd are the 1st Special Operations Squadron, which flies the MC-130E Combat Talon; the 17th Special Operations Squadron, with the MC-130N/P Combat Shadow; and the 31st Special Operations Squadron, based at Osan Air Base, South Korea. The 31st operates the MH-53J Pave Low III helicopter.

♦ **The 720th Special Tactics Group** is based at Hurlburt. This group also has units scattered all over the United States, Europe, and the Pacific Rim; it operates the special operations Combat Control Teams and pararescue forces. Its mission includes air traffic control for establishing air assault landing zones, close air support for strike aircraft, and Spectre gunship missions. The unit also establishes casualty collection stations in combat areas and provides trauma care for casualties. Its squadrons include the 21st Special Tactical Squadron at Popl Air Force Base, North Carolina; the 22nd Special Tactical Squadron at Hurlburt; the 24th Special Tactical Squadron at Fort Bragg, North Carolina; and the 10th Combat Weather Squadron based at Hurlburt.

♦ **The U.S. Air Force Special Operations School** is located at Hurlburt. The school provides special operations education to Department of Defense personnel, government agencies, and allied nations. More than 7,000 students attend the Air Force Special Operations School each year. Like the Naval Special Warfare Training School and the John F. Kennedy Special Warfare Center and School, the U.S. Air Force Special Operations School provides instruction on special operations, regional affairs, cross-cultural communications, civil action, antiterrorism awareness, unconventional warfare, psychological warfare, and so on. Many sensitive and classified materials flow through this institution. Out of the 18 courses of study available, 7 are rated "secret" and 6 are rated higher, at "top secret."

◆ **The 18th Flight Test Squadron** is headquartered at Hurlburt Field and provides expertise to improve the capabilities of special operations forces worldwide. The center conducts operational and maintenance-suitability tests and evaluations of new equipment, concepts, strategies, and tactics. Many of its operations are joint command and joint service projects.

AFSOC's two Air Reserve components include units from the Air National Guard and the Air Force Reserve.

The AFSOC Reserve Units

◆ **The 193rd Special Operations Group** is an Air National Guard unit based at Harrisburg International Airport in Pennsylvania. This unit is responsible for AFSOC's airborne radio and television broadcasts. Using the reconfigured EC-130E Commando Solo aircraft, this unit is deployed for PYSOPS missions in wartime and humanitarian assistance in times of peace.

◆ **The 919th Special Operations Wing** is an Air Force Reserve unit based at Duke Field, Florida. The 919th operates the MC-130E Combat Talon I. This reserve unit trains for rapid deployment of special operations forces day or night, at low levels into hostile areas of operation. As part of the 919th, the 5th Special Operations Squadron is also a reserve unit. It flies the HC-130N/P Combat Shadow tanker. This unit wings its way into hostile skies to provide air refueling for special operations aircraft and air resupply of ground units.

The AFSOC Aircraft

More than any other special forces group, the Air Force relies on cutting-edge technology to accomplish its tasks. Today, that technology primarily consists of specialized and unique fixed-wing and rotary-wing aircraft, along with the advanced electronics, computers, navigation systems, and avionics packed inside its flight decks. AFSOC includes in its inventory many of the most advanced aircraft available to the U.S. military. Surprisingly, many of these high-tech, advanced airplanes have evolved from low-tech platforms. The Air Force Special Operations Command springs from a long tradition of trail blazers who have reconfigured existing, low-tech cargo and transport aircraft in unique new ways, creating formidable warplanes capable of conducting covert operations, day or night, in the most hostile settings.

The aircraft come in two varieties—fixed-wing (like the AC-130 Spectre) and rotary-wing (helicopters like the MH-53 Pave Low).

The Spectre Gunship

The AC-130U Spectre gunship is the flagship of the Air Force Special Operations fixed-wing fleet. At a cost of $72 million per unit, this latest version of the Vietnam-era Spectre was designed and built exclusively for special operations. Evolved from the basic four-engine C-130 Hercules cargo and transport plane, the AC-130U's primary mission is close air support (CAS) for special warfare units on the ground—and the gunship has a vast arsenal of weapons to accomplish its task. In the nose is a GAU-12/U 25-mm Gatling cannon that is traversable and is capable of firing 1,800 rounds per minute from altitudes of up to 12,000 feet. Munitions for this gun include high-explosive incendiary and target practice rounds.

The Spectre also has a 40-mm *Bofors gun* and a 105-mm *Howitzer cannon.* The Bofors is mounted on the port side and can fire explosive, incendiary cartridges or more conventional munitions. The cannon is an M1Ai field artillery piece modified to fire from an aircraft and located on the port side of the gunship. The cannon fires high explosive and white-phosphorous projectiles.

One benefit of the AC-130 is that, unlike high-speed jet aircraft, which require a forward air controller for ordinance delivery near friendly forces, it can be controlled by the fire support officer aboard the aircraft. This unique capability makes the gunship user-friendly for forces on the ground. Fire support comes from the Battle Management Center (BMC) located in the Spectre's fuselage.

Special Ops Jargon

The **Bofors gun** and the **Howitzer cannon** are both holdovers from the Vietnam era, when they were first mounted inside the fuselage of early model AC-130 Spectre gunships.

From inside the BMC, personnel operate state-of-the-art sensors, navigation, and fire-control systems. From here, technicians view the battlefield through all-light-level television (ALLTV) monitors. Using a laser illuminator assembly (LIA), an infrared detection set, and a multimode radar target-detection system, the Spectre crews can attack a target night or day, in adverse weather, or even when the target area is swathed in smoke. With dual target attack capability, a Spectre can engage two different targets at the same time and fire both the Bofors and the Howitzer at two separate targets simultaneously. The BMC's personnel and electronics are protected by composite armor of silicon carbide and Spectra fiber.

The AC-130U has a fully pressurized cabin and advanced navigational features, including an inertial navigation system (INS) and a global positioning system (GPS). Defensive systems include a countermeasures-dispensing system that releases chaff and flares to counter radar and infrared-guided antiaircraft missiles. To cover the aircraft's heat signature, the AC-130U has infrared heat shields mounted underneath the engines to disperse the heat.

FUBARs

During Operation Desert Storm, the Spectre gunships provided air base defense and close air support for ground forces. Air Force Special Operations Command suffered the single greatest American air loss of the Gulf War when an AC-130H went down and the entire 14-man crew was killed.

With a top speed of 300-plus miles per hour and a ceiling of 30,000 feet, the range of the AC-130U is unlimited if refueled in the air. Today, 13 of these formidable warplanes are flown by the 16th Special Operations Wing's 4th Special Operations Squadron.

The AC-130H Spectre gunship is the predecessor to the more advanced U-model. The H-configuration is armed with 20-, 40-, and 105-mm cannons and includes the low-light television and infrared sensors of the more advanced U version. The AC-130H has a top speed of about 300 miles per hour, an operational ceiling of 30,000 feet, and a range of 2,200 nautical miles. That range becomes unlimited with air refueling.

The AC-130 Spectre gunship.

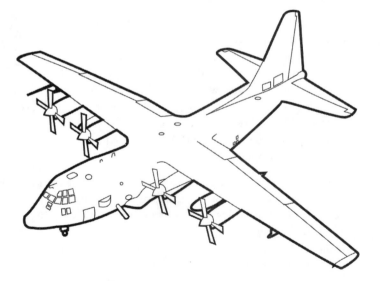

The Combat Talon

The MC-130E/H Combat Talon and the Combat Talon II are both designed for long-range clandestine or covert delivery of special operational forces. Evolved from the C-130 Hercules like the Spectre gunships, the Combat Talons are equipped with FLIR and terrain-following avoidance radar, along with specialized aerial-delivery equipment.

With integrated inertial navigation and GPS, the Combat Talon can make a complicated air drop with greater accuracy and at higher speeds than any conventional C-130. The Combat Talon can also penetrate hostile airspace at low altitudes, and the crews are specially trained in night and bad-weather operations.

The MC-130P Combat Shadow is an aerial tanker that extends the range of special operations helicopters by providing air-refueling capabilities. Such operations are carried out in formation, at night, and at low levels to reduce the chances of detection and interception. The Shadow is a visual flight rule (VFR) aircraft and can be operated only when the pilots can see the ground. The secondary mission of the MC-130P is the delivery of special operations forces, and the tanker can carry small-boat teams along with their craft—Zodiacs or combat rubber raiding craft (CRRC).

Shop Talk

During Operation Desert Storm, the Combat Talons made one third of all air drops in the first three weeks of the war. They also dropped 11 BLU-82/B 15,000-pound bombs. In Afghanistan, Combat Talons also dropped the deadly "Daisy-cutter" bombs on Osama Bin Laden's cave complexes.

The Rivet Rider Commando Solo

The EC-130E Rivet Rider Commando Solo, known formally as the Volant Solo, is flown by the 193rd Special Operations Group and is used primarily for psychological operations. This aircraft was the "Voice of the Gulf" during Desert Storm, broadcasting the facts about the war to Iraqi troops and convincing many to surrender. The EC-130E was also used as a broadcasting platform during the Haitian Crisis of 1994. The EC-130E uses standard AM/FM radio, HF/shortwave, television, and tactical military communications frequencies while flying outside of the lethal range of enemy aircraft and antiaircraft defenses. This aircraft is also capable of jamming enemy communication signals, and it can pinpoint the origin point of jamming attempts made by the enemy. The EC-130E incorporates enhanced navigation systems as well as VCR and DVD systems and transmitters capable of broadcasting color television on a multitude of worldwide standards through the VHR and UHF ranges.

The Pave Low

The primary rotary-wing aircraft (helicopter) operated by AFSOC personnel is the highly sophisticated MH-53J Pave Low III, the latest generation of Pave Low aircraft to reach operational status. The Pave Low's mission is to carry out low-level, long-range covert entry into hostile territory for infiltration, resupply, or extraction of special operations forces. This is accomplished day or night, even under the worst weather conditions. The Pave Low is a new evolution of the Sikorsky HH-53 "Jolly Green Giants" of the Vietnam era, but the Pave Low has been augmented with state-of-the-art technology and has been modified for long-range use with an air-refueling boom projecting from its nose.

The largest and most powerful helicopter in the Air Force inventory, the Pave Low is equipped with forward-looking infrared radar (FLIR), inertial GPS, Doppler navigation systems, a terrain-following/avoidance radar, on-board computers, and integrated advanced avionics. In 1999, new advances were added to the Pave Low "M" model, including the Interactive Defensive Avionics System/Multi-Mission Advanced Tactical Terminal (IDAS/ MATT)—a color, multifunctional, night vision–compatible digital map screen located on the helicopter's instrument panel. The display console gives the crew a more concise, enhanced view of the battlefield and access to real-time events. Hostile threats or navigational barriers such as telephone poles and lines, even those over the horizon, are clearly displayed with this new feature, which downloads data directly from a satellite. For protection, the Pave Low has armor plating and an assortment of weapons systems, including two 7.62-mm miniguns and a 50-caliber machine gun mounted at the rear of the helicopter on the exit ramp.

The MH-53J/M is large, at 92 feet long and 25 feet high, with a rotary diameter of 72 feet. Its top speed is just under 200 miles per hour, with a range of 550 nautical miles— unlimited with air refueling. The Pave Low can ferry 38 fully equipped combat personnel or 14 litters of equipment and supplies. Its external cargo hook is capable of 20,000 pounds of additional lift. The Pave Low has a crew of six: two officers and four enlisted—two flight engineers and two aerial gunners.

The Osprey: Combat Bird of the Future

The CV-22 Osprey is an experimental, tilt-rotor vertical-life aircraft that takes off like a helicopter but flies like a conventional, fixed-wing aircraft. This is achieved by tilting the engines—which are placed at the end of each short wing—vertically for take-off and landings, and then tilting the rotors forward for conventional flight. The development of the V-22 began in 1981 for the U.S. Marines. The CV-22 is the AFSOC forces' special operations variant of the Osprey.

The CV-22 differs from the Marine Corps version, with the addition of a third seat in the cockpit for a flight engineer and the addition of an air refueling probe. The AFSOC version also has a complete suite of electronics like that installed in the Pave Low. At a cost of $50 million per unit, the CV-22 will in time replace the entire MH-53 Pave Low and MH-60G Pave Hawk helicopters currently in service.

The Osprey is not particularly large, with a wingspan of just under 46 feet, a length of 58 feet, and a height of 21 feet, 9.5 inches. The Osprey can easily outpace any helicopter ever built with its top speed of 510 miles per hour. But the payload is slightly reduced to 24 fully equipped troops, 12 litters, or 20,000 pounds of internal load. The crew of the Air Force variant is four: two pilots and two flight engineers. The Osprey has another operational problem to surmount: No land-based vehicle in the current special operations force inventory can fit inside of it.

FUBARs

Unfortunately, a spate of fatal accidents have plagued the Osprey, especially the Marine Corps variant. The Marines have suffered fallout from these crashes. Several officers have been disciplined for doctoring maintenance and performance records for this highly innovative, but as yet unperfected aircraft.

With its ever-changing, ever-evolving fleet of aircraft, the United States Air Force Special Operations Command is ready to meet the challenge of the shifting nature of twenty-first-century unconventional warfare requirements.

The Least You Need to Know

- The Air Force Special Operations Command evolved from the Army Air Corps Air Commandos of World War II.

- Air Commandos units served with distinction in World War II, Korea, and Vietnam, where the gunship was developed.

- AFSOC, founded in 1990, is the youngest member of America's elite special forces groups.

- AFSOC is composed of seven active duty and two reserve units.

- AFSOC operates a large inventory of fixed-wing and rotary-wing aircraft in support of special warfare operations for all branches of the Armed Services.

- The AC-130 Spectre gunship—and its many variations—is the premier-fixed wing aircraft for Air Force special operations.

- The MH-53 Pave Hawk helicopter—and its variations—is the primary rotary-wing aircraft used by AFSOC.

- In the future, the new CV-22 Osprey will join the AFSOC inventory.

The Air Force Special Ops Training Regimen

In This Chapter

- ◆ Introducing the Special Tactics Squadrons
- ◆ Proud history
- ◆ Training for the Special Tactics Squadron
- ◆ Training to become a pararescue jumper
- ◆ Training to become a combat controller

Air Force special operations aren't the exclusive domain of pilots, navigators, flight engineers, and electronic warfare specialists. The Air Force fields a highly mobile, very formidable ground assault strike force, with forward air traffic control capabilities, called the Special Tactics Squadrons (STSs).

Training for these strike teams is intense and ongoing. These elite units have worked closely with Army Special Forces, Rangers, and SEAL teams in special reconnaissance, combat search and rescue, and direct action missions. These STSs have become an integral part of the United States Special Operations Command. In this chapter, I'll explore the rigorous training and career paths taken by all Air Force Special Operations candidates.

Into the Air Force Special Tactics Squadrons

Operating under AFSOC, the STSs are comprised of combat controller teams (CCTs) and pararescuemen (affectionately known as "PJs," a holdover from the time when they were known as "pararescue jumpers") who are proficient in insertion tactics. They are trained to establish assault zones with an air traffic control capability. These assault zones could be a simple landing zone (LZ) for helicopters or a hostile airport seized and ready for use by follow-on fixed-wing or helicopter forces.

CCTs specialize in air traffic control. They can place numerous forms of light—visible and infrared—on a target, for smart munitions to follow onto the target, and they are primarily responsible for ground-based fire control of the AC-130 Spectre gunships and helicopters of AFSOC. While the CCTs are busy painting targets, PJs can provide emergency medical treatment and evacuate the wounded. Like the other groups of America's special operations forces, when not in combat, PJs can be found working in trauma units or on EMS vehicles in many high-crime urban areas, where they hone their skills by working on crime victims.

There are currently six STS units worldwide, with approximately 300 combat controllers and pararescue jumpers on active duty. The 21st STS is stationed at Fort Bragg, North Carolina; the 24th STS is stationed at Pope Air Force Base, North Carolina; the 22nd STS is stationed at McChord Air Force Base, Washington; the 23rd STS is stationed at Kadena Air Base, Japan; and the 321st Special Tactics Squadron is based at the British Royal Air Force base at Mildenhall, England. Each squadron has three teams. Each team is comprised of 18 enlisted men and 2 officers. Half of each team consists of qualified combat controllers; the other half is made up of pararescue personnel.

> **Shop Talk**
>
> Special Tactics Squadrons provided air traffic control for coalition forces during Desert Shield/Storm, and they were the spearhead of the raid on Patilla Airport during Operation Just Cause.

A Bit of History

The need for CCTs surfaced in the early air campaigns of World War II, when parachute insertions often became disasters—with the troops scattered and some of them landing up to 30 miles away from their target zone. To solve this problem, the Army trained a company-size group of scouts who were parachuted into the zone before the main force. This unit, called Pathfinders, used lights, flares, or smoke pots to signal the aircraft that they were over the target. Pathfinders proved their value during the invasion of Italy and were instrumental in the D-Day invasion of Europe as they prepared the way for the 82nd and 101st Airborne Divisions.

On September 18, 1947, the U.S. Air Force was officially established, and this new branch of the armed services assumed responsibility for tactical airlift support of Army forces. The Pathfinders were renamed combat control teams, and a new unit was activated in 1953. Since then, CCTs have seen action worldwide—in the Lebanon crisis of 1958, the Congo Uprising of 1960, the Cuban Missile Crisis of 1962, the China-India confrontation of 1962–1963, and the protracted war in Vietnam.

It was in Vietnam that the CCTs and the gunships of the Air Force began to work in concert. Combat control teams were used in clandestine missions along the Ho Chi Minh Trail, where they located enemy convoys and called in the gunships to wipe them out. CCTs saw action before Operation Eagle Claw, when a lone combat controller was dropped into the Iranian desert to find a suitable location for the staging area that came to be known as Desert I.

Today, CCTs are ground combat forces assigned to the STS. Not only are they trained CCTs, but they also are fully qualified to conduct combat operations on the ground to secure the landing area. If the LZ must be cleared first, the CCTs are trained in the removal of obstacles and are equipped with demolitions that allow them to accomplish the task. Their primarily responsibility remains the planning, organization, supervision, and establishment of air traffic control at forward airheads. Special Tactics Teams (STTs) operate portable and mobile communications equipment and air navigation aids required to control and support air traffic in a combat area. CCTs possess limited weather observation capabilities and control ground vehicular traffic in the airfield area.

Straight Shooting

To establish a landing zone in the Iranian desert for Operation Eagle Claw, Maj. John T. Carey Jr. was airdropped by a CIA aircraft into the wasteland. Equipped with only a motorcycle, flares, and a pair of night-vision goggles, Major Carey guided the U.S. aircraft into the landing zone.

Special Tactics Squadron Training

Joining the STS begins with the basics. A candidate must be in sufficient physical condition to pass the Physical Abilities and Stamina Test (PAST). Male Air Force officers and enlisted men from active duty and reserve units are qualified for STS service. However, each must get through the PAST to begin combat control and pararescue training.

The PAST Test

PAST begins with a 25-meter underwater swim. If the candidate breaks the surface of the water, he has failed. After the underwater swim comes a 5-minute rest, followed by the

1,000-meter surface swim, which much be completed in 26 minutes. If the candidate pauses in the water, he fails. This swim is followed by a 30-minute rest.

Next comes the 1.5-mile continuous run, with a maximum time limit of 10 minutes, 30 seconds. After a 10-minute cool-off time, four calisthenics challenges begin, with a 3-minute break between each exercise. Then a candidate is required to do 8 chin-ups in 60 seconds, 50 sit-ups in 2 minutes, 50 push-ups in 2 minutes, and 50 flutter kicks. All of these physical trials come with no break in between. Flutter kicks are important and are used in underwater training later.

Having successfully completed PAST, the enlisted candidates enter the Indoctrination Course at Lackland Air Force Base in San Antonio, Texas. The officers usually require some additional physical retraining before they can meet the challenges ahead. This includes obstacle courses, forced marches, runs, and more swims to make the more mature officer the physical equal of the younger enlisted men. Officer candidates for STS training must also file lots of additional paperwork, including an essay about why they want to be combat controllers and three letters of recommendation from their superior officers. Then they face a tough board of field-grade officers who select the top 15 or 20 candidates out of every 100 to proceed with STS training.

The Indoctrination Course

When they arrive in San Antonio, the candidates face 12 grueling weeks under the hot Texas sun called the Indoctrination Course. A combination of the Q course, BUD/S, and airborne training, candidates go through the Pararescue/Combat Control Indoctrination course (also known as *OL-H*) with the knowledge that they are being observed and assessed constantly. They must prove to their instructors that they have what it takes to enter the high-stakes world of Air Force special operations and join an STT. To the candidates who undergo this grueling regimen, the indoctrination course is informally known as "Superman University," or "Superman U."

Special Ops Jargon

Graduates of the Indoctrination Course refer to their training as "Operations Location-Hotel," or **OL-H.** The course is designed to select and screen potential pararescue and combat controllers and then train them for their specialty fields.

The 12 weeks spent on the OL-H course are only the beginning of a 55-week journey through some of the military's most extensive and intensive training. Indoctrination is meant to push the candidates beyond their physical and mental limits. Like BUD/S and the Q course, OL-H is there to weed out those who cannot cut it. After two weeks of pure physical training, Motivation Week begins—this is the Air Force version of Hell Week and is just about as much fun. This seven-day period of mental and physical challenge usually cuts the class size considerably. STS training has an attrition rate as high as 90 percent.

Water confidence tests are an important part of Indoctrination. Candidates must be comfortable in the water and must be able to perform a variety of complex tasks. The STS course also concentrates on marksmanship skills—using the M-4A1 carbine version of the M-16, and the M-9 pistol—physiological training in altitude and dive chambers, and academics. As with the other branches of America's special forces, slow learners need not apply, no matter how good of a physical shape they are in. Muscles can be built and endurance limits can be extended, but not even the Air Force has found a way to increase a candidate's brain function or capacity!

Specialty Training: "The Pipeline"

The pipeline lasts between a year to a year and a half, and it is designed to transform an airman or officer into a highly motivated, highly skilled, high-tech warrior. That transformation begins at the U.S. Army Combat Divers School in Key West, Florida, where candidates learn to use scuba and closed-circuit SCBA gear to infiltrate a target area. This training is essential for STT members because so many of their assignments involve supporting the Navy SEALs. Water exercises are conducted day and night in the open ocean. Candidates learn how to enter and debark from a submerged submarine and learn the basics of underwater demolition techniques.

That's followed by a visit to the U.S. Navy Underwater Egress Training at Pensacola Naval Base, Florida. Here the candidates learn the proper techniques to safely escape from a sinking or submerged aircraft. Part of that training consists of learning to use the Helicopter Emergency Egress Device System (HEEDS), a small SCUBA tank with 5 minutes of air. Crews wear this tank in their survival vests in case they are trapped underwater. Candidates also experience the Helicopter Underwater Egress Trainer, dubbed the "helo dunker" by nervous candidates. During Helicopter Underwater Egress training, strapped-in candidates ride the interior of a mock helicopter as it plunges 10 feet into a giant tank of water, where it promptly sinks. The trainees are expected to unfasten their seat belts and exit the submerged fuselage—blindfolded! To make things interesting, the instructors roll the helicopter so that it lands upside down, further disorienting the candidates.

Three weeks of basic airborne training at Fort Benning, Georgia, follow the underwater training. Upon graduation, candidates are awarded the Silver Wings that mark them as airborne-qualified warriors. However, basic airborne training is not enough to make it to an STT—candidates must next attend the U.S. Army Military Freefall Parachutist School at Fort Bragg.

Straight Shooting

During free-fall parachute training, emergency procedures (EPs) are taught. Candidates learn how to deal with parachute malfunctions, cut-aways, and entanglements. Training must become second nature because when you're plunging at 180 feet per second, every moment counts!

At this facility, candidates learn the basics of military free-fall (MFF) jumping and the more advanced techniques of high-altitude, high-opening (HAHO) parachute jumping. They also become familiar with the modern *Ram-Air Parachute System* (RAPS). These methods allow parachutists to infiltrate the theater of operation undetected. During the first week of this training, candidates spend time in the Military Free Fall Simulator Facility, a $5 million, 11,000-square-foot complex at Fort Bragg with an enclosed wind tunnel. The fan generates winds up to 135 miles per hour. Suspended in a column of air, the students learn and practice body-stabilization techniques while the simulator re-creates the effects of free falling at a speed of nearly 200 feet per second!

Special Ops Jargon

Ram-Air Parachute Systems use the MC-5 ram-air parachute, which are rectangular instead of circular and are quite maneuverable. Ram-air chutes are preferred for special operations, in which a pinpoint landing on the target zone is often critical for the success of the mission.

After a week of ground training, candidates move to Yuma Proving Grounds in Arizona, where they jump several times a week—sometimes two or three times a day—learning every type of jump, from every altitude, in every kind of weather, using every type of equipment available to military airborne units. Near the end of five weeks, the candidates make 16 free-fall jumps, including two day jumps and two night jumps with oxygen and hundreds of pounds of full-field equipment.

Then it's off to the cold mountains of Coville and Kaniskau National Forests, outside Spokane, Washington, where the 22nd Training Squadron conducts the combat survival training; basic survival techniques for remote areas. Trainees learn how to build a shelter, procure food and locate water, land navigation, perform ground-to-air signaling, and undergo helicopter hoist training. They also experience the Survival Escape Resistance and Evasion (SERE) training. This course takes an additional three weeks and is the last time that officers and airmen will train together. After graduation they will part ways to concentrate on their specialties.

Pararescue Jumper Training

Airmen in the pararescue program attend the Special Operations Combat Medic Course at Fort Bragg. For 24 weeks they will have comprehensive medical training designed for managing trauma patients prior to evacuation and providing medical treatment for less serious injuries. Candidates are assigned to hands-on training in emergency rooms and hospital settings—usually a four-week stint in a high-crime area of New York City, where they will see knife wounds, gunshot wounds, blast trauma, burns, vehicular accident trauma, and the like.

During Phase I of this training, Emergency Medical Technician Basic (EMT-B) skills are learned. During Phase II, which lasts an additional 17 weeks, instructions in minor field surgery, pharmacology, combat trauma management, and advance airway treatment are taught. After they receive their EMP-P (Emergency Medical Personnel) certifications, future STS members head for Kirtland Air Force Base in New Mexico and the 90-day Pararescue Recovery Specialist Course.

The Pararescue Recovery Specialist Course is divided into three phases: the Ground Phase, the Medical Phase, and the Air Phase. During the Ground Phase, candidates learn field craft, woodcraft, and accelerated survival techniques for hostile environments. They learn about identifying edible plants, trapping wildlife, preparing food in the wild, performing advanced land navigation, and a host of other outdoor skills. This course climaxes with a 10-day field and mountain operation in the wilds of the Pecos Mountains.

Straight Shooting

Pararescue teams must be certified by the American Heart Association in basic life support and advanced cardiac life support, as well as basic emergency medical technician treatment and all paramedic levels with the National Registry of Emergency Medical Technicians in the United States.

The Medical Phase begins when the candidates are issued the standard ALICE (All-Purpose Lightweight Individual Carrying Equipment) field pack. This rucksack is used by all the Army Special Forces ODA teams, Rangers, and the combat controllers on the Special Tactics Squadron teams, but the ones the PJs get are filled with medical supplies. Each PJ's rucksack must be arranged exactly the same, so that any PJ can work out of another man's sack, even in darkness. The PJs learn to use the Rapid Extraction Deployment System (REDS). Similar to the "jaws of life," REDS are used to cut away an aircraft fuselage to extract a casualty. Candidates must also learn basic search techniques and before graduation will plan, mount, and conduct a rescue mission and "rescue" a survivor.

The final phase of the Pararescue and Recovery Course is the Air Operations Phase. Candidates become familiar with a wide inventory of Air Force aircraft, along with various aircraft systems operations. They learn how to perform an aerial search pattern and are taught alternate insertion/ extraction methods, including the use of helicopter rope ladders, hoists, rappelling, and fast roping. Candidates learn how to deploy into water from 10 feet above sea level at a speed of 10 knots. Advanced parachuting into water is also covered in this phase of the training. During this phase, a candidate will make 10 land jumps,

Shop Talk

Pararescues are familiar with the Parachutist Rough Terrain System, a padded suit that protects the neck, armpits, kidneys, elbows, crotch, and knees. Nicknamed the "tree suit," it is designed for parachute jumping in heavily wooded areas and includes a pocket with rope, in case the jumper is tangled in high branches.

2 tree jumps, and 5 scuba jumps—4 to 6 of these jumps will be carried out at night. This completes pararescue training. Graduates are awarded the maroon beret and wear the Air Force crest "That Others May Live."

Combat Controller Training

The first step in becoming a combat controller takes place at Keesler Air Force Base in Mississippi, at the Combat Control Operator Course, a 15½–week course taught by civilian and military air traffic controllers. Candidates learn basic flight rules, radar approach control (RAPCON) procedures, air navigational aids, tower and airport operations, aircraft performance statistics, weather forecasting, and air traffic control. Graduates of this course are fully prepared to take the Federal Aviation Administration's Control Tower Operator Exam.

The next step is the Combat Control School at Pope Air Force Base, North Carolina. For the next 87 days, candidates learn combat tactics, how to use a wide range of communications and navigational equipment, demolitions, fire support, assault-zone air traffic control, and landing zone preparation. This phase of training concludes with a field exercise. While at CCT school, physical conditioning is stressed, and PT is conducted throughout the 87 days of active training. This physical training may include 6-mile runs, long-distance swims, quick marches with a full field pack, weight training, and calisthenics.

After the future CCTs have learned the basics, it's time for them to practice what they've absorbed. To do this, they travel to Camp McKall, North Carolina, to those same sand hills where many Q Course exercises are carried out by the Army Special Forces. There they run through the Q Course several times, learn how to use a laser designator to paint a target, and how to prepare a landing zone. Near the end of this course, candidates plan a mock mission, are inserted by parachute into the zone, and carry out their orders under intense and realistic conditions over 10 days. At the end of this simulation, they march back to the Combat Control School, combat-equipped and carrying 70 pounds in their rucksacks, including the *SOFLAM laser target designator*. These men live up to the traditional motto of the Air Force CCTs: "First there."

Special Ops Jargon

The laser target designator of choice for the U.S. Air Force Special Tactics Squadrons is the **Special Operations Force Laser Acquisition Marker (SOFLAM)**. It is lightweight and can paint a target from a safe distance away for follow-on air assault using "smart bombs."

The candidates who complete this course can move on to assignment in conventional operations. STS candidates must complete additional training to become Special Operations Tactical Air Control (SOTAC) qualified. To accomplish this, they undergo Army Ranger training and learn additional infantry-related skills so that when they are attached to an Air Force

Special Tactics Team or work with Special Forces or SEAL teams, they can keep pace with the highly trained and skilled men beside them and be mission assets, not liabilities.

The final phase of STS training is a one-month course called Initial Familiarization (IFAM). It is here that the CCTs and PJs come together to form a cohesive team. In a series of intense exercises, these individuals become members of a lethal unit—a close-knit team of Air Commandos. Much of the training takes place at Eglin Air Force Base and aboard C-130s, AC-130s, and Pave Low helicopters. The men learn to operate the land vehicles used by Air Force special ops forces and learn to load these vehicles into a Combat Talon for air transport. This all leads to a final exercise in which the STS teams are attached to Ranger units. Together with these infantrymen, they plan, rehearse, and execute a simulated airfield seizure. After graduation, the officers and enlisted men are ready to join the ranks of the Air Force Special Operations Command's Special Tactics Squadron, men who live by the traditional motto that dates back to the dark days of World War II: "Anytime, anyplace."

The Least You Need to Know

- The Special Tactics Squadron is the ground force component of the United States Air Force.

- Special Tactics Squadron members work in teams—half are combat controllers and half are pararescue jumpers.

- Pararescue involves extensive training in rescue operations, parachute jumping, medicine, navigation, and weapons proficiency.

- Combat controllers are trained to seize airfields and make them operational for follow-on forces, establish helicopter and fixed-wing landing zones, and paint targets on the ground for destruction by air-dropped laser-guided smart bombs.

- It takes over a year of extensive training to become a member of a Special Tactics Squadron.

Part  6 The First Special Operational Detachment—Delta

The 1960s and 1970s saw a dramatic rise in incidents of international terrorism. In Europe, communist cells and socialist-inspired revolutionary movements resulted in hijackings, kidnappings, bombings, and murder. In the Middle East tensions were also rising, as Palestinian nationalists used violence to further their struggle against the State of Israel and the West.

To counter terrorist activities, the United States Army created a covert unit trained and equipped to combat terror. In this part, you will discover the secret origins of Delta, read about their operational history, and uncover their super-secret recruitment and training procedures.

Terror Is Their Business: Delta Force

In This Chapter

◆ The rising thread of terrorism
◆ America's responds with Delta and Blue Light
◆ Delta's counterterrorism operations

The smallest, most elite, most secretive component of the U.S. Army Special Operations Command is Delta, America's premier counterterrorism force. Delta was created in an effort to stem the rising tide of international terrorism in the 1970s. The rise of Islamic fundamentalism, the Palestinian *Fatah* groups, and violent anti-American, anticapitalist terrorism in Germany, Italy, Greece, and Spain forced the United States military to take on what are traditionally thought of as "police powers."

The U.S. Army established Delta in 1977. It's first test came only two years later, during the hostage crisis in Iran. Since that time Delta's successes have been few and not widely known, while their failures have been loudly trumpeted. Now, after 25 years of active duty, few Americans know what Delta does or how it is organized because Delta is one of the most secretive of all Special Operations Forces.

Terrorism on the Rise

The world watched television screens in horror when, in 1972, the celebration of the Olympic Games in Munich, West Germany, was violently interrupted by a Palestinian terrorist attack that cost the lives of Israeli athletes and shook the foundation of civilized society and behavior. For Americans, this savage incident was a first troubling glimpse into the world of international terrorism. In the rest of the world, things were different. The Old World had been living with Basque separatists, Greek militants, Armenian nationalists, and Muslim terrorists since the end of World War II. Already, terrorists had seized several commercial airliners, and the Israelis had been forced to mount a dramatic rescue of their citizens held by militant Islamic fundamentalists at the Entebbe Airport in Uganda. But, for Americans at least, the cold-blooded slaughter of the Israeli athletes in Germany was something new—and quite disturbing.

FUBARs

Terrorists operate in Western countries because of the fact that open societies allow them a remarkable degree of freedom to carry out their brutal activities.

Israel and several European nations had already crafted a response to growing terrorism. Each nation dealt with the problem of terrorism based on its own perception of how various political, economic, social, and religious factors affected its own national security and sovereignty. The British turned to their well-established special operations units, such as the Special Air Service. The Germans formed *Grenzschutzgruppe 9* (GSG-9) around the time of the Munich slaughter. The French set up the *Groupe d'Intervention de la Gendarmerie National* (GIGN) to deal with their terrorist problem.

On the other hand, the United States buried its collective head in the sand and took a wait-and-see attitude that put the nation several paces behind the Europeans—and, as it later turned out, miles behind the terrorists themselves. Meanwhile, the Europeans were moving forward with their training and arming of elite antiterrorist groups. In October 1977, the Germans enacted a measure of revenge when a 30-man GSG-9 team—with the help of two British SAS commandos and GSG-9 chief Col. Ulrich Wegener—raided Mogadishu Airport in Somalia and rescued Westerners held hostage by terrorists.

Within a few years, hijackings of commercial airliners became commonplace, and Americans began to feel a mounting sense of frustration and helplessness in the face of such wanton brutality. That brutality was brought home through a series of terrorist attacks overseas that specifically targeted Americans. In West Germany, U.S. military personnel found themselves targets. In May 1972, the Red Army Faction of the Baader-Meinhoff Gang bombed six targets, including a U.S. military officer's club in Frankfurt and the headquarters of the United States Army, Europe, in Heidelberg. It had finally began to dawn on military and political leaders that the United States had better begin to prepare itself for a similar spate of attacks in the Middle East, Europe, and even back home in America.

America Responds: Delta and Blue Light

After the administration of President James Earl Carter made it clear that it wanted an American counterterrorist organization with special operations capabilities, U.S. Army Chief of Staff, Gen. Bernard Rogers, added his voice to the chorus of supporters for such a "police" unit. Rogers was helped by Lieut. Gen. Edward C. Meyer, Deputy Chief of Staff for Army Operations, who laid out the plans and the policy for the formation of such units within the U.S. Army command structure. Gen. William DePuy, commander of the Training and Doctrine Command, wanted to field a force like the SAS and had the means to train them. Though a conventional soldier, DePuy was respectful toward special warfare units and understood that conventional "shoot-from-the-hip" tactics would not suffice to combat terrorists. Such tactics were too reactive; DePuy wanted a proactive group like the British commandos, who had the capability and resources to stop terrorism before it happened.

But the real architect of Delta was then-Commandant of the Special Forces School at Fort Bragg, North Carolina, a veteran of the guerilla war in Vietnam named Col. Charles "Chargin' Charlie" Beckwith. It was Colonel Beckwith who requested that Delta be moved into Fort Bragg. Joining the military chorus was Col. Othar Shalikashvilli, then-commander of the 10th Special Forces group based at that time in Fort Devens, Massachusetts, who assembled his senior commissioned and noncommissioned officers and told them that the job Colonel Beckwith was planning was "more important than the job we have to do." He encouraged the best and brightest men on his staff to join the new unit. Despite this enthusiasm, there were also complaints—especially from the Army Rangers, who claimed that the new Delta unit duplicated some of their own functions, and the commander of the 5th Special Forces Group, Col. Robert Mountel.

After the activation order was handed down, the Army decided that it would need an interim force to do the job of Delta until the first units were trained and ready in two years. It was Col. Robert Montell's 5th Special Forces Group that was assigned to fill the position until Delta was truly activated. Colonel Montell selected 40 Special Forces troopers and trained them in hostage rescue and quick-response tactics. This group was code-named Blue Light.

Straight Shooting

Green Beret Col. Robert Montell fought against the formation of Delta. But when the unit was activated, the Army decided that it needed an interim unit to do the same task until Delta was ready. Ironically, it was Montell's 5th Special Forces Group that got the job!

Delta in Action

Meanwhile, Colonel Beckwith's 1st Special Forces Operational Detachment-Delta was activated on schedule, in October 1977. However, Beckwith still had to select and train his unit. It took him over two years because Beckwith was both selective and thorough. The colonel knew that he had to find the best personnel available in the special operations community because the members of Delta would have to be able to blend into the civilian world yet possess the necessary martial skills to accomplish any mission. Delta personnel would find that their education was far-reaching and unorthodox—they learned everything from fast-roping from a helicopter to climbing up the side of a building, to carrying out burglary and safe-cracking techniques, to rescuing hostages, to hot-wiring a car.

The name Delta derived from old-fashioned Army Special Forces terminology. Six ALPHA detachments (or A-Teams, which are now known as Operational Detachment ALPHAs) make up a company-size BRAVO detachment (or B-Team), commanded by a major. A CHARLIE (or C team) detachment is battalion-size and commanded by a lieutenant colonel. When Delta was created, it was commanded by a full colonel, Charlie Beckwith, and was structured along completely separate lines. So, following the Alpha, Bravo, Charlie logic, it became a Delta detachment. The rest is history—classified history, mostly!

Delta's First Mission: Operation Eagle Claw

On November 4, 1979, the very first Delta unit had completed its training and certification exercises and was ready to go. Six months later, Delta launched its first mission—to rescue the American hostages held for months at the U.S. Embassy compound in Iran.

The disaster that resulted from this operation has been recounted in Chapter 10, "The Coming of the U.S. Special Operations Command." However, it must be said that Delta had little to do with Operation Eagle Claw's failure. Blaming Delta for the aircraft collision at the secret site called Desert One is equivalent to blaming the passengers of a commercial airliner for the pilot error that causes a crash! Yet Delta paid a high price for the FUBAR that resulted in the Iranian desert—it was the unit's very first deployment, and it ended in a very public disaster.

> **Shop Talk**
>
> Operation Eagle Claw's Delta team was dressed in casual attire—Levis, boots, and black-dyed field jackets. The members' only national markings were taped-over U.S. flags. Inside the embassy, they were to rip off the tape and reveal their identity to the hostages. Needless to say, Delta personnel never got that far.

When the mission was aborted, in-country Delta members and Special Forces teams—including Dick Meadows, veteran of many covert operations—who entered Iran with phony identities and doctored "Scottish" and "Irish" visas (Meadows himself carried an Irish passport as part of his fake identity), had to exfiltrate themselves. The dazed team on the ground at Desert One rode an MC-130s home, their clothing singed and their lungs filled with smoke from the explosion and fire from the aircraft collision. In the chaos, U.S. Navy Sea Stallion helicopters containing classified documents were left behind. The Iranian debacle was not the coming-out party that Colonel Beckwith and Delta were hoping for!

Political Fallout

The wreck and the political fallout from Operation Eagle Claw began a decade of frustration and inactivity for Delta, but there were some positive results. One was the establishment of a Joint Special Operations Command (JSOC) in 1980, a change that Colonel Beckwith had lobbied long and hard for. As a reward, Beckwith was promoted and placed in command of JSOC, the organization he had pushed to create. More changes were in store for Delta, including the codification of procedures, mission profiles, personnel selection, and training. Colonel Beckwith himself wrote the study, called "Task, Conditions, and Standards for Delta," known in the force as "the Black Book."

Despite the failure of Eagle Claw, Delta expanded. From a unit strength of about 100 men in 1979—comprising two small A and B squadrons, plus support—Delta grew to a relatively stable force of 300 men during the 1980s. Yet Delta remained flexible. Four troops of approximately 16 men make up a Delta squadron, with each troop able to reconfigure itself into 8-, 6-, 4-, 3-, or even 2-soldier teams. Such a structure gives Delta the edge in any situation, and each smaller unit is capable of performing the same basic missions as the 16-man squadron.

In the 1980s, Delta moved its headquarters from a former post stockade at Fort Bragg to a new, state-of-the-art, high-tech special operations training facility (SOT), nicknamed "Wally World" after the fictional theme park featured in the movie *National Lampoon's Vacation*. But all was not well. During the administration of Ronald Reagan, the men of Delta trained and drilled but were seldom deployed. They were often assembled for a rescue operation that was ultimately cancelled by high command. Meanwhile Delta personnel watched in helpless frustration as American hostages were seized in Beirut by Muslim fanatics and were detained for long periods of time—sometimes years.

> **CAUTION**
>
> ### FUBARs
>
> In the 1980s, a highly publicized scandal involving members of Delta and misused and misappropriated funding eroded the morale and further damaged the reputation of this beleaguered unit. Several officers spent hard time in Levenworth Penitentiary for their "black-budget" criminal activities.

Delta Gets a Second Chance: Operation Urgent Fury

On October 19, 1983, the Marxist prime minister of the Caribbean Island of Grenada, Maurice Bishop, was shot by his former associates, who then formed a radical Revolutionary Military Council with cozy ties to the Soviet Union and Fidel Castro's Cuba. Bishop himself had invited the communists in, and they promptly constructed a large military communications facility and a large airport with a 10,000-foot runway and complex hangar facilities capable of servicing Russian warplanes. The situation was further complicated by the presence of 600 American students attending the island's medical school, students who could be seized and used as pawns in a game of international chess.

President Ronald Reagan authorized direct military action against the new communist government in the region, and Operation Urgent Fury was launched. As part of this operation, Delta personnel were ferried in Black Hawk helicopters to a target area close to the new airfield at Point Salines, where they were to carry out a "direct action" mission ahead of two Ranger battalions parachuting in at dawn. The base was ringed with automatic weapons and packed with Grenadan and Cuban troops. Though not a classic FUBAR, Delta lost several troopers when a Black Hawk was downed by Soviet-made antiaircraft guns. At the same time as the Rangers were parachuting onto the Soviet-built airfield, Delta elements attacked Richmond Hill Prison, supported by C Company, 1st Ranger Battalion.

Although Delta managed to achieve some of its objectives, it had no realistic intelligence estimates about the size of the airport's defensive force—a critical error. The unit's second chance at glory ended with a draw.

Straight Shooting

The exact casualty figures for Operation Urgent Fury are still classified. Only after ABC News obtained actual footage of the helicopter shoot-down *eight years after the invasion of Grenada* did the Army acknowledge that it lost an aircraft. Unofficially, it is believed that 11 Delta troopers were injured.

Delta Training Pays Off

On the evening of April 18, 1983, a pair of suicide bombers drove a truck laden with explosives into the U.S. Marine Corps barracks in Lebanon. Despite warnings and a similar attack on the U.S. Embassy earlier that year, the barracks complex was not on high alert. Strict rules of engagement forbid the Marine sentries who guarded the entry points from carrying loaded weapons. The results: 241 Marines and 40 French paratroopers dead. This incident ultimately forced the U.S. government to withdraw its troops from Lebanon.

In October of that same year, members of the 10th Special Forces Group were billeted in a downtown hotel while on FID duty training the Lebanese Army. Col. Richard Potter, former deputy commander of Delta, heard similar warnings and took precautions: He moved his entire command to a Lebanese army base miles outside the city. The suicide attack was thwarted. It was a quiet testament to Delta training that saved hundreds of lives. Meanwhile, in a 15-year period, from 1970 to 1986, over a thousand American citizens were murdered by terrorists, wounded by their bombs, or taken hostage.

During the next several years, Delta would be prevented from acting effectively by international red tape. During the seizure of the cruise

FUBARs

Strict rules of engagement (ROE) restrict Marine sentries from loading their weapon without specific instructions from a commissioned officer. When the truck bomb crashed the gate, the guards had nothing in their rifles to stop it.

ship *Achille Lauro* by Palestinian extremists, an American tourist was murdered. Delta was on the way but was prevented from acting by the Italian authorities. An ugly international incident followed as SEAL Team Six members tried to seize the terrorists after U.S. Navy F-14 Tomcats forced down the aircraft that they were escaping in at an Italian airport. The SEALs surrounded the plane, and the Italian police surrounded the SEALs. Ultimately, the SEALs stood down. Less than a month later, a commercial airliner was hijacked in Malta by Palestinian terrorists. Delta tried to intervene but was prevented from setting foot in the country. Instead, Egyptian commandos rushed the plane. In the ensuing firefight, the terrorists and 57 hostages lost their lives.

Meanwhile, Delta provided crucial security and counterterrorism training for the 1984 Los Angeles Summer Olympics. Some of Delta's operations took place in a rapid-response security vehicle—complete with an armed security detail—in a van disguised as a Budweiser beer truck. Talk about blending into the environment! In this same period, Delta executed a successful hostage rescue at an airport in Venezuela.

Delta Rescues a Radio Star

Kurt Muse was a radio star, of sorts. With the help of fellow Rotary Club members in Panama, Muse ran a clandestine, subversive radio station that was the bane of dictator Manual Noriega's existence. Though an American citizen, Muse had business in Panama, and he and his pals decided that the Panamanian strongman's iron-fisted ways were bad for the freedom of all Panamanians—and generally bad for business, too. Muse was devious. At times, he broadcast confusing and misleading orders over military frequencies to Panamanian Defense Forces, and at other times he spread white propaganda in his highly informative broadcasts. Kurt Muse was doing good work, disrupting Panamanian forces and keeping the newly installed dictator off balance, until a woman turned him in. Muse was dumped into a cell in Panama's notorious Modelo Prison, right next to Noriega's military headquarters, to await trial and probable execution.

When the United States invaded Panama in Operation Just Cause, it was Delta's job to break Muse out. This they did in the early morning hours of December 19, 1989. A Delta assault team landed on the roof of the prison in an MH-6 helicopter flown by a pilot from SOAR, while someone inside the prison disabled the emergency electric generators, cutting off all power. The team fought its way down from the rooftops, blasted the door off Muse's cell, and whisked him away as a Spectre gunship pounded Noriega's military command headquarters next door. The helicopter was knocked out of the air by ground fire but made a relatively soft landing in a crowded street between two tall apartment buildings. An armored Black Hawk and an M-113 personnel carrier came to the rescue of the hurt Little Bird. Although four Deltas were injured, none of the wounds was serious. It was a textbook operation and a rousing success.

Delta in the Desert

Operation Desert Storm in 1990 provided new missions for the Delta teams. When Iraqi-fired, Soviet-made Scud missiles began to rain down on Israel and Saudi Arabia, the fragile political coalition built by President George H. Bush threatened to fracture. The Scuds had to be stopped, but it was an almost impossible job. Scuds are fire-and-forget missiles with minimal internal guidance systems. They were quite primitive but mobile. A Scud could be fired, and the truck that launched it could be away from the scene in mere minutes—too quickly for coalition fighters and bombers to destroy it. Many likely Scud-launching sites were easily reached by MH-53 Pave Low helicopters of the Air Force 1st Special Operations Wing or the MH-60s flown by the 160th Special Operations Aviation Regiment—the famed "Nightstalkers." But some of the target sites were deeper into Iraqi airspace and called for more drastic insertion methods.

Delta assault teams made HAHO (high-altitude, high-opening) parachute jumps onto the target areas from 30,000 feet or higher. During this procedure, the jumper opens his chute almost as soon as he is out of the aircraft and then maneuvers his double-canopy parachute until he is precisely over the drop zone. A jumper can travel up to 50 or 60 miles using this parachuting technique. The teams were to locate Scud trucks and notify Special Operation Command, which would use an E-2C Sentry to vector in fighter aircraft to hit the target—which was usually "painted" with a laser target designator by the reconnaissance team.

One assault team landed in the middle of a concentration of Iraqi tanks, armored personnel carriers, and troops. The members quickly called in air support, and A-10 Thunderbolt

IIs (affectionately called "Warthogs" by the pilots who fly them) turned the desert into a killing field. Air strikes continued throughout the day, with British Tornadoes joining the fun. The Deltas never located one Scud, but they did get shot up in a firefight, lost a man, and were later extracted. Most Scud-busting missions ended in failure because the launch trucks were almost impossible to find, even with the most sophisticated high-tech detection devices. Human intelligence also couldn't travel far enough, fast enough to prevent the Scuds from launching.

Delta in Somalia

By the 1990s, the culture of Delta was firmly established. Delta continued to operate in secret, and according to Mark Bowden's masterful book *Black Hawk Down*, "The Army would not even speak the word 'Delta.' If you had to refer to them, they were 'operators' or 'The Dreaded D' .... They were noble, silent, and invisible." Yet, according to other reports, spotting a Delta team member in Africa was not that hard because they all looked the same—rippling muscles, thick neck, deep tan, a big Casio watch, and hair longer than regulations. The "D-Boys" almost always dressed like civilians.

Delta team members were involved in the most intense, violent, and sustained firefight that U.S. forces experienced since the Vietnam War when, on October 3, 1993, a mixed team of Rangers and Delta units went into the streets of Mogadishu to capture the lieutenants of Somali warlord Mohammed Addid. The warlords had made humanitarian assistance to the Somali people nearly impossible, and close to half the population of that African nation lived close to starvation. Addid was the worst of the warlords who preyed on the Somalis and was targeted by Army command. The mission was supposed to be routine: Capture a bunch of Addid's henchmen and then return to base—all in less than 30 minutes. It turned into anything but routine when Soviet-made rocket-propelled grenades downed two supposedly invulnerable Black Hawk helicopters. Within 24 hours, 18 Americans and between 700 and 1,000 Somalis were dead.

The mission was a FUBAR because Secretary of Defense Les Aspin would not allow armor to be shipped to Somalia and refused the Rangers the use of a Spectre gunship because the aircraft was "too public." The fallout resulted in Aspin's resignation and America's ignominious withdrawal from Somalia.

Into the Future

International terrorism shows no sign of abating. Instead, as the events on September 11, 2001, indicate, it is becoming more widespread and more deadly. For 25 years, the men of Delta have countered this threat with every means at their disposal. They have had some quiet successes and many highly publicized failures. However, as the volatile situation in the Middle East continues to boil over into violence, and terrorists come to threaten American lives and property at home, the mission of the 1st Special Operational Detachment-Delta is more important than ever. Whenever terrorists threaten the Ameri-can way of life, the men of Delta are ready and eager to stop them—and stop them dead.

The Least You Need to Know

◆ Delta was created to combat the rising tide of international terrorism in the 1970s and 1980s.

◆ Although its first operation, Eagle Claw, ended in disaster, Delta regrouped and came back from the brink more formidable than before.

◆ Delta teams have served in the Middle East, Grenada, Panama, the Persian Gulf, Somalia, and Afghanistan.

◆ As international terrorists continue to threaten America, Delta's mission is even more urgent than before.

Chapter 20

The Delta Force Training Regimen

In This Chapter

- ◆ An invitation to join Delta
- ◆ The physical trials before training begins
- ◆ The Delta interview process
- ◆ Delta training

Only Army personnel qualify for Delta counterterrorism training. Even then, only a few meet the stringent mental, physical, psychological, and leadership qualifications necessary to join this elite unit.

Every year, over a hundred potential candidates are screened and tested. Only a few make it through the selection process, and others are weeded out during the rigorous and demanding training process. The few who manage to graduate into the ranks of the 1st Special Forces Operational Detachment-Delta will undoubtedly find themselves on the front lines of the covert life-and-death war against international terrorism. In this chapter, we'll explore the recruitment and training process that turns a promising candidate into a full-fledged member of America's premier antiterrorism force.

Who Joins Delta?

As a rule, nobody joins the 1st Special Forces Operational Detachment-Delta—Delta picks its recruits. If Delta members want a potential candidate to enter their close-knit (and tight-lipped) community, they will introduce themselves and ask the candidate to take the tough qualification course. Delta recruitment personnel travel to special forces training centers, troop posts, and staff college or NCO advance training centers to introduce prospective candidates to Delta and its mission. The recruitment drives precede Delta's scheduled assessment courses, and only the top students are invited in for a try.

Delta has rigid entry requirements but is open to officers and NCOs of the active-duty Army, Army Reserve, and Army National Guard—civilians cannot apply. The applicant must be no younger than 22 years old, a U.S. citizen, and male. Other requirements involve past military service and education; if a candidate can meet the stringent basic requirements, he will most likely get the opportunity to prove himself to the folks at Delta. Specially qualified candidates who possess a unique talent, skill, or training that is particularly needed receive a personal invitation to volunteer for the unit. Special language skills, particular ethnic origin, schools attended, and past military experience can all be assets. All applicants must pass a background check as a condition of admission to training. Records are checked for discipline problems, alcohol or drug abuse, and psychological abnormalities. The applicant receives a complete physical and an eye examination, followed by a battery of psychological, emotional, and stress tests.

Special Ops Jargon

The eye exam and physical that Delta candidates receive commonly are known as the **SCUBA/HALO** physical and resemble the thorough physical exams that aviators receive.

The Physical Trials

About 100 candidates enter the month-long physical and psychological testing process each year. Once the doctors give a candidate a thumbs-up, he must pass six grueling physical challenges within a designated period of time, including a 40-yard inverted crawl, usually under an obstacle, in under 25 seconds; 37 sit-ups in a minute; 35 push-ups in a minute; completion of a dodge-and-jump course in 25 seconds or less; a 2-mile run in 16 minutes; a 100-meter swim while fully clothed and booted; dashes; chin-ups; flutter kicks, and so on. This is followed by an 18-mile speed-march to test a candidate's endurance. And the instructors mean *speed*—a 10-minute mile or less!

By this point, the rigors of the selection process cause a few candidates who lack the right stuff to drop out. Those who survive travel for their next round of testing—the combination 40-mile speed-march, compass navigation course, and survival exercise. This round takes place at a site in the rugged terrain of Camp Dawson, West Virginia, or the even more inhospitable, arid geography around Nellis Air Force Base, Nevada.

When a candidate arrives at Camp Dawson or Nellis Air Force Base, he is handed a 50- or 60-pound rucksack packed with energy bars, MREs, gallons of water, maybe sun block for the skin or Vaseline to protect the lips, a compass, a map, some extra clothes, and very little else. Then he's escorted to a truck filled with the other wannabes. The truck drives the recruits into a remote area where, one by one, the candidates are ordered out. On the ground, they get a short list of spoken instructions and then are ordered to hike to a specific point on the map ASAP. Then they're left in the dust as the truck rumbles off. The land navigation test has begun.

The testing takes place on particularly inhospitable terrain, with hills, valleys, dry and filled creek and stream beds, thick woods, tangles of cacti, twists and turns in the landscape, and absolutely no roads. Gazing at the topographical map, the candidate must decide the best course to get from where he is to where he should be. After hours in driving rain, under a burning desert sun, or across miles of steep hills and deep valleys, he arrives at the map point, where an instructor hands him the coordinates of his next destination. Off the candidate goes, with no words of encouragement, to the next dot on the map—miles and miles away.

> **Shop Talk**
>
> The 40-mile land navigation test is really a psychological exam meant to put the maximum amount of mental pressure on the candidate. To succeed, the potential Delta member must proceed fearlessly and meet and beat every obstacle without knowing precisely what is expected of him.

This happens several times. At each destination, the candidate finds only more instructions. Finally, after over 24 hours of hard hiking, when a candidate is on the point of mental and physical exhaustion, he arrives at another mark on the map and is told that the examination is over. He does not know whether he passed or failed, only that he can rest. Perhaps a dozen or more of the original hundred will pass this mental and physical endurance and navigation test. Those who do will face an even harder exam—the interview.

The Interview

The interview has been described by past candidates as a four- to five-hour grilling by a board of Delta veterans to determine the suitability of the candidates. The board members have heard and seen it all and cannot be snowed—they smell baloney a mile away. And few human beings can keep the baloney flowing for five whole hours, while any and all types of questions are thrown at them in rapid succession. These questions have no right or wrong answers, but they are meant to give the board a sense of the individual as a whole—his values, education, military skills, potential to learn and grow, ability to handle himself in a crisis, and so on.

At the end of this long, rigorous process, only about 10 percent of the original candidates are accepted into the Delta training program. That's fine with the leaders of the 1st Special Operations Detachment-Delta because they emphasize the quality, not the quantity, of the personnel entering their unit.

> **Straight Shooting** _____
>
> The objective of the interview by a board of Delta veterans is to find a candidate who will both work well with a team and be capable of operating independently, taking sensible actions and making rational decisions without the benefit of instructions from a higher military authority.

Delta Training: Enter the SOT

Those who are accepted into Delta training begin the two-year education course at Fort Bragg's Special Operations Training facility (SOT), a multimillion-dollar military education complex that began operations in the mid-1980s. The facility's mission is to teach new methods and refine old techniques used in the fine art of counterterrorism. Candidates learn the distinct phases of a successful counterterrorism operation: insertion, preparation, and execution.

- *Insertion* simply means arriving at the scene of the terrorist attack. This sounds simpler than it is. Delta units must arrive at the scene in a timely fashion, even if the action takes place thousands of miles away in a foreign country. Political and cultural considerations may preclude direct action—these must be smoothed over or dealt with if the Delta team is to proceed with a "takedown" or apprehension. As the team moves into place, copious amounts of intelligence must be assembled, evaluated, and disseminated by supporting agencies or even foreign espionage and special operations units.

- During the *preparation* phase, a critical consensus must be reached. Who is in charge of the operation? In the critical period after a terrorist attack or hostage situation has begun, authorities don't have time to waste butting heads with competing federal agencies, intransigent local officials, or resistant foreign governments. During the preparation phase, target surveillance begins in earnest while command and control functions and facilities are established.

- In the *execution* phase, all the preparation and the intelligence comes together for the climax. Usually it is an assault of the objective, with the desired results being the capture or elimination of the terrorists, the safe return of any hostages, and the prevention of property damage.

The first stage of Delta training is meant to determine just where the potential candidate is likely to fit into these three phases. Usually the trainee has enough talent, brains, and past experience to fill a number of these roles—and he will be expected to do so as an active member of a Delta team. That past experience is important. A former Ranger with sniper skills might become a Delta sniper; a demolitions man might go into demolitions; and a good small-arms, hand-to-hand fighter might become a Delta team "door-kicker."

> **Shop Talk**
>
> Delta's arena is counterterrorism, not antiterrorism. *Antiterrorism* refers to the skills and methods used to prevent a terrorist attack—which, in extreme cases, may include the assassination of a potential terrorist. Delta goes into action only *after* the terrorist incident has already occurred—to *counter* the *terrorism.*

Changing Acquired Behavior

During SOT training, candidates are broken of some of the operational habits acquired in the other services. These habits may be fine in conventional combat situations, but are often detrimental to counterterrorism operations. Troopers learn various methods of entry, seizure, and exfiltration from a terrorist situation. They learn to rappel into high windows, to kick down a door or blow it off its hinges, to fast-rope out of a helicopter onto a roof and then fight their way through the building to the lower floors. Most important, they learn the methods and techniques of close-quarters fighting—a delicate business because the individual team members must know where their mates are or risk friendly fire casualties.

Troopers learn to pick their targets carefully and quickly and how to place a minimum of two shots into an eye-socket kill zone from up to 50 feet away. This type of shot, in which the Deltas aim for a "T" shaped area that encompasses the forehead down to the mouth, is known as the *double-tap*. Trainees learn how to secure an area, restrain everyone in the room with plastic flex-cuffs, and move on to the next target zone. During the classic "takedown," targets and hostages alike appear as a dull smudge in the smoke and confusion of the entry, which is usually preceded by a stun, flash/bang, or gas grenade.

During a takedown, Delta troopers wear a variety of modern, sophisticated body armor. Headgear is a matter of personal choice. A few Deltas chose to be protected by a black Kevlar "Fritz" helmet and flame-resistant balaclava—others prefer lightweight, unarmored Pro-Tech plastic hockey-style helmets. Delta members often wear a standard pilot's Nomex flight suit—either green or sand color, depending on the

Special Ops Jargon

The technique of shooting a terrorist in the eye socket with two rounds, from up to 50 feet, is known in the business of counterterrorism as the "**double tap**."

mission environment. These flight suits are ideal for Delta missions. They are light, flexible, and flame-resistant. Earphones and a microphone provide the trooper with instant tactical communication with command and the rest of the unit. Eye protection ranges from shatter-proof goggles to a protective chemical mask. Armored shorts to protect the groin, Gore-Tex boots, Kevlar vests, and dark Nomex coveralls complete the bulky outfit. Onto that uniform is strapped the general equipment required to accomplish the task, including flashlights, radio receivers, a variety of grenades, ammunition, first-aid equipment (a medical pouch), knives, and so on. The training includes instruction in numerous infiltration methods for moving into isolated target areas, including parachuting into the area using high-altitude, low-opening (HALO) and high-altitude, high-opening (HAHO) techniques. They learn to use scuba and SCBA gear, as well as miniature submersible vehicles for long-distance underwater travel. Rappelling and fast-roping out of helicopters is a basic skill, and Delta teams also learn to use various types of all-terrain fighting vehicles. Cross-training with Rangers, SEALs, SAS, and other foreign and domestic counterterrorism units is common. The goal is to produce a well-rounded trainee who can operate under many conditions.

Assault on the "Killing House"

An integral part of a Delta team member's training involves repeated assaults on a field exercise complex built in the middle of the SOT complex. This facility is dubbed "the Killing House." It is here that simulated attacks are carried out in head-to-toe body armor—even on the hottest, most uncomfortable North Carolina days. Troopers carry a special-purpose Mossberg automatic shotgun or a 9-mm Heckler & Koch MP5 submachine gun—a weapon used by most of the counterterrorism forces of the world. More recently, the MP5 has been replaced by the M-4A1 M16 carbine in the SOPMOD—Special Operations Peculiar Modification—configuration. Indeed, many weapons and equipment manufacturers clamor to equip Delta members in the same way that athletic attire and sneaker companies try to outfit professional sports stars—and as with pro-athletes, these "perks" often come free of charge.

Each assault on the Killing House is different. The rooms are crowded with furniture, and mannequins and pop-up targets substitute for bad guys and hostages. The hostages, the bad guys, the furniture, and even some of the walls and doors are moved so that no two assaults are similar and the Delta trainees can't resort to habit to accomplish their "mission." Following assault after assault, shoulders, knees, elbows, shins, and faces are bruised and battered, and ears are ringing from the noise of flash grenades and blank rounds. During a Killing House assault, each individual unit member is taken through the paces and then repeats his actions. Later, roles are reversed or switched so that each trooper can meet the mission requirements of the man next to him, in case that Delta member should fall in combat. Instructors often play the role of terrorists, wielding the bad guys' weapon of choice, an AK-47.

Delta teams have mere seconds to carry out a successful takedown, and they learn quick methods to neutralize an area. After the action is over, troopers are taught how to be debriefed and how to file detailed after-action reports. These reports must be accurate because, in a real-world situation, they may be used for evidence in a future trial. During Killing House training, troopers are taught not to shoot indiscriminately or fire from the hip. Each shot must be taken with care and judgment—and with accuracy. Delta members learn quickly how to fire and move, drop to a crouch, and then fire again.

The training continues for two solid years. Much of what Delta team members learn is still highly classified, and one can only imagine what candidates experience during the long, complex, and rigorous training regimen. What we do know is that at the end of the long tunnel trainees emerge transformed into modern, technological warriors skilled in the techniques required of a modern counterterrorist operative.

The Least You Need to Know

- The 1st Special Operational Detachment-Delta is the premier counterterrorism unit in the American armed services.

- Delta candidates are recruited from active-duty U.S. Army, U.S. Army Reserve, and National Guard units.

- Before a candidate can begin Delta training, he is carefully screened, psychologically tested, physically challenged, and subjected to a thorough background check.

- It takes two years of rigorous training at the special operations training facility to produce an active-duty Delta team member.

Special Forces Weapons

The task of America's elite special operations forces is, to put it simply, to kill people and break things. To accomplish these objectives, unconventional warfare specialists employ a vast array of firearms, equipment, explosives, and vehicles. This appendix takes a closer look at some of the weapons, equipment, and explosives, currently in general use by the U.S. Special Operations Command.

A Word About Terminology

First, let's get the terminology right. A rifle is a weapon; a gun is—something else. It's something that has little to do with combat, at least according to military jargon. Infantrymen carry *rifles*—not guns—into combat. Of course, they may also carry a submachine gun, a light machine gun, a squad automatic weapon, a Light Antitank Weapon (LAW), or a wide array of other weapons, but never a gun. Any soldier who doesn't learn the difference quickly will find himself repeatedly running around the jogging track, clutching his military weapon in one hand and his private parts in another while constantly reciting, "This is my rifle, this is my gun, one I use to kill with, the other to have fun," or some variation of that popular training ditty.

Of all his personal weapons, an infantryman will rely on his personal firearm more than any other piece of military equipment. The men of special warfare are no different. Individual weapons—rifles, machine guns, mortars—are used to engage hostile forces. However, before that can happen, recruits to the conventional armed forces and candidates for special operations units must become proficient in a wide array of modern weapons. That proficiency comes from training, and that's where MILES comes in.

The Military Integrated Laser Engagement System (MILES) is used with M16s and M60 rifles in training exercises. One part of this unit fits on the front of the gun barrel; the other is worn by the recruit. When the rifle fires a blank, the laser designator is activated. If the weapon is aimed properly, the laser on the opposing soldier beeps, signaling that he is a casualty. More than one hit, and he's battlefield dead. MILES is Laser Tag, with a purpose. The system is a valuable training tool but will not work accurately in deep foliage or in smoke and fog.

The M16 Combat Rifle

The most common weapon in the arsenal of the United States and its allies is the *M16* combat rifle, now in its fourth decade of service. Since the Vietnam era, the M16 has been the basic weapon of all branches of the U.S. Army—and perhaps the most recognizable symbol of America's military might. The current model in service is the *M16A2*. Built by Colt Manufacturing in Hartford, Connecticut, and licensed for production around the world, this new model has been modified since the Vietnam-era prototypes, which had a failure-to-feed problem that cost the lives of more than a few soldiers fighting in Vietnam. The M16A2 weighs in at nearly 8 pounds when empty. It uses 5.56-mm ammunition (NATO-compatible) and can be fitted with a bayonet and a variety of scopes.

The current special operation forces version of the M16A2 is the *M4A1 (CAR-15)*, which is basically an M16 with a collapsible metal tub stock, a shorter barrel, and a modified sight deck. The M4A1 is lighter (5.7 pounds unloaded) and shorter, but it fires the same basic ammunition. It is accurate up to 460 meters. Like the standard model, the M4A1 has selectable semiautomatic and an automatic three-shot "burst mode" (but not the full-auto feature of the original M16 models), has a 30-round magazine, and fits a number of special forces add-ons, such as the *M203* 40-mm grenade launcher, a family of low-light and thermal imager systems, and laser-pointing and sighting devices. It can even fit a sound suppressor. This weapon has proven its worth on the battlefield and on special operations teams. The M4A1 is used widely by every special forces group. The CAR-15 comes complete with a shotgun under the main muzzle.

A favored night vision system is the AN/PVS-4 Night Vision Individual Weapons Sight—a second-generation starlight sighting system that can be hand-held for night observation, but can also be mounted on the M14 and M16 rifles, the M60 machine gun, and the M72A2 Light Antitank Weapon (LAW).

Grenade Launchers

A favorite add-on for the M4A1 is the Colt *M203 Grenade Launcher*. The M203 isn't much more than a short aluminum tube with a breech block and trigger assembly. The

M203 bolts onto an M16/M4A1 under the barrel and can fire a 40-mm cartridge with one of several "warheads." The trajectory of the grenade launcher allows the user to lob a grenade over a barrier, and it is accurate to within 200 to 300 meters. Cartridges include the high-explosive (HE) antipersonnel round, illumination rounds to light up the battle-field, tear gas, deadly white phosphorus, and flachette rounds.

Another type of grenade launcher is less portable but more deadly. The *Mark 19, 40-mm Grenade Launcher* is a heavy-weapon version of the M203, used for base security and on boats. Because of its incredible firepower, this fully automatic, rapid-fire grenade launcher is used by all branches of the U.S. military and special warfare groups today. Capable of firing over 60 rounds per minute of high-explosive white phosphorous, tear gas, illumination, or high-explosive dual-purpose (HEDP) rounds, this weapon can quite literally blanket an area with 40-mm grenades.

The U.S. Army Rangers continue to use the *M67 90-mm Recoilless Rifle*, an older weapon abandoned by every other conventional and special operations force. The Rangers are vir-tually the only unit in the U.S. military still using the reliable M67 in combat.

Rifles

Rifles used exclusively by special warfare units include the *Haskins .50-caliber Sniper Rifle* and the *M24 Sniper Rifle*. The Haskins, which can kill an enemy with a single shot at ranges of over a half mile or more, has a tremendous recoil that is only partially absorbed by twin hydraulic shock absorbers built into the stock. It is almost always used with a special tele-scopic, thermal, infrared, or laser sight. It weighs about 20 pounds and is a single-shot, bolt-action weapon used mostly with a bipod. The cartridge is a half inch long and flies far and accurately to its target. Delta uses the heavy-barreled *40XB Sniper Rifle*, which is specially manufactured for Delta by Remington Arms.

The *M24 Sniper Weapons System* (SWS) was introduced in 1988 as a replacement for the old M21 sniper rifle. Based on the Remington 700 Sniper Rifle, the M24 has an aluminum/fiberglass/Kevlar composite bed and stock, and it fires the M118 Special Ball round. The M24 SWS is equipped with a 10 × 24 Leopold M3 Ultra scope. In recent years, the *M82A1 Barretts* have been issued to some Army Special Forces teams.

The *Stoner SR-25* is a semiautomatic 7.62-mm rifle that can deliver a round out to 1,000 yards with total accuracy. Built by Knight Manufacturing Company, the SR-25 looks and feels like an M16—on purpose, as it turns out. Designed by Eugene Stoner, the design genius behind the original Armalite AR-15, which spawned the M16 family of military rifles, the SR-25 uses many of the same spare parts as the M16. It includes a scope-mounting rail and can mount a sound suppressor.

Shotguns are employed by America's special warfare units for a variety of situations, usually associated with forced-entry techniques. SEAL teams use them on point, and Delta uses them for quick access through locked barriers. Twelve-gauge rifle slugs are used, but the twelve-gauge "sabot" slug allows for deeper penetration of the target and can be employed against vehicles or aircraft engines as well as in forced-entry engagements.

The M9 Baretta

The M9 Baretta 9-mm pistol is the sidearm of choice, especially for special forces units, which really need a good, easy-to-maintain, and reliable semiautomatic pistol. The M9 is compact and light and can easily be concealed—a real plus in unconventional warfare scenarios. Virtually every member of America's special forces command is issued a *9-mm M9 Baretta Model 92F*. In service for more than 10 years, the M9 replaced the sturdy Browning .45-caliber, which saw military service for over 80 years and is still the handgun of choice for Delta teams. The M9 comes equipped with a 15-round magazine and uses a double-action trigger mechanism. It is an excellent general-purpose firearm.

In August 1991, Heckler and Koch and Colt Manufacturing were awarded contracts to develop an offensive handgun weapon system (OHWS) for exclusive use by the USSO-COM. It was to consist of three components: a .45-caliber pistol; a laser-aiming module, and a sound and flash suppressor. After 30 or more prototypes were developed, the final contract went to Heckler and Koch in January 1994. The result was the *Heckler & Koch MK23* pistol, referred to as the *Special Operation Forces Offensive Handgun*. This weapon has an effective recoil-reduction system that reduced overall recoil by 40 percent. It contains a 12-round magazine, a barrel that is threaded to accept attachments such as the *.45-Caliber Suppressor* manufactured by Knight Armament Company—called the "KAC sound suppressor" by special operations units—and a decocking lever that allows the hammer to be lowered quietly, a great feature for covert operations.

The MK23 frame has groves to attach the *ITI LAM* scope. The ITI LAM contains visible and infrared lasers for aiming, as well as an infrared illuminator and a lamp for visible white light. It is easy to operate and offers a range of capabilities not available with any other night-vision device of its size and compactness.

Submachine Guns

When the mission parameters call for smaller, lighter weapons with good stopping power for close-quarters fighting, special warfare units prefer the *Heckler and Koch MP5* family of submachine guns. The MP5 is simple to use and quite accurate—the result of a fixed barrel that is cold-forged with the cartridge chamber. The recoil is smooth, allowing for easy use. The MP5 is an automatic weapon firing from a closed bolt. The weapon fires a

9-mm Parabellum pistol round, carried in a 30-round magazine with dual-magazine capability. Modes of fire include sustained (firing as long as the trigger is suppressed), semi-automatic (single shot each time the trigger is pulled), and three-round burst. The MP5 is the weapon of choice for the U.S. Navy SEALs, Delta, the British SAS, Air Force Special Operations Command, and the U.S. Army Special Forces. It weighs just 9 pounds loaded, and a little over 7 pounds empty. The *MP5-SD3* model comes with an effective sound-suppression system.

Squad Automatic Weapons

When you want to saturate the target with munitions, there is nothing better than a squad automatic weapon (SAW). The special operations forces of the United States have adopted the conventional military's standard light machine gun, the *M249 5.56-mm Squad Automatic Weapon* (SAW). The M249 weighs only 22 pounds and fires the same 5.56-mm ammunition as the M16A2, the M4, and other NATO weapons. It can fire the ammunition from a feeder belt, the M16/M4 30-round magazine, or a 200-round plastic box magazine. The weapon can be loaded from either the right or left sides for easy positioning in tight places. A single gunner can operate the M249, firing from the ground using the bipod or while standing. This weapon can also be mounted on a HMMWV (Hummer). It lacks the stopping and penetration power of heavier machine guns and is ineffective against light unarmored vehicles, thick walls, or even sandbag emplacements. But a new generation of 5.56-mm sabot cartridges may solve this problem.

The *M24G 7.62-mm Light Machine Gun* is a heavier machine gun—topping off at nearly 25 pounds—that is used by special operations units for forward base protection and security strong points, although this weapon is normally mounted on a HMMWV. The M24G fires the 7.62-mm cartridge, which has a longer range and stopping power than the lighter 5.56-mm round found in most NATO weapons. The drawback is that it is not as easily man-portable, and it takes two men to operate it efficiently. Older machine guns such as the M60 are also used by America's special forces, but in recent years this reliable weapon has been utilized primarily in special operations training.

Grenades and Demolitions

Despite what we've all seen in the movies, modern high-explosive materials are safe and easy to handle. Old-fashioned *dynamite* (nitroglycerine and gun cotton) was volatile and tended to leak nitroglycerine, but *TNT* (or a basic mixture of fuel oil and fertilizer) is both safe and effective for demolitions work.

C-4, the first of the famous "plastic explosives," looks like Silly Putty but has a kick. You can shape it with your fingers in perfect safety because it is not dangerous until a blasting cap is attached to it and activated—then watch out.

Primacord (detonation cord, or simply "det" cord) is a material that looks like a fuse or a flexible plastic-like rope, but it contains high explosive PETN and is used to connect main charges. The cord is set off with a blasting cap or another charge, and it explodes at a linear rate of about 4 miles per second—quite handy for making a lot of little charges blow up at the same time.

Blasting caps come in two types: electric and fused. Both are little tubes of aluminum or copper filled with a three-stage mixture of specialized explosives, an ignition charge, a priming charge, and a base charge. Blasting caps are very dangerous to handle and can go off if not treated with respect.

One explosive favored by the U.S. military is the *M18A1 Claymore mine*, which really isn't a mine at all. Developed in the Vietnam era, the Claymore is a simple package of C-4 explosive and a few hundred little steel ball bearings. Fitted with an electric blasting cap, a Claymore detonates and sends the metal balls flying in the general direction of the bad guys, with devastating results. Used especially to defend temporary positions, the Claymore is not buried like a conventional mine. It is set up on the ground, in a tree, or anywhere it is needed with little metal legs, with the business end facing the enemy.

Hand grenades have evolved considerably from the old World War II–era "pineapples," as the Mk II fragmentation grenade was called by front-line troops. Though the old Mk II was efficient and lethal, their unique "pineapple" shape caused them to roll in unpredictable directions--sometimes back at the person who tossed it! Today's round and flat-sided grenades can be rolled across the floor with a reasonable degree of accuracy, and they come in a dozen different "flavors"—nonlethal types such as gas (usually tear gas, used in hostage-taking situations), smoke (in many colors, used primarily to signal or mark a landing zone), and flash/bang grenades (concussion/stun) that make a bright flash and a lot of noise to shock the enemy but do not usually kill. Lethal varieties include incendiary and white phosphorous grenades and the most common grenade in the U.S. military arsenal, the *M67* fragmentation grenade.

Airborne Drones

Advanced reconnaissance is still the surest way to avoid sending a force into a death trap. Special operations forces employ many tactics to scope out the battlefield ahead of insertion—deep reconnaissance, reconnaissance in force, and direct action reconnaissance are all effective, but they all involve putting troops in harm's way.

A new reconnaissance resource is the pilotless drone. Carrying sophisticated cameras, radar, and, in some cases, missiles, these drones are controlled by operators hundreds of miles away, far in the sky and out of antiaircraft missile range.

The U.S. Special Operations Command employs three types of pilotless drones. The *Predator* is the most common model. Flying slow and low, the Predator carries a radar system able to detect objects as small as 4 inches across from up to 15 miles away.

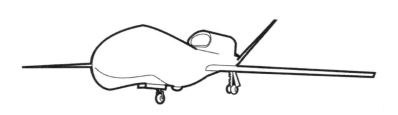

Predator drone.

The *Gnat* is a tiny drone that carries a high-resolution radar system and can remain aloft for up to 48 hours.

The *Global Hawk* is the most sophisticated drone presently in use. Able to stay aloft at about 60,000 feet for up to 24 hours, the Global Hawk also contains still-classified avionics, surveillance, and radar packages, and a de-icing system for its wings. This drone was first deployed in Afghanistan.

With an arsenal of sophisticated weapons systems at their disposal, the men of the United States Special Operations Command can deal with any combat situation at any time, any place on the globe.

B

Guide to Military Acronyms

ACG   Air Commando Group

AFSOC   Air Force Special Operations Command

ALICE   All-Purpose Light Individual Carrying Equipment field pack

ALLTV   All Light Level Television

ANG   Army National Guard

ARCS   Air Resupply and Communications Service

ARG   Amphibious-Ready Group

ARVN   Army of the Republic of Vietnam

ATV   All-terrain vehicle

BAC   Basic Airborne Course

BDU   Battle dress uniform

BMC   Battle management center

BUD/S   Basic Underwater Demolition/SEALs

CA   Civilian Affairs

CAC   Close air support

CBT   Combating terrorism

CCT   Combat control team

CCTS   Combat Crew Training Squadron

CD   Counterdrug operations

CENTCOM   U.S. Central Command

CINSOC   Commander-in-Chief, U.S. Special Operations Command

CONUS   Continental United States (48 contiguous states)

CP   Counterproliferation

CRD   Chemical Reconnaissance Detachments

CRRC   Combat Rubber Raiding Craft

CSAR   Combat search and rescue

CST   Close Support Team

CT   Counterterrorism

DA   Direct action

DDS   Dry deck shelter

DLI   Defense Language Institute

DZ   Drop zone

E&E   Escape and evasion

EC   Electronic countermeasures

ECWCS   Extended Cold Weather Clothing System

EP   Emergency procedure

EUCOM   U.S. European Command

EW   Electronic warfare

FAC   Forward air controller

FID   Foreign internal defense

FLIR   Forward-looking infrared radar

FOB   Forward operation base

GMV   Ground mobility vehicle

GPS   Global positioning system

HA   Humanitarian assistance

HAHO   High-altitude, high-opening parachute jump

HALO   High-altitude, low-opening parachute jump

HD   Humanitarian demining

HEEDS   Helicopter Emergency Egress Device System

HMMWV   High Mobility Multipurpose Wheeled Vehicle ("Hummer")

HSB   High-speed boat

IDAS/MATTS   Interactive Defensive Avionics System/Multi-Mission Advanced Tactical Terminal

IDP   Internally displaced person (refugee)

IFAM   Initial familiarization

INS   Inertial Navigation System

JCS   Joint Chiefs of Staff

JRTC   Joint Readiness Training Center

JSOC   Joint Special Operations Command

LDNN   Lien Doi Nguoi Nhai (Vietnamese navy demolition teams)

LIA   Laser Illuminator Assembly

LRP   Long-range patrol

LZ   Landing zone

MATC   Mini-Armored Troop Carrier

MATS   Military Air Transport Service

MERC   Mobility Enhancing Rational Components

MFF   Military Free Fall parachute jump

MILES   Multiple Integrated Laser Exercise System

MOUT   Military operations in urban terrain

MRE   Meals, ready to eat

NAVSPECWARCOM   Navy Special Warfare Command

NAVSPECWARDGRU   Navy Special Warfare Development Group

NCDU   Naval Combat Demolition Unit

NTC   National Training Center

ODA   Operational Detachment Alpha

ODB   Operational Detachment Bravo

OL-H   Air Force Special Operations Indoctrination Course, or "Operations Location–Hotel"

PACOM   U.S. Pacific Command

PASGT   Personal Armor System, Ground Troops

PAST   Physical Abilities and Stamina Test

PAVN   People's Army of North Vietnam

PBL   Patrol boat, light

PBR   Patrol boat, river

PERC   Performance-enhancing ration component

PJ   Pararescue jumper

PLF   Parachute landing fall

PRTS   Parachutist Rough Terrain System

PSYOPS   Psychological operations

PT   Physical training

RAPCON   Radar Approach Control Procedures

RAPS   Ram-Air Parachute System

REDS   Rapid Extraction Deployment System

RIB   Rigid inflatable boat

ROE   Rules of engagement

RRF   Ranger Ready Force

RSSZ   Rung Sat Special Zone

SAC   Strategic Air Command

SAW   Squad automatic weapon

SAWC   Special Air Warfare Center

SBS   Special Boat Squadrons

SCBA   Self-contained breathing apparatus

SCUBA   Self-contained underwater breathing apparatus

SDV   Swimmer Delivery Vehicle

SEAL   Sea, Air, Land

SERE   Survival, Evasion, Resistance, and Escape

SFAS   Special Forces Assessment and Selection

SFG   Special Forces Group

SOCCE   Special Operations Command and Control Element

SOCCENT   Special Operations Command, Central

SOCEUR   Special Operations Command, Europe

SOCKOR   Special Operations Command U.S. Forces Korea

SOCOM   U.S. Special Forces Command

SOCPAC   Special Operations Command, Pacific

SOCSOUTH   Special Operations Command, South

SOF   Special Operations Force

SOFLAM   Special Operations Force Laser Acquisition Marker

SOPMOD   Special Operations Modifications

SOT   Special Operations Training facility

SOTAC   Special Operations Tactical Air Control

SOUTHCOM   U.S. Southern Command

SPECWARCOM   Special Warfare Command

SR   Special reconnaissance

STS   Special Tactical Squadron

STT   Special Tactical Team

SVD   Russian Dragonov sniper rifle

TEL   Transporter Erector Launcher

TFR   Terrain-following radar

TRANSCOM   U.S. Transportation Command

UAV   Unmanned aerial vehicle

USASOC   U.S. Army Special Operations Command

UX   Unconventional warfare

UXO   Unexploded ordinance

VFR   Visual Flight Rules

WMD   Weapons of mass destruction

Further Reading and Viewing

This appendix provides a sampling of books and films about special warfare operations and special operations forces.

Nonfiction

Ambrose, Stephen E. *D-Day*. New York: Simon & Schuster, 1994.

————. *Band of Brothers*. New York: Simon & Schuster, 1989.

Atkinson, Rick. *Crusade: The Untold Story of the Persian Gulf War*. New York: Houghton Mifflin, 1993.

Bank, Col. Aaron (Ret.) *From OSS to the Green Berets: The Birth of Special Forces*. Novato: Presidio Press, 1986.

Beckwith, Col. Charlie A. (Ret.), with Donald Knox. *Delta Force: The Army's Elite Counter-Terrorism Unit*. Novato: Presidio, 1983.

Bohrer, David. *America's Special Forces: Weapons, Missions, Training*. Wisconsin: Motorbooks International, 1998.

Bowden, Mark. *Black Hawk Down: A Story of Modern War*. New York: Penguin Books, 1999.

Clancy, Tom, with John D. Gresham. *Airborne: A Guided Tour of an Airborne Task Force*. New York: Berkley Books, 1997.

———. *Special Forces: A Guided Tour of U.S. Army Special Forces.* New York: Berkley Books, 2001.

Clansy, Tom, with Gen. Carl Stiner (U.S. Army, Ret.) and Tony Koltz. *Shadow Warriors: Inside the Special Forces.* New York: Putnam, 2002.

Dooley, George E. *Battle for the Central Highlands: A Special Forces Story.* New York: Random House, 2000.

Garner, Sgt. Maj. Joe R., with Avrum M. Fine. *Code Name: Copperhead.* New York: Simon & Schuster, 1994.

Griswald, Terry, and D. M. Giangreco. *Delta.* Wisconsin: Motorbooks International, 1992.

Halberstadt, Hans. *U.S. Navy SEALs.* Wisconsin: Motor Books International, 1993.

Kessler, Ronald. *Inside the CIA.* New York: Simon & Schuster, 1992.

LaBarge, Lieut. Comm. William H., USN. *Desert Voices: Personal Testimony from Gulf War Heroes.* New York: HarperCollins, 1991.

Landau, Alan M., and Frieda W. Landau. *Airborne Rangers.* Wisconsin: Motorbooks International, 2000.

Lewis, Jon E. *True Stories of the Elite Forces.* London: Carroll and Graf, 1993.

Livingstone, Neil C. *Rescue My Child.* New York: Simon & Schuster, 1992.

Marcinko, Richard, with John Weisman. *Rogue Warrior.* New York: Simon & Schuster, 1992.

Marquis, Susan L. *Unconventional Warfare: Rebuilding U.S. Special Operations Forces* (The Rediscovering Government Series). Washington, D.C.: Brookings Institute, 1997.

McRaven, William H. *Spec Ops: Case Studies in Special Operations Warfare, Theory and Practice.* Novato: Presidio Press (Reissue), 1998.

Murphy, Edward D. *Heroes of World War II.* Novato: Presidio Press, 1990.

———. *Korean War Heroes.* Novato: Presidio Press, 1992.

———. *Vietnam Medal of Honor Heroes.* Novato: Presidio Books, 1994.

Pushies, Fred J. *U.S. Air Force Special Ops.* Wisconsin: Motor Books International, 2000.

——— *U.S. Army Special Forces.* Wisconsin: Motor Books International, 2001.

Santoni, Al. *Everything We Had.* New York: Random House, 1983.

Stubblefield, Gary, and Hans Halberstadt. *Inside the Navy SEALs.* Wisconsin: Motor Books International, 1995.

Walker, Greg. *At the Hurricane's Eye: U.S. Special Forces from Vietnam to Desert Storm.* New York: Ivy Books (Reissue), 1994.

Waller, Douglas C. *The Commandos: The Inside Story of America's Secret Soldiers.* New York: Dell (Reissue), 1995.

Encyclopedias and Reference Books

Chambers, John Whiteclay II, editor-in-chief. *The Oxford Companion to American Military History.* Oxford: Oxford University Press, 1999.

Crawford, Steve, Editor. *The SAS Encyclopedia.* Miami: Lewis International Incorporated. 1998.

Dunnigan, James F., and Albert A. Nofi. *The Pacific War Encyclopedia.* New York: Checkmark Books, 1998.

Farwell, Byron. *The Encyclopedia of Nineteenth-Century Land Warfare.* New York: W. W. Norton and Company, 2001.

Holmes, Richard. *The Oxford Companion to Military History.* Oxford: Oxford University Press, 2001.

Lang, George M. H., Raymond L. Collins, and Gerard F. White. *Medal of Honor Recipients, 1863–1994*, two volumes. New York: Facts on File, 1995.

Laur, Col. Timothy M., and Steven L. Llanso. *Encyclopedia of Modern U.S. Military Weapons.* Edited by Walter J. Boyne. New York: Berkley Books, 1995.

Library of America. *Reporting World War II, Part One: American Journalism 1938–1944.* New York: Library of America, 1995.

————. *Reporting World War II, Part Two: American Journalism 1944–1946*. New York: Library of America, 1995.

————. *Reporting Vietnam, Part One: American Journalism 1959–1969*. New York: Library of America, 1998.

————. *Reporting Vietnam, Part Two: American Journalism 1969–1971*. New York: Library of America, 1998.

Special Forces Handbook. Boulder: Palladin Press, 1965.

Special Forces Operational Techniques, Department of the Army Field Manual. Boulder: Palladin Press, 1965.

Taylor, James, and Warren Shaw. *Dictionary of the Third Reich*. London: Penguin Books, 1997.

Tucker, Spencer C., editor. *Encyclopedia of the Vietnam War*. Oxford: Oxford University Press, 2000.

Further Viewing

Air America (1990). Directed by Roger Spottiswood. Mel Gibson, Robert Downey Jr., Nancy Travis. Fictional exploits based on the CIA smuggling flights in and out of Laos during the Vietnam War. Mediocre.

Apocalypse Now/Apocalypse Now Redux (1979/2001). Directed by Francis Ford Coppola. Marlon Brando, Martin Sheen, Robert Duvall, Laurence Fishburne, Dennis Hopper, Harrison Ford. Though an undeniable classic in both its original form and the new, reissued "director's cut," this film uniformly (and stereotypically) portrays Vietnam-era Army Special Forces officers as unbalanced psychopaths. From Sheen's "Willard," who goes wild during a solo drinking binge in a Saigon hotel room while "waiting for a mission"; to Brando's mad "Colonel Kurtz," who leads his Montagnard army on a personal campaign against the Viet Cong, the Green Berets here are all bloody-minded killers itching for combat. Even more regrettable is the manner in which director Coppola, actor Robert Duvall, and screenwriter John Milius (who should have known better) portray the Air Cavalry. Though this film is a true classic, do not view it for a realistic portrayal of the U.S. Special Forces in *any* war!

Black Hawk Down (2001). Directed by Ridley Scott. Josh Hartnet, Ewan McGregor, Eric Sena, Sam Shepherd. Perhaps the finest depiction of America's Special Operations Forces ever filmed. Superb.

The Cockleshell Heroes (1955). Directed by José Ferrer. José Ferrer, Trevor Howard, Dora Bryan. Lifeless tale of the British Special Boat Service in World War II. Mediocre.

The Deer Hunter (1978). Directed by Michael Cimino. Robert De Niro, Christopher Walken, Meryl Streep. Powerful, elegiac, epic war film about three western Pennsylvania youths who go to Vietnam for "one good fight." Notable here because of the use of a Green Beret soldier as an almost medieval symbol of the grim reaper. He appears at a wedding party, with dire consequences for the groom. A masterpiece.

The Delta Force (1986). Directed by Menachem Golan. Chuck Norris, Lee Marvin, Joey Bishop. Fatal combination of Menachem Golan and Chuck Norris spells doom for this shoddy, violent, pointless comic-book adventure. Spawned several sequels, which are even worse. Abysmal.

Dogs of War (1980). Directed by John Irvin. Adapted from the novel by Frederick Forsyth. Christopher Walken, Tom Berenger, JoBeth Williams. Tense, moody, and violent, this film outlines, step by step, the way ex-Special Operations Forces turned mercenary plan, mount, and execute a military assault in an African hellhole. Excellent.

First Blood (1982). Directed by Ted Kotcheff. Sylvester Stallone, Brian Dennehy, Richard Crenna. Overly sensitive ex–Green Beret John Rambo, trying to shake the horrors of Vietnam, is persecuted by a rural sheriff with tragic consequences. Needless to say, this film didn't help redeem the reputation of Vietnam-era Green Berets. Two sequels (listed later). Mediocre.

The Frogmen (1951). Directed by Lloyd Bacon. Richard Widmark, Dana Andrews, Gary Merrill. Tense and realistic drama about the Navy's Underwater Demolition Teams in the Pacific Theater of World War II. Very good.

The Green Berets (1967). Directed by John Wayne and Ray Kellogg. Starring John Wayne, David Janssen, Jim Hutton, and Aldo Ray. Love it or hate it, a fairly realistic portrayal of Green Beret activities in Vietnam. Hokey dialogue and unrealistic scenery (Georgia swamps substitute for Vietnam) mar an otherwise interesting, gung-ho war epic. Mediocre.

The Lost Battalion (2001). Directed by Russell Mulcahy. Ric Schroder, Phil McKee, Jamie Harris. Powerful drama based on the true story of a unit from the 77th U.S.

Division, American Expeditionary Force, that was surrounded and repeatedly attacked by German troops in World War I. Notable here for its depiction of General Ludendorff's fierce *Sturmtruppen* (storm troopers). Very good.

Merrill's Marauders (1962). Directed by Sam Fuller. Jeff Chandler, Ty Hardin, Andrew Duggan. Gritty, fairly realistic war film from tough-guy director Fuller, highlighting the exploits of the famed Special Operations jungle fighters of World War II. Jeff Chandler, in his final role, plays Brig. Gen. Frank Merrill. Very good.

Navy SEALs (1990). Directed by Lewis Teague. Michel Biehn, Charlie Sheen, Joanne Whalley-Kilmer. Interesting film about the modern Navy SEALs on a mission in Beirut. While the characters are strictly one-dimensional, this film offers a glimpse inside the workings of a SEAL team. Good.

Proof of Life (2000). Directed by Bruce Beresford. Russell Crowe, Meg Ryan, David Morse. Sturdy ex–Special Air Service commando Crowe helps Ryan recover her husband, an engineer kidnapped by South American narco-thugs. Plausible drama about hostage rescue marred by mawkish love-story-that-isn't between Crowe and Ryan. Fair.

Rambo: First Blood, Part II (1985). Directed by George P. Cosmatos, from a script by James Cameron. Sylvester Stallone, Richard Crenna, Charles Napier. Rambo returns to Vietnam, with predictable results. One of the first Vietnam War revisionist films. If only the government suits had unleashed Rambo! Fair.

Rambo III (1988). Directed by Peter MacDonald. Sylvester Stallone, Richard Crenna, Kurtwood Smith. Ex–Green Beret Rambo goes to Afghanistan to help freedom-loving Muslims battle the evil Soviet oppressors. Oops! This comic-book adventure portrays the now-defunct Soviet Union as an evil empire—complete with *Star Wars*–like music and HIND helicopters buzzing around like TIE fighters. Silly, but surprisingly good fun.

Glossary

1st Air Commando Group America's first modern Air Force Special Operations unit, established in World War II to support British forces fighting the Japanese in Burma, India, and China. This unit was followed by the 2nd and 3rd Air Command Groups.

1st Ranger Battalion America's first modern special forces unit, which began training in June 1942 in Carrickfergus, Northern Ireland.

1st Special Services Force (FSSF) Joint American and Canadian airborne unit in World War II, also known as the Devil's Brigade. This unit was created at the insistence of Winston Churchill.

160th Special Operations Aviation Regiment (SOAR) The "Nightstalkers." The most secretive and technologically advanced unit of the Army's Special Forces, SOAR provides aviation support for Special Forces teams, inserting SF units by air into their theaters of operation; night or day and in any kind of weather.

Abrams, Gen. Creighton Commander of all U.S. forces in Vietnam, and opponent of the Army's Special Forces. Abrams used the Rheault incident as an excuse to kick the 5th Special Forces Group out of Vietnam in 1971.

Abwehr German military intelligence in World War II. The *Abwehr* was divided into three branches. *Abwehr* I handled espionage and intelligence, *Abwehr* II controlled special operations, and *Abwehr* III dealt with counter-intelligence.

AC-130 "Specter" gunship   Armed version of the Lockheed C-130, four-engine transport airplane flown by the Air Force Special Operations Squadrons. The Specter is equipped with night-targeting sensors and a mix of heavy weapons, including a Bofors cannon and a "Gatling" machine gun.

after-action review (AAR)   Group assessment and evaluation of a special operation after the mission is complete.

Air Force Special Operations Command (AFSOC)   Based at Eglin Air Force Base, Florida, AFSOC is composed of helicopter and transport aircraft units. Its primary mission is to transport special operations units from other commands to their areas of operation and to provide resupply and support operations.

Air Resupply and Communications Service (ARCS)   Created in February 1951, ARCS was primarily responsible for Air Force covert operations during the Korean conflict—or, in the jargon of the era, "special air missions."

American Brigades   Nazi troops who dressed as American soldiers to infiltrate American lines during the Ardennes Offensive of 1944.

Apache Force   Combined force of U.S. Army Special Forces men and indigenous troops who performed advanced reconnaissance, and helped orient American or South Vietnamese entering a new combat area.

Army of the Republic of Vietnam (ARVN)   The armed forces of South Vietnam, America's ally in the Vietnam War.

Bank, Col. Aaron   U.S. Army officer and veteran of the OSS units of World War II who championed the creation of American Special Forces units after the war. When the first American Special Forces units were formed at Fort Bragg in the early 1950s, it was Colonel Bank who trained and commanded them.

Basic Airborne Course   Three weeks of parachute jump school instruction designed to make special forces personnel airborne-qualified. BAC is taught at Fort Benning, Georgia.

Basic Underwater Demolition/SEALs (BUD/S)   A tough, physically and mentally challenging training program that candidates must complete to join the Navy's Sea, Air, Land (SEAL) teams.

Bay of Pigs Invasion   On April 17, 1961, Cuban exiles supplied and trained by the CIA landed in La Bahia de Conchinos (the Bay of Pigs) on Cuba's southern coast in a futile attempt to overthrow dictator Fidel Castro. Members of the invasion force were annihilated or captured in the worst intelligence failure in American history.

Beckwith, Col. Charles "Chargin' Charlie"   U.S. Army officer who spearheaded the creation of the 1st Special Operational Detachment (Delta) and was the unit's first commander.

black budget   Secret funding to pay for intelligence.

Blackburn, Brig. Gen. Donald D.   Planner behind the Son Tay raid during the Vietnam War. Blackburn trained Filipino guerillas to fight the Japanese in World War II.

Blue Light   Code name for an Army counterterrorist unit formed in Europe during the 1970s.

Brandenburg Division   German special forces unit in World War II. The Brandenburgs began as a political organization but later were absorbed into the *Abwehr* (German military intelligence).

"Budweiser"   Nickname for the gold eagle-and-trident emblem of the Navy SEALs.

C-4   Military-grade plastic explosive.

Carpetbaggers   Army Air Corps squadron in World War II that flew black painted B-24 Liberator bombers on low-level, long-range nighttime missions to gather intelligence and deliver covert, three-man OSS Jedburgh Teams behind German lines.

Central Intelligence Agency (CIA)   America's foremost instrument for intelligence gathering.

Central Intelligence Group (CIG)   Under the leadership of Col. William W. Quinn, the Central Intelligence Group functioned from 1946 until the National Security Act of 1947 transformed it into the Central Intelligence Agency.

Chemical Reconnaissance Detachment (CRDs)   Units specially trained to deal with all chemical and some biological warfare actions and emergencies.

Chindits   Special indigenous force raised in India by British Gen. Orde Wingate. Chindits specialized in making air assaults deep inside Japanese territory in Burma and then fighting their way back toward British lines, destroying everything in their path.

civic action   The promotion of social, medical, and economic improvement programs for indigenous peoples. An important component of the Army Special Forces. Civic actions in Vietnam were intended to "win the hearts and minds" of the Vietnamese people.

Civic Affairs/Psychological Operations Command (CA/PSYOPS)   Headquartered at Fort Bragg, the U.S. Army's CA/PSYOPS Command is responsible for civic action programs and provides psychological warfare services for the rest of America's Special Forces.

Civilian Irregular Defense Group (CIDG)   U.S. Special Forces program to teach counterinsurgency tactics to the many indigenous tribes and peoples of South Vietnam.

CO   Commissioned officer. Military officer with a rank of lieutenant or higher.

Cold War   The general term for the state of political tension between the Soviet bloc countries and the United States–led western nations, which existed between 1945 and the collapse of the Soviet Union in 1991.

Combat Control Operator Course   Fifteen and a half–week course taught by civilian and military air traffic controllers. Air Force Special Tactics Squadron candidates learn basic flight rules, radar approach control procedures, air navigational techniques, tower and airport operations, aircraft performance, and the basics of air traffic control.

combat controllers (CCTs)   Air Force Special Tactics Squadron members proficient in covert insertion tactics and trained to establish assault zones with an air traffic control capability for follow-on forces.

commando   Word of Portuguese origin used to denote citizen soldiers during the First and Second Boer Wars in South Africa. Adopted by the British in World War II, *commando* became a synonym for "special forces."

Commando Order   Orders issued by Adolf Hitler mandating that any Allied commandos taken prisoner be executed.

Coordinator of Information (COI)   An intelligence-gathering organization headed by William Donovan. The COI was a precursor to the Office of Strategic Services and the Central Intelligence Agency.

counterinsurgency   The military, paramilitary, political, psychological, and civil actions taken by a government to defeat internal revolution.

County Fair   Name given to the United States Marine Corps pacification and civil action program in Vietnam.

Cramer, Capt. Harry G.   First American killed in Vietnam, on October 21, 1956. Cramer was a member of the 14th Special Forces Operational Detachment of the 77th Special Forces Group. His name heads the list on the Vietnam Veterans' Memorial in Washington, D.C.

Darby's Rangers   Elements of the First Ranger Battalion commanded by Col. William O. Darby. Darby's Rangers were active in the European theater of World War II.

Defense Language Institute (DLI)   Navy training facility at Monterey, California, where SEALs learn to speak dozens of foreign languages so that they may operate covertly inside a foreign country and culture.

Delta (the 1st Special Forces Operational Detachment)   Elite U.S. Army counterterrorist unit modeled after the British Special Air Service. One of the newest and most secretive component of America's Special Forces.

Detachment 2   Special unit that placed operatives called "Rabbits" behind enemy lines with B-29s air insertions. These operatives carried SCR-300 radios and provided critical intelligence about North Korean and Chinese troop deployment during the Korean War.

Detachment 101   Unit of the OSS operating in Burma in World War II under the command of Col. Carl Eifer.

Devil's Brigade   Name given to the joint American/Canadian First Special Service Force in World War II.

Dien Bien Phu   Communist forces in Vietnam annihilated 2,200 French "paras"— elite troops of the French Expeditionary Corps—in a two-month siege of this base camp. This defeat marked the end of France's involvement in southeast Asia.

domino theory   Cold War philosophy stating that if one country fell to communism, neighboring countries would be threatened with a chain reaction of communist takeovers, falling like dominoes.

Donlon, Capt. Roger Hugh Charles   Commander of the Special Forces camp Nam Dong. He was awarded the first Congressional Medal of Honor in the Vietnam War.

Donovan, William Joseph "Wild Bill"   Coordinator of Information under Franklin Roosevelt and later head of the Office of Strategic Services.

down range   Military slang for hazardous overseas duty.

drop zone   Open area on the ground where parachute insertions or supply drops are made.

Dulles, Allen W.   Established the first active unit of the Special Intelligence Branch of the OSS in Europe. Later became the first director of the Central Intelligence Agency.

Eagle Scouts   Combined units of American Special Forces and South Vietnamese indigenous troops capable of deep reconnaissance, orientation, and combat missions. Eagle Scouts were a quick-reaction team that could be transported to the theater of operation by helicopter.

Ellis, Lieut. Col. Earl "Pete"   Visionary Marine Corps officer who predicted the Pacific War against the Japanese two decades before the surprise attack on Pearl Harbor.

Executive Order 11905   Order issued by President Gerald Ford in the 1970s stating that no United States government employee can participate in assassination attempts against foreign leaders.

Fallschirmjäger Battalion 500/600   Special forces units comprised primarily of disgraced Waffen SS personnel and officers who were given a second chance to redeem themselves.

force multiplier   Any small unit (such as a Special Forces team) capable of training, fielding, and leading 300 to 500 indigenous warriors into combat.

force protection   General term for measures taken to prevent terrorist attacks against U.S. government facilities, military personnel, and military bases.

foreign internal defense   Special operations missions to strengthen the internal security of friendly nations, one of the most basic responsibilities of the U.S. Army Special Forces.

forward-looking infrared radar (FLIR)   Expensive but effective radar system that locates targets by heat.

Freiwilligen Gebirgs   The "Prinz Eugen" Division, a Waffen SS unit made up of ethnic Germans who volunteered or were conscripted from the occupied countries of the Balkans.

Galahad   The 5307 Composite Unit of Merrill's Marauders that operated in Burma against the Japanese in World War II under the command of Gen. Joseph Stillwell.

G-Bands   Special Forces jargon for indigenous guerilla groups.

Goldwater-Nichols Act   Law enacted by the U.S. Congress in 1986 that restructured America's military commands under a group of unified commanders-in-chiefs (CINCs) who are responsible for a particular mission or geographical region.

Great Locomotive Chase   One of the most spectacular special forces operations of the Civil War. Mounted by James J. Andrews, a Union spy from Kentucky, the raid failed, but the survivors became the first troops ever to be awarded the Congressional Medal of Honor.

Grenzschutzgruppe 9 **(SGS-9)**   Formidable German counterterrorism unit formed in the 1970s.

Grierson, Col. Benjamin   Leader of a union Ranger unit during the Civil War.

Groupe d'Intervention de la Gendarmerie National **(GIGN)**   French counterterrorism unit.

Halyard Mission   U.S. Army Air Corps special operation in World War II. Air crews dropped OSS agents into Yugoslavia, where they contacted partisan units and arranged for the return of downed Allied aircrews.

Hamlet Program   Name given to the U.S. Army's pacification and civil action program in Vietnam. This program was separate from those civil action programs conducted by the Army Special Forces.

Hoa Lo   The notorious "Hanoi Hilton," a North Vietnamese prison camp in Hanoi where American POWs were kept in isolation, tortured, and brutalized.

HUMINT (human intelligence)   Information gathered by humans operating on the ground, inside or within plain sight of the target area.

hydrographic reconnaissance   Beach surveys conducted in advance of an amphibious invasion.

indigs   Special Forces shorthand for "indigenous peoples."

internally displaced person (IDP)   Special Forces jargon for "refugee."

Jagdkommando Division   Elite special force within the ranks of the Waffen SS in World War II.

Jarai bracelet   Brass band given by Montagnard tribes to trusted members of the Army's Special Forces. Wearing these bracelets became a status symbol among the troops serving in Vietnam.

Jedburgh Teams   Legendary three-man teams that trained in England and later parachuted into occupied France to direct partisan resistance against the Nazis.

John F. Kennedy Special Warfare Center and School   Located at Fort Bragg, North Carolina, the JFKSWCS is the Army's special operations university. The JFK school provides a complete spectrum of special operations training. The center is the repository of all U.S. Army Special Forces knowledge and includes an extensive archive and museum.

Joint Special Operations Command (JSOC)   Based at Fort Bragg, North Carolina, JSOC is responsible for counterterrorism training and operations of the U.S. Army's Delta Force, Navy SEAL Team Six, and elements of the Federal Bureau of Investigation's Hostage Rescue Team.

K-Bar   Combat knife adopted by the Special Forces from the U.S. Marine Corps.

Lewis bomb   A special explosive developed and used by the SAS.

Lien Doi Nguoi Nhai (LDNN)   The South Vietnamese Navy Underwater Demolitions Teams.

Lodge Bill   Public Law 597, passed in June 1952, mandating the formation of U.S. Special Forces units capable of conducting unconventional warfare operations behind enemy lines.

Long Range Desert Group (LRDG)   Special unit of British desert fighters active in Africa during World War II.

Ludendorff, Gen. Erich   German World War I commander who created the twentieth-century's first special forces, the *Stosstruppen* (shock troopers).

M4   Short-barreled, lightweight version of the standard military M16 automatic rifle used for special operations.

M16   Standard U.S. Army automatic rifle.

MAGIC   Code name for information culled from German radio communications during World War II.

Malayan Emergency   1948 uprising by Chinese communists inside Malaya. The revolution was thwarted by new methods of counterinsurgency applied by the British government.

Marcinko, Comm. Richard   Author and controversial leader of SEAL Team Six. Marcinko was also a founding member of Red Cell.

Marion, Col. Francis   The legendary "Swamp Fox" and America's first guerilla leader. Marion and his men battled British forces stationed in America's South during the War for Independence.

McClure, Brig. Gen. Robert A.   Chief of the Office of Psychological Warfare who advocated the creation of U.S. Special Forces units in the 1950s.

Meadows, Maj. Richard "Dick"   Special Forces officer in Vietnam and leader of the ground assault team during the Son Tay raid. Meadows was trapped behind the lines in Teheran during the failed hostage rescue mission called Operation Eagle Claw.

meals ready to eat (MRE)   Basic U.S. military ration package. Comes in about a dozen varieties, lasts forever, and can be eaten without cooking.

Merrill's Marauders   Ranger units trained and organized under the overall command of Gen. Frank D. Merrill in World War II.

military operations in urban terrain (MOUT)   Military term for street fighting, the most hazardous and costly type of combat action.

Mini-Armored Troop Carrier (MATC)   Small amphibious landing craft similar to the amphibious landing craft that the Marine Corps has used for decades, only much smaller.

Mobile Strike Force Command   "Mike Force" companies were deployed in the Vietnam War to exploit contacts with the enemy, to aid in the extraction of compromised teams, and to perform reconnaissance-in-force missions.

mobility-enhancing rational components (MERC)   Nutritionally rich food bars designed for quick eating.

Montagnards   Indigenous tribal people of Vietnam and America's allies during the Vietnam War. Their name comes from the French for "mountain people" because they dwelled in the mountainous Central Highlands.

Moore, Robin   In 1963, through the intervention of Robert Kennedy, American author Robin Moore was granted permission to join the U.S. Army Special Forces as a civilian. His 11-month stint at Fort Bragg and Vietnam resulted in the 1965 novel *The Green Berets*.

Morale Operations Branch (MO)   Part of the OSS that created "black" propaganda— propaganda that appeared to originate from Germans or Japanese citizens.

Mosby's Rangers   Confederate guerilla unit formed by Virginia lawyer John S. Mosby during the Civil War.

Multiple Integrated Laser Exercise System (MILES)   Training simulator in which laser transmitters mounted on rifles are used against laser detectors worn by individual soldiers or mounted on vehicles. The military version of Laser Tag.

National Security Act of 1947   Legislation that authorized the creation of the Central Intelligence Agency to collect, correlate, and evaluate intelligence relating to national security matters.

National Security Agency (NSA)   Secretive U.S. government agency responsible for encrypted communications, electronic surveillance, and espionage. Also known as the "Puzzle Palace" or "No Such Agency."

National Training Center (NTC)   A rugged, expansive, high-tech desert training center at Fort Irwin, California.

Naval Combat Demolition Unit (NCDU)   Unit formed at Fort Pierce, Florida in May 1942 using expert swimmers trained in demolitions and advanced reconnaissance tactics. These NCDT teams first saw action in the European theater in support of the Normandy invasion.

Naval Special Warfare Command (NAVSPECWARCOM)   Based in Coronado, California, with detachments stationed around the world, NAVESPECWARCOM controls the Sea, Air, Land teams and their support groups.

Naval Special Warfare Development Group I (NAVSPECWARDGRU)   Based at Dam Neck, Virginia, the Naval Special Warfare Development Group was formerly known as SEAL Team Six. NAVSPECWARDGRU is responsible for counterterrorist operations in the maritime environment.

NCO   Noncommissioned officer. A soldier, sailor, airman, or Marine with a rank below lieutenant or ensign.

Nunn-Cohen   Legislative act that created and funded the U.S. Special Operations Command (SOCOM). Sponsored by Sam Nunn (D–GA) and William Cohen (R–ME), passed in 1987.

O course   Obstacle course designed to test physical strength, speed, and agility of SEAL candidates, who are required to improve their performance and running times over the weeks or be eliminated.

Odessa   Secret organization formed after World War II by former special forces commander Otto Skorzeny to smuggle ex-SS members and Nazi war criminals to South America.

Office of Naval Intelligence (ONI)   Primary arm for military intelligence gathering before the Second World War.

Office of Strategic Services (OSS)   Intelligence-gathering and covert operations agency established in World War II under the directorship of William "Wild Bill" Donovan.

Operation Brightlight   From 1970 to 1972, SEALs staged raids to free American POWs imprisoned in the Mekong Delta. Although many ARVN troops were rescued and caches of weapons were destroyed, not one American was ever liberated.

Operation Eagle Claw   Name given to America's disastrous attempt to rescue the U.S. Embassy hostages held prisoner in Iran, which resulted in the destruction of several aircraft and the death of eight American servicemen.

Operation Earnest Will/Prime Chance   Twin SEALs operations in the Persian Gulf, mounted from a floating platform. These operations were designed to keep the sea lanes open during the Iran/Iraq War.

Operation Just Cause   U.S. military operation launched in December 1989 to oust Panamanian dictator Manuel Noriega from power.

Operation Mongoose   Code name of the Miami-based CIA campaign to assassinate Fidel Castro in the 1960s. Mongoose was supervised by Attorney General Robert F. Kennedy.

Operation Prime Chance   From 1987 to 1989, the Nightstalkers protected ships passing through the Persian Gulf, flying their helicopters 30 feet above sea level at night using night-vision goggles and forward-looking infrared (FLIR) devices to spot hostile boats.

Operation Thunderbolt   The 1976 Israeli Special Forces raid of Entebbe Airport in Uganda, where 103 hostages from a hijacked airliner were being detained. All but one of the hostages was rescued.

Operation Torch   The Allied landings in North Africa during World War II.

Operation White Star   Special Forces operation in which Col. Arthur D. "Bull" Simons led 107 Special Forces soldiers into Laos, where they recruited thousands of Meo tribesmen to fight the communists.

Operation Zapata   Secret CIA-controlled program to overthrow Cuban dictator Fidel Castro, resulting in the disastrous Bay of Pigs invasion on April 17, 1961.

Operational Detachment Alpha (ODA)   Twelve-man U.S. Army Special Forces team combining combat, language, engineering, medical, and communications skills. Formerly known as an "A-Team."

Operational Detachment Bravo (ODB)   U.S. Special Forces company headquarters unit. OBD controls and coordinates several ODAs in the field.

operational tempo (OpTempo)   Measure of the demand placed on a military unit—that is, the number of days that a unit is deployed away from its main base.

pararescue   Members of an Air Force Special Tactics Squadron trained to perform covert insertion, combat search and rescue, and trauma medicine.

Pararescue/Combat Control Indoctrination Course (OL-H)   A combination of the Q course, BUD/S, and airborne training that all Air Force candidates must pass to join the Special Tactics Squadron.

Pararescue Recovery Specialist Course   Rigorous course for Air Force pararescue specialists that teaches candidates the basics of airborne insertion, search-and-rescue indoctrination, and basic medical skills.

Pave Hawk   Sikorsky MH-60 K/L helicopter modified for use by the Special Forces. Includes an in-flight refueling boom and special terrain-following radar.

Pave Low   Sikorsky MH-53J helicopter modified for long-range missions at night and at low levels.

People's Army of Vietnam (PAVN)   Conventional North Vietnamese military. PAVN troops were nicknamed "Mr. Charles" by the American forces.

performance-enhancing ration component (PERC)   High-nutrition beverage mix or food bar specially developed for the U.S. Army Special Forces, now used by most special warfare units.

Persian Gulf War   Conflict that resulted from Iraqi dictator Saddam Hussein's invasion of Kuwait in 1990. The war had two distinct phases. The buildup of American and United Nations forces in the region was called Operation Desert Shield; the bombing of Iraq and the land war to liberate Kuwait that followed the buildup was called Operation Desert Storm.

Personal Armor System, Ground Troops (PASGT)   Lightweight helmet and vest made of Kevlar synthetic fiber.

Physical Abilities and Stamina Test (PAST)   Tough physical endurance test that candidates must pass to be admitted to the Air Force Special Tactics Squadron training program.

poop and snoop   Slang for long-range, long-duration reconnaissance missions deep into enemy-held territory.

Project Delta   Code name for the first unit of indigenous Vietnamese specifically trained by U.S. Special Forces to perform special operations.

Project Gamma   A cross-border, intelligence-gathering operation during the Vietnam war, targeted on Cambodia.

Project Omega   Combined unit created for reconnaissance-in-force missions in Vietnam. Similar to Project Sigma, but smaller. Omega included a reconnaissance element, a reaction force, and an advisory command.

Project Sigma   Combined unit created for reconnaissance-in-force missions. Sigma consisted of 900 Civilian Irregular Defense Group troops and 125 U.S. Army Special Forces personnel, and included a reconnaissance element, a reaction force, and an advisory command.

Q course   Special Forces Qualification Course. Candidates who successfully complete the three phases of the Q course receive their Green Berets.

Ranger   Elite units of airborne-qualified troops trained for hazardous and challenging missions.

Ranger Ready Force (RRF)   A designated battalion that must be ready to deploy anywhere in the world within the specified 18-hour window.

Ranger Stakes   A series of 11 tasks to test a Ranger candidate's proficiency with communications equipment and light infantry weapons.

Red Cell   Semicovert unit of the Navy SEALs. Red Cell evolved out of the Naval Security Coordination Team to assist U.S. Navy commands all over the world improve their base, harbor, and ship security procedures, to better guard against terrorism, sabotage, and theft.

Rheault, Col. Robert B.   Commander of the 5th Special Forces in Vietnam. Following an intelligence scandal involving men under his command, Rheault was relieved of command and faced a court martial on charges of murder. He was acquitted after the Central Intelligence Agency refused to cooperate with the investigation.

roadrunner teams   In the Vietnam War, roadrunner teams gathered intelligence on enemy movement and disposition. The teams consisted of four indigenous soldiers who conducted long-distance deep-reconnaissance missions in communist-held territory, usually disguised as Viet Cong or PAVN troops.

Robin Sage   Large-scale U.S. Army Special Forces exercise that serves as the final exam for SF candidates.

Rogers, Maj. Robert   Leader of the British Rangers during the French and Indian War.

Royal Naval Commandos   Sometimes called "Beach Commandos," these British units were sent ashore in advance of an amphibious landing force to clear the beaches of enemy obstructions and mine fields.

Ruddy, Sgt. Maj. Francis   U.S. Army Special Forces soldier who laid his green beret on President John F. Kennedy's grave at Arlington National Cemetery on November 25, 1963.

Rung Sat Special Zone (RSSZ)   Enemy stronghold during the Vietnam War. A vast swamp and one of the most difficult places to conduct military operations in southeast Asia. SEALs deployed hunter/killer teams that targeted VC boat traffic and land concentrations in this zone.

Sadler, Staff Sgt. Barry   U.S. Army Special Forces soldier, recording star, and author. Sadler became famous for his song "The Ballad of the Green Berets." Wounded in Vietnam, Sadler returned to civilian life to become the author of 21 adventure novels. He was murdered in Guatemala in 1989.

SCBA   Self-contained breathing apparatus. New generation of bubbleless, self-contained rebreathing units that "scrub" the air so that the diver can rebreathe it. This efficient system significantly extends the period of time that a diver can remain underwater.

Schwarzkopf, Gen. H. Norman   Commander of all Allied forces in Operation Desert Shield/Desert Storm, the liberation of Kuwait in 1990–1991.

SCUBA   Acronym for self-contained underwater breathing apparatus. World War II–era underwater breathing technology.

Scud missiles   Primitive, Soviet-designed missiles with no internal guidance system. Iraq fired hundreds of Scuds at Israel and Saudi Arabia in an attempt to destabilize the Gulf War coalition forged by President George H. Bush.

SEAL Team Six   Unit formerly responsible for counterterrorist operations in the maritime environment, now deactivated. The origin of SEAL Team Six can be traced to the fallout from the 1980 failed hostage-rescue attempt in Iran called Operation Eagle Claw.

Secret Intelligence Branch (SI)   OSS branch created to conduct espionage operations.

single contingency operation   Military activity undertaken to achieve a single goal.

Skorzeny, Maj. Gen. Otto   Probably the most effective special forces commander of World War II. An officer in the Waffen SS, Skorzeny is best known for the rescue of Italian dictator Benito Mussolini in September 1944.

snake eater   Pejorative used to describe the Green Berets of the Vietnam era.

Son Tay raid   Special Forces raid on North Vietnamese prisoner-of-war camp outside Hanoi on November 21, 1970, commanded by Col. Arthur D. Simons. Although the Green Berets failed to liberate the prisoners—who had already been moved—the raid resulted in improved treatment of all American POWs for the rest of the war.

Special Air Service (SAS)   British commando unit created in World War II. Today the SAS is one of the most formidable special forces groups in the world.

Special Boat Squadron (SBS)   Formed through a marriage between the Special Air Service and the Commando Special Boat Section, this British unit operated in the Greek islands during World War II.

Special Forces Assessment and Selection (SFAS)   Demanding regimen designed to test a candidate's mental and physical fitness to join the Army Special Forces. Less than three percent of applicants finish this tough and rigorous screening process.

Special Forces Command (SFC)   The home of the U.S. Army Special Forces today.

Special Operations Branch (SO)   Unit of the OSS that ran guerilla campaigns in Europe and Asia. The SO worked in conjunction with the British Special Operations Executive.

Special Operations Command (SOCOM)   Unified command created as part of the provisions of the Nunn-Cohen Amendment. Today SOCOM controls all of the Special Operations Forces of the Army, Navy, and Air Force.

Special Operations Command and Control Element (SOCCE)   A small unit of officers and enlisted technical specialists established at a task force headquarters to coordinate and control special operations within the local CINC's overall battle plan.

Special Operations Component, U.S. Forces Korea (SOCKOR)   Special operations command responsible for action in Korea. Although there are no units in the country, they can quickly be dispatched to Korea from Okinawa or other Pacific locations.

Special Operations Component of U.S. Central Command (SOCCENT)   Headquarters of U.S. Special Forces Operations Command responsible for actions in the Middle East and central Asia.

Special Operations Component of U.S. European Command (SOCEUR)   Headquarters of U.S. Special Forces Operations Command responsible for actions in the Balkans and eastern Europe.

Special Operations Component of U.S. Pacific Command (SOCPAC)   Headquarters of U.S. Special Forces Operations Command responsible for east and southeast Asia.

Special Operations Component of U.S. Southern Command (SOCSOUTH)   Headquarters of U.S. Special Forces Operations Command responsible for Latin America.

Special Operations Executive (SOE)   British civilian agency tasked with undermining the Nazi occupation of Europe through guerilla warfare and psychological operations.

Special Operations Force Laser Acquisition Marker (SOFLAM)   The laser target designator of choice for the U.S. Air Force Special Tactics Squadrons. A lightweight laser that can paint a target from a safe distance. Smart bombs follow the laser signature to the target.

Special Operations Forces (SOF)   Collective term for Army, Navy, Air Force, or joint military forces assigned to a special forces command.

Special Operations Modifications (SOPMOD)   Any upgrade, attachment, or modification to the standard M4 Carbine.

Special Operations Support Command (SOSCOM)   Unit of the Army's Special Forces responsible for logistical support. SOSCOM provides spare parts, special weapons, ammunition, and other necessary supply services for front-line Special Forces units.

Special Operations Training Facility (SOT)   Military education complex in Fort Bragg, North Carolina, that teaches methods and techniques used in counterterrorism operations. SOT is where Delta team members are trained.

Special Proficiency at Rugged Training and Nation-Building (SPARTAN) United States–based civil action program conducted by the Army Special Forces. SPARTAN helped improve the lives of poor populations in Arizona, Florida, and Montana.

special reconnaissance (SR) Any special operations mission requiring covert reconnaissance and surveillance behind enemy lines.

Special Tactics Squadrons (STT) Air Force Special Operations Command ground troops, used to seize air fields and provide combat air traffic control for follow-up forces.

Stiner, Gen. Carl W. Commander of the U.S. Special Forces Command (USSOCOM) during the Persian Gulf War of 1990–1991.

Stirling, Capt. David British commando who created the Special Air Service in World War II.

Strategic Services Unit (SSU) Short-lived intelligence-gathering organization created from the ashes of the OSS after World War II. SSU was commanded by Brig. Gen. John Magruder, former Deputy Director of the OSS.

strike force operations U.S. Special Forces patrols deep into communist-held territory during the Vietnam War.

Survival, Evasion, Resistance, and Escape (SERE) Special training course for personnel who are at risk of becoming prisoners of war. An arduous course that subjects students to real mental and physical abuse.

Swimmer Delivery Vehicle Teams (SDVs) Specially trained and BUD/S qualified teams that operate a variety of submersible craft used for SEAL team insertions.

terrain-following radar (TFR) Specialized radar linked to automatic flight control that allows an aircraft to fly with relative safety at night and during bad weather, or at an extremely low altitude ("nap of the Earth") to elude detection.

Title 10 Section of the U.S. code dealing with the national defense establishment rules and regulations, and legal and financial authority.

Tonkin Gulf Incident On August 2, 1964, three North Vietnamese torpedo boats unsuccessfully attacked the U.S. Navy destroyer *Maddox* in the Tonkin Gulf. This incident was used to justify the expansion of the ongoing war in Vietnam.

Tonkin Gulf Resolution Legislation passed by the U.S. Congress in 1964, authorizing President Lyndon Baines Johnson to do whatever was necessary to stop communist aggression in Vietnam. Johnson used this resolution to dramatically escalate the war in Vietnam.

T-rations Precooked meals packaged in aluminum trays. Also called "T-rats."

tripwire patrols   Special Forces patrols to root out Viet Cong units that infiltrated South Vietnam from Laos and Cambodia.

ULTRA   Code name for information culled from Japanese radio communications during World War II.

Underwater Demolition Teams (UDTs)   The brainchild of U.S. Navy Lieut. Commander Draper L. Kaufman, who organized the first teams in 1943. UDTs cleared obstacles such as mine fields and barriers that barred the way for an amphibious assaults in World War II.

unmanned aerial vehicle (UAV)   Remote-controlled drone aircraft used for reconnaissance and surveillance.

U.S. Army Special Operations Command (USASOC)   Based at Fort Bragg, North Carolina, USASOC is the largest component command of SOCOM, composed of the Army Special Forces Command, the 75th Ranger Regiment, the 160th Special Operations Aviation Regiment, the John F. Kennedy Special Warfare Center and School, the U.S. Army Civic Affairs and Psychological Operations Command, and the United States Army Special Operations Support Command.

U.S. Transportation Command (TRANSCOM)   Unified command including Air Mobility Command, the U.S. Navy's Military Sea Transportation Service, and the U.S. Army's Military Traffic Management Command.

Viet Cong   Communist guerillas who lurked undetected among the populace of South Vietnam, mingling with both the rural and urban populations during the Vietnam War. U.S. troops nicknamed these soldiers "Charlie."

Vietnamization   President Richard M. Nixon's plan for South Vietnam to take on more responsibility for their own defense against the communist North Vietnamese.

weapons of mass destruction (WMD)   Any nuclear, chemical, biological, or radiological weapon.

X-2   Elite branch of the OSS with the highest security clearance. Members of X-2 were permitted access to MAGIC and ULTRA intercepts and could veto Special Operations Branch activities without explanation.

Zodiac boat   Squad-size rubber raft used in special operations.

Index

Symbols

B

H

S

X–Y–Z